Eucharist and Ecclesiology

Eucharist and Ecclesiology

Essays in Honor of Dr. Everett Ferguson

EDITED BY
Wendell Willis

☙PICKWICK *Publications* • Eugene, Oregon

EUCHARIST AND ECCLESIOLOGY
Essays in Honor of Dr. Everett Ferguson

Copyright © 2016 Wipf and Stock Publishers. All rights reserved. Except for brief quotations in critical publications or reviews, no part of this book may be reproduced in any manner without prior written permission from the publisher. Write: Permissions, Wipf and Stock Publishers, 199 W. 8th Ave., Suite 3, Eugene, OR 97401.

Pickwick Publications
An Imprint of Wipf and Stock Publishers
199 W. 8th Ave., Suite 3
Eugene, OR 97401

www.wipfandstock.com

PAPERBACK ISBN: 978-1-4982-8292-5
HARDCOVER ISBN: 978-1-4982-8294-9
EBOOK ISBN: 978-1-4982-8293-2

Cataloguing-in-Publication data:

Names: Willis, Wendell, editor.

Title: Eucharist and ecclesiology : essays in honor of Dr. Everett Ferguson / edited by Wendell Willis.

Description: Eugene, OR: Pickwick Publications, 2016 | Includes bibliographical references.

Identifiers: ISBN 978-1-4982-8292-5 (paperback) | ISBN 978-1-4982-8294-9 (hardcover) | ISBN 978-1-4982-8293-2 (ebook)

Subjects: Lord's Supper. | Church. | Ferguson, Everett, 1933–.

Classification: BV823 E82 2016 (print) | BV823 (ebook)

Manufactured in the U.S.A.   12/15/16

Unless otherwise indicated, all translations from the Bible are from the Revised Standard or the New Revised Standard Versions.

Revised Standard Version of the Bible, copyright 1952 [2nd edition, 1971] by the Division of Christian Education of the National Council of the Churches of Christ in the United States of America. Used by permission. All rights reserved.

New Revised Standard Version Bible, copyright 1989, Division of Christian Education of the National Council of the Churches of Christ in the United States of America. Used by permission. All rights reserved.

Dedication

THIS BOOK IS DEDICATED to Dr. Everett Ferguson and to those scholars who took part in a 2013 colloquy to celebrate his eightieth birthday. It is also dedicated to the Seminar on Second Century Christianity (formerly the Southwest Seminar on the Development of Early Catholic Christianity), which originated in response to Vatican II, and of which Dr. Ferguson was a founder, and many of the contributors are active members. This seminar has been, and remains, a model of ecumenical and open discussion of significant concerns in understanding the Christian faith.

I wish to express thanks to Abilene Christian University for hosting the colloquy at which these essays were first presented and to those who contributed financially to make it possible. This volume is the first publication sponsored by the Center for the Study of Ancient Religious Texts located at Abilene Christian. Special thanks must be extended to all who participated and especially those who contributed papers for discussion. I am also very appreciative of the valuable guidance provided by Brian Palmer who worked tirelessly on this project representing the publisher, Wipf & Stock. Personally I also express deep appreciation to my graduate assistant, Aaron G. Brown, who spent many hours proofing the copy (all essays several times). He did conscientious and effective work in getting the volume prepared, although of course he bears no responsibility for any errors I too missed!

Contents

Preface | ix
Abbreviations | xi
Contributors | xv

Part 1: Plenary Presentations

1. "Cheap Grace" The Problem of "Inter-Communion"
   —*Gary D. Badcock* | 3

2. Bible and Eucharist in an Incarnational Model
   —*Denis Farkasfalvy, O. Cist.* | 19

3. Church and Eucharist in the Orthodox Tradition
   —*Paul D. Meyendorff* | 33

4. Eucharist and Church: Response —*Everett Ferguson* | 48

Part 2: Presented Essays

5. No One Has Ascended to Heaven but the One Who Has Descended from Heaven, the Son of Man Who Is in Heaven (John 3:13)
   —*Roch Kereszty, O. Cist.* | 59

6. Eastern Orthodox Social Ethics and the Anaphora of St. Basil the Great —*Philip LeMasters* | 76

7. The Words of Institution: Their Function in the Earliest Biblical Traditions —*Allan McNicol* | 87

8. Toward Locating Eucharistic Theology in the Fourth Gospel —*Curt Niccum* | 108

9. From Passover to Eucharist: The Didache and Early Christian Eucharistic Observance —*Jeffrey Peterson* | 125

10. Before There Was a Eucharist: Worship in the House Ekklesia —*Dennis Smith* | 144

11. Wait for One Another: The Significance of the Eucharist for a Theology of Patience —*Arthur M. Sutherland* | 159

12. The Koinonia of Christians—and Others —*Wendell Willis* | 172

Preface

THE ESSAYS IN THIS volume were originally presented in a 2013 colloquy at Abilene Christian University in recognition and celebration of the eightieth birthday of our esteemed colleague, Dr. Everett Ferguson, Professor Emeritus. They have been revised for this publication.

Dr. Ferguson was a faculty member at Abilene Christian University (earlier College) from 1962 until his retirement in 1998. A prolific scholar, Dr. Ferguson is known and esteemed world-wide in the academy for his work in the study of Patristic literature (for example, his definitive *Baptism in the Early Church* published in 2009 by Eerdmans). He has also contributed many works in service to the church, examples include his books of devotional readings using early Christian authors (*Inheriting Wisdom*, published 2004 by Hendricksons).

This colloquy was planned to feature two aspects of Christian faith that have been prominent in Dr. Ferguson's research, the Eucharist and the church. In the twentieth century the understanding of the Eucharist had been a major focus and often a crux in the ecumenical talks that occurred that century—as the plenary speeches well illustrate. Because the Eucharist is the most uniquely Christian practice, it becomes a central concern in understanding ecclesiology as practiced in the many communities who affirm a relationship to Jesus Christ as their Lord. For this reason, the colloquy had three plenary addresses by leaders in the Orthodox churches (Dr. Paul Meyendorff), the Roman Catholic church (Fr. Abbot Denis Farkasfalvy) and the Protestant church (Dr. Gary Badcock). Their presentations are presented as a group in the first section of this book. While each spoke as a committed and academic member of their religious community, they also each would not want to be regarded as official representatives of their church. Dr. Ferguson has graciously offered a response to these plenary presentations, and gives a valuable and succinct review of the history of teachings on the Eucharist.

The relationship of church and Eucharist was also the object of focused research and discussions. At the colloquy there were working sessions at which such research was presented. Eight of these papers, selected among several presented in the colloquy, are included in the second part of this book. These essays examine the important evidence in the New Testament for the Eucharist and aspects of Patristic engagement with it. It must be noted that these essays have all been revised for publication without the authors engaging (or largely even having access to) the essays of each other. Much of such interchange took place in the colloquy, but must remain unreported here.

Because the colloquy and the presenters all believe that it is vital in the present time for both the formation and role of the church that the relationship of the varied Christian communities to each other be examined with candor as well as charity, we believe this book can become a useful work for seminary study and inter-church conversations. It is sent forth in that expectation, relying upon God's blessing and use for our work.

—Wendell Willis

Abbreviations

AB	Anchor Bible
BCH	*Bulletin de correspondance hellénique*
BDAG	Frederick W. Danker et al., eds., *A Greek-English Lexicon of the New Testament and Other Early Christian Literature*. 3rd ed. Chicago: University of Chicago Press, 2000
BibIntSer	Biblical Interpretation Series
BK	*Bibel und Kirke*
BTB	*Biblical Theology Bulletin*
BZNW	Beihefte zur Zeitschrift für die neutestamentliche Wissenschraft und die Kunde der älteren Kirche
CBQ	*Catholic Biblical Quarterly*
CJ	*Classical Journal*
CP	*Classical Philology*
CS	*Christian Studies*
Dae	*Daedalus*
Ecc	*Ecclesiology*
EDNT	*Exegetical Dictionary of the New Testament*. 3 vols. Edited by Horst Balz and Gerhard Schneider. Grand Rapids: Eerdmans, 1990–93

ABBREVIATIONS

EJ	*Eranos Jahrbuch*
ET	*Evangelical Theology*
ExAud	*Ex Auditu*
GOTC	*Greek Orthodox Theological Review*
Greg	*Gregorianum*
JSNT	*Journal for the Study of the New Testament*
JSNTSup	Journal for the Study of the New Testament Supplemental Series
LCC	Library of Christian Classics
LCL	Loeb Classical Library
Mid-Stream	*MidStream*
NovT	*Novum Testamentum*
NRSV	New Revised Standard Version
NovTSup	Novum Testamentum Supplements
NTS	*New Testament Studies*
OrChrAn	Orientalia Christiana Analecta
PColon	Köllner Papyri
POxy	Oxyrhynchus Papyri
PRSt	*Perspectives in Religious Studies*
PTMS	Princeton Theological Monograph Series
QD	*Questiones Disputatae*
QL	Questiones Liturgiques
RQ	Restoration Quarterly
RSV	Revised Standard Version
RTR	*Reformed Theological Review*
SBT	Studies in Biblical Theology
SJT	*Scottish Journal of Theology*
SNTSMS	Society for New Testament Studies Monograph Series

SocF	*Sociological Forum*
SR	*Sciences Religieuses*
ST	*Studia Theologica*
SVTQ	*St Vladimirs Theological Quarterly*
TANZ	Texte und Arbeiten zum neutestamentlichen Zeitalter
TDNT	Theological Dictionary of the New Testament
ThD	*Theology Digest*
TJ	*Trinity Journal*
TynBul	*Tyndale Bulletin*
VCSup	Vigiliae Christianae Supplements
Wor	*Worship*
WUNT	Wissenschaftliche Untersuchungen zum Neuen Testament und die Kunde der älteren Kirche
ZNW	*Zeitschrift für die neutestamentliche Wissenschaft*
ZPE	*Zeitschrift für Papyrologie und Epigraphik*

Contributors

Gary D. Badcock, Peache Professor of Divinity, Huron University College, London, Ontario, Canada

Denis Farkasfalvy, O Cist, Adjunct Professor of Theology, University of Dallas, Dallas, Texas

Everett Ferguson, Professor Emeritus, Abilene Christian University, Abilene, Texas

Roch Kereszty, O Cist, Adjunct Professor of Theology, University of Dallas, Dallas, Texas

Philip LeMasters, Professor of Religion, McMurry University, Abilene, Texas

Allan J. McNicol, Professor of New Testament Emeritus, Austin Graduate School of Theology, Austin, Texas

Paul Meyendorff, Alexander Schmemann Professor of Liturgical Theology, St Vladimir's Orthodox Theological Seminary, Yonkers, New York

Curt Niccum, Professor of Bible, Abilene Christian University, Abilene, Texas

Jeffrey Peterson, Jack C. and Ruth Wright Professor of New Testament, Austin Graduate School of Theology, Austin, Texas

Dennis E. Smith, LaDonna Kramer Meinders Professor of New Testament Emeritus, Phillips Theological Seminary, Tulsa, Oklahoma

Arthur M. Sutherland, Associate Professor of Theology, Loyola University Maryland, Baltimore, Maryland

Wendell Willis, Professor of Bible, Abilene Christian University, Abilene, Texas

PART I

Plenary Presentations

I

"Cheap Grace"

Ecumenism and the Problem of "Inter-Communion"

—*Gary D. Badcock*

HISTORICALLY, EUCHARISTIC THEOLOGY HAS served not only as a stable point of reference in Christian theology, but also as one of the key points around which controversy and tensions have tended to focus. Here both the substance of the faith, and the contradictions of theological theory, come to expression. The theology of the Eucharist was, for instance, used by Irenaeus of Lyons in the second century to ward off Docetism, on the grounds that it is precisely the *body* of the Lord that is communicated in it. Given the centrality of the Eucharist to early Christian worship, any implied denial of the words of Christ, "This is my body . . . ," could be taken to be a danger and a lie, something alien to the Apostolic tradition and hostile to the true import of the gospel of Christ. Again, in the context of the scholastic revival of the twelfth and thirteenth centuries, the hold of the new scientific and metaphysical theories introduced from the Aristotelian tradition were nowhere more emphatically sealed than by the development of the doctrine of "transubstantiation." Transubstantiation had become definitive Latin teaching by the early thirteenth century, after the eucharistic controversy of the twelfth, and on this basis was explored and extended by such theologians as Thomas Aquinas in the thirteenth century. Again, at the time of the Protestant Reformation, the theology of the Eucharist served as a focal point for divergent understandings of the meaning of justification, and therefore of sin, grace and salvation. Everything at issue, indeed, could be understood through the lens of divergent views of the Eucharist: the Eucharist as the church's *sacrificium* on the one side, and the Lord's body and blood offered to faith as pledge of Christ's righteousness on the other.

In our time, however, debates about the Eucharist bring to focus a rather different, and in fact in many ways an entirely distinctive set of theological questions, clustered around ecclesiology. This is in and of itself an important observation, for it reveals the importance of the ecclesiological question in recent theology. The twentieth century saw, among other things, the "rediscovery" of the Christian East by the Christian West, the rise of the World Council of Churches, and the developments surrounding the Second Vatican Council, so that by the nineteen sixties, it seemed that earlier divisions between Christians, which had once been understood to relate to the whole nature of the gospel, now had come overwhelmingly to be concentrated in one question—ecclesiology.[1] We are thus heirs of a century of ecumenical engagement that has brought about a transformation in Christian thought; indeed, in many ways we stand at a unique juncture in Christian history, in a situation that would have astonished our forebears. However, for all the effort, we have not arrived at a common eucharistic table; indeed, that goal is as elusive today as it was a half-century ago. This has led some even of the ecumenical movement's most prominent representatives to conclude that failure beckons, and that ecumenical passion is now largely spent—Paul Avis, for instance, has ruefully written that today, "Inertia and apathy confront ecumenism on every side."[2] Perhaps it would be fairer to say simply that some of the most important questions have not yet been raised, and that there is much work to be done in entirely new phases of ecumenical labour. It is unrealistic to expect that a situation of division which has developed over long centuries should be resolved within the space of a few decades. Furthermore, new forms of Christianity have emerged, having little sense of an organic relation to the older Christian tradition (e.g., the house churches of Asia or the many global forms of Pentecostalism), with memberships that exceed those of many of the older, ecumenically engaged churches. These also must somehow be drawn into the ecumenical project. The fact that at the Eucharist, the church remains

1. Congar, *Diversity and Communion*, 2.
2. Avis, *Reshaping*, 20.

scandalously divided, therefore, merely reflects at this one point of intensity what is actually the case, and what ought not to be swept under the carpet.

It is in this context that I wish to consider a dominant, peculiarly Protestant approach to the overcoming of eucharistic division—the practice of "inter-communion." It is difficult, of course, to speak of the Protestant world as a whole, since Protestantism is comprised of many hundreds of sects and sub-sects, not all of which say the same things or value the same practices. However, the relation between Eucharist and ecclesiology within the various Protestant churches is nowhere better expressed than in the widespread practice seen in Protestant churches of showing eucharistic hospitality to Christians of other traditions. Such hospitality is today not infrequently enjoyed by Roman Catholics in Protestant settings, even though for Roman Catholics such practice is strictly illicit and the sacrament is officially deemed to be fundamentally flawed. The same hospitality would no doubt also be extended to Orthodox Christians in certain settings, though there a similar prohibition is also in effect. Protestants themselves, of course, are technically excommunicated still by the Catholic and Orthodox, though there is the category of "pastoral necessity" that some individual Roman Catholic priests employ to permit a Protestant to receive. The general situation tends to entail today that Protestant Christians very often take offence that the same eucharistic hospitality shown to Catholics is not extended to them. Thus inter-communion tends to be, perforce, an inter-Protestant matter, and it is this particular feature of the Protestant tradition that is our immediate concern in what follows.

I use the term "inter-communion," rather than its sibling, "open communion," because it seems to me to represent more accurately the peculiar theological meaning of the practice. Rather than the Catholic or Orthodox "full communion" that involves at heart the idea of belonging to a single ecclesial body gathered around the bishop, in a church with a single sacramental structure, Protestant inter-communion conversely insists, generally on the basis of baptism and faith, that members of one church can share the Eucharist with members of another church, all the while retaining their distinct identities as members of quite separate institutional churches, with different ministries and often with discrete points of doctrine and practice that are not only mutually incompatible, but that as often as not are explicitly defined as such.

There are, of course, a variety of mechanisms by which this interchange at the sacramental level may be achieved, from informal arrangements that prevail among Christians at the local, congregational level; to more formal bilateral agreements existing between, let us say, Lutherans and Anglicans in a number of jurisdictions; to the common view that the true church is *invisible,* and therefore that the visible structures that we bump up against in "inter-denominational" relationships and rivalries ought not to matter ultimately, since they cannot be assumed to matter ultimately to God. However, what is common to them all is the notion that there can be one denomination, which itself exists as a "communion," that celebrates something in the eucharistic meal commonly called "communion," and that can share the latter but not the former with members of another denomination, which again exists as a separate "communion." Thus, amid the resulting thicket of theological ambiguity, one can share the one sacrament of the body of Christ, without any expectation of visibly existing as one body in Christ. Let us ponder the significance of this practice.

To begin with, there is historical precedent—of a sort—within Protestant theology for the practice in view, though the point of it needs to be carefully qualified over against contemporary Protestant polity. It was, for instance, commonly understood in the sixteenth, seventeenth and even the eighteenth centuries that an Englishman abroad in Germany or Switzerland could rightly communicate in another Protestant church—in the case of the Englishman, allowing only for occasional scruples, this might regularly have involved an Anglican receiving communion in churches ordered without episcopal ministry. By the nineteenth century, English attitudes had hardened, particularly in connection with the Oxford Movement; by then, the religious position of the Englishman abroad had changed fundamentally, and the expectation that an Anglican gentleman should never receive the Eucharist from a Presbyterian—or worse still, a Congregationalist—became a commonplace. The original practice, curiously, is reflected in the ordinary expectations laid upon the British Crown. Most Anglicans, for instance, seem unaware that when Her Majesty the Queen (who is formally not simply a member but the *Head* of the Church of England) visits Scotland, she attends Presbyterian worship and is a communicant in the Church of Scotland. The practice in view is not a constitutional ruse, intended to keep unruly Scots happy with an English sovereign; it rather reflects the older expectation of which I have been speaking, an expectation embedded in Protestant liturgical practice at its origins.

There is, however, a key difference between these older forms of Protestant inter-communion, and what we (for the most part) know today.

Our tendency is to think that the point of such practice was essentially one of mutual recognition, and so that the effect was to sanctify the *differences* between the Reformation churches, rather than to unite them. In fact, however, the reality is rather different, and its implication much more interesting. The rationale was (as is often the case) most clearly set out by John Calvin in the ecclesiological sections that dominate the overall structure of the *Institutes of the Christian Religion*. According to Calvin, who at this point is by no means unrepresentative of the broad sympathies of the magisterial Reformers, the distinguishing "marks of the church" are "the preaching of the Word and the observance of the sacraments," and where these are present, "there . . . no deceitful or ambiguous form of the church is seen; and no one is permitted to spurn its authority, flout its warnings, resist its councils, or make light of its chastisements—much less to desert it and break its unity."[3] He goes on to argue that Christ himself "esteems the communion of his church so highly that he counts as a traitor and apostate . . . anyone who arrogantly leaves any Christian society, provided it cherishes the true ministry of Word and sacraments . . . even if it otherwise swarms with many faults" (IV.1.12).

What is especially important about these claims is that they were clearly intended to cover not only the commonplace situation of a Christian who finds himself or herself in a "dead" church—a problem that we all perhaps know too well—but also that of a Reformed Christian living, for instance, in Lutheran territories. This may not seem a stretch at first sight, but Calvin actually regarded much of the Lutheran teaching on the Eucharist of his time as deeply flawed, and in some of its expressions thought it so misguided that it was worse than the teaching of "the papists," as he himself puts it.[4] Yet for all that, he rejects the possibility that one should attempt to worship separately from the one, established church in those territories, or in any way to undermine its unity. The regulative idea turns out to be that there should be only one church in each jurisdiction. Now here, as ever, tensions emerge in his theology: if this were really so, for instance, then why separate from Rome? Even Calvin was generous enough to admit that there were churches that remained worthy bearers of the name "church" in the Roman fold. But the greater problem for our purposes is that, as

---

3. Calvin, *Institutes* IV.1.10.

4. Calvin thought the doctrine of the physical ubiquity of Christ's body taught by some leading exponents of Lutheran orthodoxy in the mid-sixteenth century to verge on Eutycheanism. In an extraordinary outburst, he writes that the standard Roman doctrine is "more tolerable or at least more modest" than that Lutheran account (IV.17.30).

ever, the disciples were not greater than their master, so that a tendency to schism among Calvin's followers soon becomes evident. The seeds of that particular form of ruin are present in Calvin's own theology, as certainly his Catholic critics have long observed. Indeed, the trouble emerges at the decisive point, for who is to say just how the true preaching of the Word should sound, or who is to adjudicate that question? Or, what precisely comprises a right administration of the sacraments, given how perilously misinformed he regarded certain Lutherans? It was over just such matters that his followers divided—to say nothing of what the notoriously hair-splitting Lutherans of the time thought of the Calvinists. And on we go. It is for this reason, undoubtedly, that even as "conservative" a contemporary Protestant theologian as Wolfhart Pannenberg has argued that there is need for a ministry to the unity of Christianity as a whole, centred in the office of the Bishop of Rome—just as also there is need for the office of the Bishop of Rome to be redefined and purified of its self-appointed privileges—since without it, there can effectively be no way to arbitrate such divisions.[5]

High principles were, then, one thing, whereas (and as ever) the practice that followed was to prove to be another. This in itself should scarcely surprise us, of course, for we also do not live above ambition and spiritual blindness. Furthermore, the varied ecclesial traditions that emerged in Protestantism certainly fared well enough for a season. Allied with political and economic powers that were to prove dominant on the stage of modern history, Protestant Christianity grew and expanded far beyond the small borders that were its first world. As the dynamics of modernity developed, and particularly with the emergence of the modern concept of the individual, we witness the generation of a very different, "denominational" Protestantism that, on the whole, has moved entirely beyond the idea of national, established churches to the ideal of a church founded on freedom of religious association. This is the decisive development, for it redefines the older Protestant practice of inter-communion in profound ways. Its effect is to prioritize the believing individual, and to relativize the significance of the institutional churches to which these members variously belong. This occurred nowhere more clearly than in the United States, of course, but through its influence, it is now a global Christian reality. In a certain sense, in fact, one can see in this development an expression of the

---

5. Pannenberg, *Systematic Theology*, 3:420–31. So, for instance, he writes: "We ought freely to admit the fact of the primacy of the Roman Church and its bishop in Christianity. Not the fact itself so much as the way of describing it is the point at issue, along with the question of the implied rights" (421).

ideals of the radical rather than of the magisterial Reformation, so that, in a manner of speaking, all Protestants have become, by default, the spiritual descendants of the Anabaptists. Earlier Protestant figures such as Luther or Calvin, of course, had famously denied that there is such a thing as freedom at all, and certainly individual choice does not loom particularly large in their theologies, so that the idea that the traditions to which they gave their names should have become so assimilated to something inherently alien to what they themselves stood for ought to be much more explicitly discussed than tends to be the case. But that it has happened can scarcely be disputed, and the countless sects and sub-sects of contemporary Protestant Christianity bear witness both to the "entrepreneurial" success of the model that developed, and to the failure of the earliest Protestant principle to control what modernity unleashed.

The Reformation-era expectation that a Swiss believer should share the communion meal with his or her Lutheran contemporaries, therefore, is not straightforwardly consistent with the later development of the practice of denominational inter-communion, and we should be careful to differentiate between them. The distinctiveness of the modern variant is nicely put by Lesslie Newbigin (1909–98), the British missionary to India whose career included episcopal ministry in the Church of South India, distinguished service to the ecumenical movement, and at the end of his life, a rather profound missiological engagement with the culture of the West. Though the primary reference is mission rather than Eucharist, Newbigin wrote of denominationalism as *the* fundamental problem inherent in modern Protestant ecclesiology, and his observations are certainly relevant to our theme:

> We say that in the realm of values (and religious beliefs are included in that realm), everyone must be free to have his or her own faith. Pluralism reigns. We also have a public world of what we call facts, where pluralism does not reign, where things are either true or false; and religion does not belong to that field. It does not belong to the public world. Now the denomination is the visible form that the Church takes in a society which has accepted the secularization of public life and the privatization of religion, so that the variety of denominations corresponds, if you like, to the variety of brands available on the shelves of the supermarket. Everyone is free to take his choice.
>
> The denomination, either singly or together, cannot be the bearer of the challenge of the Gospel to our society, because it is

itself the outward and visible form of an inward and spiritual surrender to the ideology of that society. And, therefore ... we have to challenge this whole acceptance of the denominational principle as being the normal form in which Church life is expressed ... I cannot avoid [this necessary thought] if I try to be faithful to the scriptures.[6]

Newbigin's critique makes a clear connection between the post-Enlightenment liberal democratic political order, and the modern Protestant denomination. Implicit in his criticism is the idea that modern Protestants are effectively in thrall to the powers of the age, in what we might call a new "Babylonian Captivity" of the church. It is interesting that he references the common sacramental formula, deriving in this case from Augustine,[7] of outward signs of inward grace, so that denominationalism is read as the outward theological sign or sacrament of what modern Protestants really believe inwardly, which is shaped not only by the gospel of Jesus Christ or by the teaching of Holy Scripture but, at a level that is truly basic, by the political ideal of freedom, by the principle of choice and by a fundamental individualism. Newbigin refers to this by analogy with the supermarket: denominational Protestantism is consumerism extended to the sphere of faith. It would be worthwhile to ponder the point Newbigin is making, since there is here a genuine case to be answered, and if he is right about it, it amounts to a reef that imperils the ship of faith.

To begin with, the case Newbigin makes could be readily extended and amplified. As "standard" a contemporary theological source as the South African missiologist David Bosch, for instance, offers an extended and disturbing treatment of the ways in which the doctrine of salvation came to be assimilated to modern social and political advances from the eighteenth century, so that the kingdom of God was conflated with the modern nation state in much of Protestantism.[8] Newbigin sees it as essential to mount a principled theological challenge to the denomination as such, since, in his view, it is not merely an impediment to the unity that is the mystery of God's will in Christ (the epistle to the Ephesians is a major source for his theology at this point), but because it is an expression—a "sacrament," if you will—of an idolatrous identification of the gospel with a particular form of political culture. To take the point further in the specific direction of that essay, one

---

6. Newbigin, "On Being the Church," 141.
7. The usual source cited is Augustine, *De Catechizandis Rudibus*.
8. Bosch, *Transforming Mission*, 268–353.

might appeal specifically to the eucharistic practice of inter-communion among Protestant denominations, which (like all eucharistic theology) sums up this whole understanding of the meaning of the gospel, of the significance of Jesus Christ for faith, and of the place of the church in the system of belief. Extending Newbigin's analysis in this way might allow us to see the extent to which inter-communion can be understood as an affirmation, not so much of common identity in the one body of Christ, but of common identity in the liberal state, since what it celebrates is precisely the kind of differentiation uniquely possible in the practice of religion in a society founded on democratic principle. On this view, for Christians and churches to which they belong to share the communion meal with others outside the boundaries of a denomination is essentially to affirm the right, and perhaps even the responsibility, of the individual to choose his or her pattern of belonging, his or her personal set of preferences in the whole arena of faith. Inter-communion is the recognition, on these terms, of the ultimate validity of freedom of religion, mine as well as yours, so that what we recognise in the practice is the legitimacy of all those personal choices made by individuals in the spiritual marketplace. It is a recognition of the primacy of personal freedom, which itself is effectively deemed through the sacramental practice of inter-communion to be a means of salvation. "Since there is one bread, the many are one body, for they all partake of the one bread," writes Paul in 1 Cor 10:17.[9] On this reading of inter-communion, the sharing of the one bread genuinely does signify sacramentally that the many are one body—but it is not in the body of Christ so much as in the body politic that they are one.

Now, it is obviously important to recognize that the Protestant churches would, on the whole, resist this critical reading of the significance of the sacrament, and insist to the contrary that the practice of inter-communion is rooted in the distinction between visible and invisible church. The visible, institutional churches are, at best, provisional realisations of the purpose of God for the people of God in the world, and so of proximate rather than ultimate importance. On this view, inter-communion becomes a coherent theological possibility, it is argued, since otherwise we would be found guilty of deeming what is merely proximate to be precisely of ultimate importance. Since we grant members of other churches the title "Christian," and so account them to be accepted by God, grafted into the body of Christ, and made by baptism the dwelling place

---

9. My translation.

of the Holy Spirit, we also rightly extend to them the sacramental sign of all of this in eucharistic hospitality. Furthermore, it would be claimed that inter-communion opens the churches over time to ever greater forms of cooperation and common life; as a means of grace, it is also a means of the grace of further unity. Thus, for instance, it is commonly said that inter-communion can be legitimately practised as a stage on the way to the realization of whatever fuller communion may, in future, be accomplished through the work of the ecumenical movement. Were more churches to engage in inter-communion, such Protestants argue—even though inter-communion may be a very imperfect halfway house—there would be better prospect for some future, fuller communion among Christians. In my own experience, I have encountered even many Roman Catholics who tend to agree with this way of putting the matter, and there are certainly millions who will participate in Protestant eucharistic worship, and even a great many priests who are perfectly prepared to welcome any baptized Christian at the altar, interpreting recent canon law with a certain laxity. The official position of the church is one thing; what prevails on the ground is quite another.

But this is also the case among Protestants, and I rather fear that among the membership, and even very often at the top, there is much more of the civil religion of which Newbigin complains in the practice of inter-communion than there is of high ecumenical principle. If this is correct, then it means that Protestants have a genuine problem on their hands. It used to be the case that Protestant theology accused the Catholic tradition of the sin of idolatry in relation to practices such as the veneration of the Host, since such things confused, it was said, the worship of God with adoration of a corporeal object. But even if these allegations were justified as they stood, idolatry comes in many forms and guises. To take the Eucharist, which contains in itself the whole meaning of Jesus' life as gift of God and as self-offering to God, and which sums up the whole mystery of the gospel and life of the church,[10] and to conflate all of this theological richness with a particular political standpoint (one that gives us not only religious freedom, but with it, incidentally, rights to pornography and abortion and all the rest) is also a form of idolatry—and it is an idolatry to which modern Protestants, I suggest, are particularly susceptible. The dangers are, I fear, latent in the common practice of inter-communion.

10. Kasper, "Aspects," 177–94.

This raises the key theological question: How do we avoid being conformed to the world, or at least, reduce the temptation to be so? The long answer is that modern Protestants need a much more robust ecclesiology than they tend to have. Here the interesting thing is that, given the extent to which the ecumenical question must frame any contemporary ecclesiology, Protestants cannot do this on their own: they will need to learn from the Catholic and Orthodox. However, there is obviously no question of developing such a comprehensive vision in what follows. Something more modest, however, may be possible, and so, I want in what remains to sketch an approach that speaks from and to our different traditions. It will involve understanding the doctrine of the church, and with it the question of the Eucharist, from two perspectives, or from the standpoint of two movements that are essential to the subject.

Interestingly, the two perspectives involved could be expanded and developed in different ways. One especially viable approach leads through the structures of Christology, as we shall see; another could conceivably be some adaptation of the *exitus-reditus* pattern of much classical Christian philosophy, theology and spirituality; another might be through reference to the twin concepts of justification and sanctification, in order to anchor the discussion much more explicitly in the language and conceptuality of Protestant soteriology. I will make reference only to the first of these, for what I wish to do is refer mainly to Pneumatology, and to make the most of its intimate connection with ecclesiology. In the classical creeds, after all, the church and the Christian life generally are handled as a function of the third article. For ecclesiology does not stand on its own in the structure of Christian doctrine. It is controlled by other regulative, more basic themes, and by the doctrine of the Holy Spirit in particular. One could go so far as to say that an ecclesiology is always an implicit Pneumatology.

There are, says Paul, different spiritual gifts (*charismata*), but the same Spirit; different ministries (*diakonion*), but the same Lord; different energies, but the same God working them (1 Cor 12:4–6). The principle of differentiation is basic to what has to be said of the work of the Spirit in the church. Diversity, or individuation, is in a manner of speaking the name of the game. Protestantism generally, like most Western theology, has a relatively weak Pneumatology, but what Pneumatology it does have tends to be clustered around the idea that encounter with the Holy Spirit takes place in the life of the individual person. The work of the Spirit is, for example, commonly associated with the gift or awakening of "saving faith," and there the question is not what the church believes, but what I believe, cling to, trust in, and commit my life to. The Bible, furthermore, is put into the hands of the people of God, so that they may read it and understand it for themselves. The same principle of individuation in the encounter with the Spirit leads to the plethora of new endeavours that, in varieties of Protestant and especially evangelical Protestant practice, lead to such an entrepreneurial approach to the life of the church, to missionary labours, church planting, and so on.

All of this, we may say, belongs to the different gifts, the different ministries and energies that the Spirit gives, and of which the New Testament speaks. Here the Spirit can seem wild and free, blowing where it wills, untamed and anarchic—for this reason highly centralized authority structures in the older churches find it hard to fathom, and the tendency is to impose some control, to stifle and quench the fire before it gets out of control. But if the cause of Christian unity is to see progress, it is essential that some language be found by which this work of the Spirit, which is characterized by such diversity and individuation, be owned by the wider Christian church, else we will be likely to find ourselves unable, for example, to accommodate those new forms of Christianity that are emerging under these auspices in places such as West Africa, which are fast becoming the new demographic centres of the Christian church globally.

This movement of the Spirit towards diversity, from the centre to the edges, is a risky venture that threatens the stability of the centre, and yet it is an essential dynamic in the life of the people of God. There is a Christological dimension here too that it is important to name, for this expression of the Spirit amid all the exigencies of history and culture, in the multitude of human personalities to whom the Spirit is given, reflects the coming of the Word of God, not merely into a portion of human nature, but into the whole sphere of the human. Even sin and death are not excluded. The incarnation of the Son of God leaves nothing of what it is to be human "unassumed," and certainly modern theology tends to emphasize that the *assumptio carnis* extends even to the embracing of human psychological, social and spiritual development, so that the incarnate Son did not know all things, and walked by faith rather than by sight. More astonishing still is that even his being made sin for us, to cite Paul (2 Cor 5:21), does not contradict his being the Holy One, of one substance with the Father, for just this one is the Lamb slain from the foundation of the world. Karl Barth speaks of this under the heading of the humiliation of the Son of God, and finds God's glory expressed nowhere more clearly or in more exalted fashion than in his identification with what is abased and inglorious, in the obedience of the Son of God and in his submission to the death of the cross. For Barth, the whole difference between true God and the false gods is that the latter are projections of human pride, whereas, as Barth puts it, "God is not proud."[11] The false gods accordingly not only do not but *can* not stoop to be the one who God is in Christ: the Servant who washes the disciples' feet, the one who takes upon himself the sin of the world. Similarly, Hans Urs von Balthasar speaks of the abyss of non-being, the "integral experience of death," as he puts it, that is uniquely experienced by Jesus—so that we are spared it.[12] In the paschal mystery, death and hell and rejection are taken up into the very relations constituting the Trinitarian life of God. In von Balthasar's extraordinary theology, in fact, the point at which the crucified Lord cries out, "Why have you forsaken me?" is the very point at which his union with the Father in obedient self-giving is most obviously demonstrated. And so God, as it were, is spent for the creature's debt—yet, as in Barth, here we find the most glorious exhibition of his deity, for the triune God from all eternity is none other than the ceaseless mutual self-surrender of the Father and the Son.

What I am attempting to argue is that we need to assume a similar generosity on the part of God in the work of the Spirit. Unfortunately, there is a tendency to suppose instead that the Spirit's work is something that must be subordinated at all points to juridical authority and rational control. Accordingly, I would suggest that the whole problem of the communion of the church tends in consequence to be understood in astonishingly superficial, theologically innocuous, legalistic terms, as by a process of linear reasoning some are said to be one with God in the church, while the one who lives by the anarchic wind of the Spirit places himself or herself beyond communion. To cite von Balthasar once more—who here again is deeply indebted to Barth—we need a genuinely theological account of communion, one that is sensitive to the fact that there is a specific "theo-logic" established by God himself that contradicts the continuities of human reasoning.[13] For it was in his self-emptying in the suffering and death of Christ, when silence swallowed the Word of God, and revelation broke off, after all, that the

---

11. Barth, *Church Dogmatics*, IV/1, 159.

12. Von Balthasar, *Mysterium Paschale*, 168.

13. The sources are numerous and lengthy, but for a brief account, ibid., 23–36; 79–83.

Word of God was most authentically spoken. What the message of the cross can contribute to ecclesiology is nothing less than what is of paramount importance for the whole subject: that the love of God, and with it, the scope of what is capable of being used by God and brought into communion with God, reaches beyond the grasp of our own community, and embraces not only those who seem alien to us, but even what seems strictly alien to God.

I do not believe that the catholic Christian traditions have yet reconciled themselves to the heights and depths of this strange "theo-logic," though they have made enormous strides in the past century. However, it is not as if the situation with Protestants is any better. For here what is missing is precisely the other movement of the Spirit with which I began, which concerns not the principle of individuation but of unity. There is "one body and one Spirit"; there is "one Lord, one faith, one baptism, one God and Father of all" (Eph 4:4–6); yet in Protestant packaging the one faith comes, like Heinz beans, with 57 varieties in every tin. Protestantism characteristically conceives of the Holy Spirit as dwelling in the heart of the believer, rather than in the church, and the church is an aggregate of individuals in whom the Spirit is at work—rather than, as in the catholic traditions, the body, in which the Spirit is given to Christ the Head, and mediated by him to the members, a body complete with its varied ministries, its sense of continuity with the visible and invisible worlds, its life of sacramental worship. Hence in the ecclesiologically impoverished world of so much Protestant theology, there is scarcely any impetus to unity, or awareness of the theological importance of the issue, because there is a basic pneumatological one-sidedness. If the trouble with the catholic traditions is a certain difficulty in acknowledging the way that the Spirit is not merely found at the centre of the church but at its edges, and even well beyond them, the trouble with Protestantism is that it cannot perceive that the Spirit is moving from the edges to the centre, that the many are one body, and that the one body is utterly basic to Christian faith, confession, worship, and practice. It is for this reason that much Protestant ecumenical engagement desires not unity, but only the affirmation of difference, and with it intercommunion as the acknowledgement of the principle of individuation on which their existence depends.

This movement from the edges towards the centre too has a Christological dimension, for Christology is not only concerned with the movement by which God comes to the human creature, taking flesh by the Holy Spirit of the Virgin Mary and being made man; it is also about the movement by which those whom he makes his own are reconciled to God in one body and brought into the fellowship of the Father's house. Not only is there a descending movement, by which true God of true God identifies with the sinful lot of fallen humanity, but there is also an ascending movement, by which Christ identifies himself in his true humanity with the lot of humankind once more, leading them by the power of his Spirit in joyful obedience, raised from the dead and freed from the powers of darkness. Here the movement is not that of the one to the many, but that of the many, in the one Lord who is the Head, to God. This is something that Protestants seem to find particularly hard to grasp—so much so that one suspects that the future road of ecumenism can only be long and hard—but it is essential to a holistic Christology and to a balanced theology of the Holy Spirit.

Now if any of this is true, then it must be possible to see it reflected in the Eucharist, for the Eucharist sums up the whole mystery of the gospel; in fact it is just because it has this capacity to sum up the mystery that it is itself sacrament, with such extraordinary profundity and richness. In the Eucharist, however, there are these two movements, the first one of *katabasis*, by which Christ comes again, placing himself in the hands of men and women afresh; the second one of *anabasis*, by which Christ draws us into one body and causes us to share in his oblation, his obedient surrender to God. Both are pneumatological events, or perhaps better, each is an aspect of the one pneumatological event by which Christ is given to the world, and by which the world is renewed in him.

And what of inter-communion? It seems to me, as I have said, that the practice is understandable as a by-product of the desire not so much for unity as for the legitimation of difference. Real unity in fact is costly. Inter-communion is cheap. As something as simple as marriage reveals, unity requires renunciation of self, the cultivation over long years of patience, understanding, charity, and not least, faith in God. Yes, there are expressions of Christian unity that can be reduced to the rather different virtues of fear, submission and violence, and the history of the Christian church is unfortunately marred by them. But for Protestants to reduce the extraordinary level of attention and devotion—which is the word—by which the unity of the catholic traditions has been (however imperfectly) preserved over centuries to such a trivial question of power would be dishonest and irresponsible. Protestants need to grow a good deal wiser at this point, reflect much more deeply at the theological level, and learn to keep in step with the Spirit, who not only gives gifts to the many, but who calls the many to be one in Christ. Were Protestants to do so, their presently incoherent desire for "inter-communion" might yield to a grasp of why *communion* matters, and to a more coherent theology by which communion, rather than inter-communion, might be set at the centre of their ecumenical policy.

BIBLIOGRAPHY

Avis, Paul. *Reshaping Ecumenical Theology.* London: T. & T. Clark, 2010.
Balthasar, Hans Urs von. *Mysterium Paschale.* Translated by Aidan Nichols. Edinburgh: T. & T. Clark, 1990.
Barth, Karl. Church *Dogmatics.* Vol. IV/1. Edited by G. W. Bromiley and T. F. Torrance. Translated by Geoffrey W. Bromiley. Edinburgh: T. & T. Clark, 1959.
Bosch, David. *Transforming Mission.* Twentieth Anniversary Edition. Maryknoll, NY: Orbis, 2011.
Calvin, John. *Institutes of the Christian Religion.* Edited by John T. McNeill. Translated by Ford Lewis Battles. Philadelphia: Westminster, 1960.
Congar, Yves. *Diversity and Communion.* Translated by John Bowden. London: SCM, 1984.
Kasper, Walter. "Aspects of the Eucharist in Their Unity and Variety: On the Recent Discussion of the Fundamental Form and Meaning of the Eucharist." In *Theology & Church*, 177–94. Translated by Margaret Kohl. London: SCM, 1989.
Newbigin, Lesslie. "On Being the Church for the World." In *Lesslie Newbigin, Missionary Theologian: A Reader.* Edited by Paul Weston. Grand Rapids: Eerdmans, 2006.
Pannenberg, Wolfhart. *Systematic Theology.* 3 vols. Translated by Geoffrey W. Bromiley. Grand Rapids: Eerdmans, 1991–93.

2

Bible and Eucharist

In an Incarnational Model

—*Denis Farkasfalvy, O. Cist.*

General Introduction

THE STUDY OF THE second century introduced me not only to Ignatius, Justin, Irenaeus, and Tertullian, but also to Baptists, Disciples, Church of Christ, and the rich evangelical variety present in the Dallas Theological Seminary, in one word: to a much more diverse and dynamic reality of Protestantism than what was known to me from my Hungarian roots through my acquaintance with the traditional churches of Lutherans and Calvinists.

This may sound as a very awkward opening statement, yet the reality to which I try to point is both embarrassing and possibly profound. My New Testament studies offered constant documentation for two processes flowing in opposite directions in church history. In both the history of the church at large and the history I witnessed as a young student in the Catholic Church I noticed an ongoing urge to go back to the sources and yet an effort of explaining and justifying the current state of affairs in various denominations by forces of historical development.

PART 1: PLENARY PRESENTATIONS

"Back to the Sources!" was the slogan of the Catholic Renewal which led to the documents of the Second Vatican Council. But a closer involvement in ecumenical relations opened my eyes to see that the post-Reformational splintering of the church with new denominations appearing was usually inspired by this same slogan. It was interesting for me to notice how in a sense my own whole faith life benefitted from various demands urging to return to the sources: *REDITUS AD FONTES*:

- my spiritual family, the Cistercian Order, was itself the product of a reform with a program of returning to the "purity of the Rule of Benedict"; then every *later reform* of the same family claimed to be a return to the twelfth-century model of Citeaux.
- in the pre-Vatican II liturgical movement the ideal was a return to the "Golden Age" of patristic liturgy in the fourth and fifth centuries.
- the biblical renewal of the 1950's held as its golden measure the "apostolic age" (which practically meant the sub-apostolic age of the late first and early second century.)
- In ecumenism, a number of superimposed models were at work creating the well-known ambiguities bordering on dishonesty in the various dialogues.

It seems to me that the Second-Century Seminar, a brainchild of Albert Outler advising to use the study of the second century as a tool by which an ecumenical path may be found came from a clear vision that everybody wants to go back to the sources and that a return to the New Testament as the "ultimate common" source fascinates all Christians. But the antechamber of the apostolic age, offering a viable entrance to it, is the second century, —an age in which for the first time the model of a return to the sources was formulated—and so its study is an excellent context for ecumenical work.

What I will present today belongs to a composite genre. It is not only some biblical and some patristic theology, but an effort of working toward a doctrinal synthesis, based on Christological foundations, defined in Nicaea and Chalcedon, but also combined with insights from modern biblical and patristic studies. I will begin with four short sections, which I will call our four foundational themes.

First Theme: Return to the Sources

My first thesis is that many or most of the attempts to return to ultimate sources are more or less vitiated by various evolutionary models, based on ambiguities or errors. All Christian theologies are held hostage by a culture which identifies the historically authentic with the original and the original with words that were exactly said or events photographically described, the famous *ipsissima verba* and *what really happened*, and so we have an indomitable passion to fall back on what is chronologically the earliest. But, at the same time we easily flip-flop the rules of the game and identify the ultimate model with the cumulative result of an evolution i.e., as the best and clearest, the perfect outcome of a process of development. So, really my first theme is that, when speaking about history of doctrines, we badly need to clarify the methodology and ask: what are we really after?

Is there a biblical model of "evolution," based on some general Christological principle, omnipresent in the New Testament, which could regulate our concept of what to return to and how? I think there is such a thing and can be expressed in several biblical formulations, of which I quote here three, one from Mark, one from John and one from Hebrews:

> [The Kingdom of God] is like a mustard seed, which, when sown upon the ground, is the smallest of all the seeds on earth; yet when it is sown it grows up and becomes the greatest of all shrubs, and puts forth large branches, so that the birds of the air can make nests in its shade. (Mark 4:31–32)

> Very truly, I tell you, unless a grain of wheat falls into the earth and dies, it remains just a single grain; but if it dies, it bears much fruit. (John 12:24)

These two open the door for recognizing a "development of doctrine" in which the Incarnate Word is a fellow traveler with humanity. But here comes the third biblical quotation:

> Jesus Christ is the same yesterday and today and forever. (Heb 13:8)

To summarize this theme, I state that the Incarnate Word of God has *a sameness but with a dynamic potentiality of addressing man in his historical existence*. Moreover, this dynamic aspect is an integral part of the understanding of the Incarnation according to its fully developed conceptualization in Nicaea and Chalcedon. The meaning and relevance of the Logos are successively revealed so that the Word may penetrate our historically unfolding existence as we progress both individually and collectively to its full realization.

Second Theme: The Dynamic Meaning of the Incarnation

This is about the Incarnation and is an application of the doctrine of Chalcedon. In agreement with what was said above, God reveals himself ultimately as "God made Man" but in God's incarnate self-revelation a twofold character must be discerned and each equally honored. In the Incarnation an eternal unchanging sameness is linked to continued growth and development. This statement is based on some, at least two, presuppositions.

a. It states the full humanity and full divinity of the Incarnate Word. Full humanity means that Jesus is human also in a dynamic sense of the term: his humanity was undergoing physical, mental, and emotional growth. Fully human meant an ongoing process of change in the assumed human nature. But change in human nature implied no change in the divine nature. Yet it meant that God was consubstantially linked to this ongoing process of human development through Jesus, and the divine person was experienced by this consubstantially united human nature in the context of a continuously developing flux. It is in a dynamic development that the human nature of Jesus was growing toward a fullness of self-realization and the experience of unity with God, as it became obedient, on its way to become a full sacrificial gift and the flesh-and-blood expression of the Son, consubstantial with the Father.

b. This is why God's self-disclosure in Jesus constitutes true history: It was the Divine Person (not just an individual nature as a separately existing human being called Jesus) who was born, grew up, lived, died and rose to glory. I think this is the full meaning of the pre-Pauline formula embedded in Rom 1:3–4:

> the Gospel concerning his Son who was a descendant of David according to the flesh, who was appointed the Son-of-God-in-power according to the spirit of holiness by the resurrection from the dead, Jesus Christ our Lord.

The summary and peak of divine revelation is, therefore, not reducible to a set of propositional truths or a doctrinal system combined with a list of codified moral precepts. Revelation cannot be identified with a time-bound slice of what Christ was at a given time with a petrified final outcome. It is the Incarnate Word's full journey in his comprehensive motion from the Father and to the Father. In Christ an individual human life has been taken up and was, in course of his human history of development, fully integrated into the divine person's unity with the Godhead.

c. Also the doctrine of the church as body of Christ must be seen under this dynamic aspect. While Jesus' individual incarnate human life was finite and finalized by being summoned up into eternity at his resurrection, in virtue of the outpouring of the Spirit, his expanding presence in human history continues and expands the process which began at the Incarnation but now continues its course to the eschatological end.

Third Theme: The Cumulative Character of Salvation History

The third theme is this: the reality of Christ, historical, glorified, ecclesial and eschatological must not be reduced to something less than the complete presence of the fullness of humanity in the glorified Christ or less than a presence of divinity in the work of the Holy Spirit, the earthly body of Christ, the church.

In God's salvation plan the phases do not nullify, do not cancel or push into oblivion the earlier ones. Rather, to state it in positive terms, Christ as expressed in his historical humanity, Christ glorified and thus manifested as the foundation stone of a world to come and Christ discerned as incarnate in his body, the church, and, finally Christ announced in proclamation through sacrament and scripture are not collapsible into one static and one-dimensional entity. There is, of course, sameness and oneness of Christ which is not merely a matter of perception: the incarnate divine son is one and indivisibly united with the Father through the Spirit. This oneness includes that unity into which one single individual human nature is glued with the Son of God. But this oneness also means God's unity with redeemed mankind, united through the Spirit into one body of Christ. In that sense Jesus Christ is the same yesterday, today and forever.

In this aeon, Christ is both fully revealed and yet on its way to a full manifestation which is still to come. The dynamic character of revelation allows, even requires, that we state both the completeness of the process of revelation terminating in Christ and the ongoing nature of revelation, still to continue in history. Since the human beings who are members of his church still make part of a changing world, they are as if "swimming" in the stream of time and historicity. Thus Christ keeps on coming to humankind, both individually and collectively, as something both old and new. At any point in time, when listening to God's word, we look back to the past and look forward to a future. We grow and develop as we move on. But since the eternal Son has fully become man and has fully run the course of his biographical history from birth to death and beyond death into glory, God's coming to man is complete on the side of the divine initiative. Yet in terms of the human response and reception, his full arrival to humanity is still incomplete and in process.

Fourth Theme: A Threefold Analogy

"On the night he was betrayed" Jesus performs an action which becomes the exemplar of a specifically Christian ritual. The linkage between the Last Supper and the Eucharist of the early church is based on sufficient number of explicit testimonies so that even on a rationalistic basis its historical authenticity is beyond reasonable doubt.

From what we said about the history of revelation, it appears that the eucharistic moment in this history is that point at which God's self-disclosure through the incarnate son comes to *completion* in his mortal body and Christ's journey takes off to both eternity and a new phase into the rest of human history. It is the moment at which Jesus' finite earthly life of some thirty years closes and thus arrives at the threshold of eternity. But this is the point at which, he is constituted "God's Son according to the Spirit of holiness" (Rom 1:4).

We understand this if we realize that the whole Christ, existing in history, eternity and in the church, is summarized in the act of Jesus' self-offering in death and the resurrection which follows, as an act in which his sacrifice is accepted by the Father. In this way every moment of his human history and the entire reality of his glorious eternal life become accessible to every created human being destined to become "church": to all those who are part of the flow of history and are called to be incorporated into his body. This is the meaning of what has been stated, that his death and rising are sacramentally celebrated, i.e., made present for participation in the Eucharist up to the end of time until he comes again.

One is tempted to turn to a geometric model in the following way. At the Last Supper in the form of the foundational act of the Eucharist, when Jesus offers his body and blood to the Father and distributes them to the disciples, Christ, with his sacrifice to be accepted and to be ratified in his resurrection, becomes the center of history. For that point of his Passover from time to eternity makes him "equidistant" i.e., equally accessible and equally important for every point of the human time line. The Johannine gospel says that this action results in his "being lifted up": to that I add that this action makes him equidistant or, maybe more correctly, equally near to all points in time. I speak in terms of a spatial and temporal metaphors but the value of the image lies in the way the metaphor conveys a meaning. To describe in other terms: Christ, the person existing in two natures offered himself to the Father for all mankind and his offering was accepted. What does this mean? It means that in the one and same act in which he accepted his death, he became fully connected with all the children of Adam, not only in their nature but also in their sinfulness. His death is, as a completed act of obedience and self-denial, an act by which he gave himself over and away to embrace and encompass all humanity so as to integrate it into the Trinitarian relationship of the Son. His resurrection makes him, as the firstborn of the dead, the first building stone of the world to come, enter into divine life. The high-priestly prayer in John's gospel summarizes this in a sacerdotal language: "I consecrate myself for them—but not only for them, but all who through their word will come to believe in me."[1]

Proposal of an Incarnational Understanding of Scripture and Eucharist

We must stop here for a moment and ponder. Accepting death, Jesus' incarnate life explicitly plunges him by an ultimate act into our sin-burdened existence as sons of Adam. At the height of his act of obedience, when we could correctly think he reveals himself as most distant from us (fully sinless and self-giving), he accepts full share in our sinfulness. For death

---

1. "For their sake I consecrate myself so that they too may be consecrated in truth. I pray not only for these but also for those who through their teaching will come to believe in me." (John 17:19–20)

entered the world through sin (cf. Rom 5:12; Wis 2:24) and he, although sinless, dies as a victim of murder. In this context one may understand and affirm that the work of our redemption reaches its summit in the Eucharist.

For an exegete, this means that the Last Supper is integral part of the Passion Narrative.[2] Moreover it also implies that Jesus' conscious acceptance of his sacrificial death goes beyond telling with certainty how Isa 53 fared in Jewish interpretation of the first half of the first century, and so how consciously it was present in Jesus's mind at the Last Supper or how many of Jesus' utterances in Gethsemane are *ipsissima verba Jesu*. The breaking of bread as body to die, the pouring out of wine as blood to be shed, the secretive gathering in the upper room, the foretelling of Judas' betrayal, the foretelling of Peter's denial, the agonizing moments in the garden and the disciples overcome by sleep cannot be reasonably dealt with as clips of a colorful story invented or standardized piece-by-piece and sown into a narrative whole by the "early church." There is a global story rooted in reality antedating the pieces of the mosaic examined in isolation by redaction criticism. Without this global reality supporting the narrative whole, there is no early church. If there is no factual basis to the pieces, there is no force and no reason by which human beings would gather into assemblies celebrating these facts in communion with Jesus who rose after such a death. Nor would there be reasons by which to explain the blitz of mere twenty five years carrying the Eucharist from Jerusalem to Corinth and Rome all across the Roman Empire, together with the message of Jesus' expiatory death and salvific resurrection and thus creating a major discontinuity in Greco-Roman and Jewish history.

Historians and theologians of liturgy need an explanation of the origins of the Christian cult. The rise and fall of Bultmann's theory about a Greco-Roman cultic myth re-enacted by Pauline churches should have raised enough caution for historians not to relegate the origin of the Eucharist to a slowly developing innovation by the Pauline churches but place it among the words and deeds of Jesus in immediate succession to the Last Supper and in continuity with the table fellowship of the disciples with Jesus.

The same applies to what is the kernel of Christian belief in the incarnation. Jesus' relationship to the Father belongs to the most intimate layer of his words about his identity. I refer here to his word of exultant

---

2. Curiously, after some hesitation, Raymond Brown did not include the Supper into his *The Death of the Messiah*.

jubilation over what others might have viewed as a fiasco but he sees it as the Father's will coming to fulfillment as his identity is revealed and only to those whom his gracious will had elected, those who are mere children in spirit, small, poor and humble: "All things have been handed over to me by my father; and no one knows the Son except the Father; nor does anyone know the Father except the Son, and anyone to whom the Son wills to reveal him." (Matt 11:27)

The revelation of the son's incarnation and that of his self-sacrifice to the Father belong together. They are not understandable but at the price of major distortions if separated from each other. The stable verbal expression of divine revelation takes place in the scriptures. On the other hand, the ongoing contact with the risen Lord, who is described in the fourth gospel as carrying the marks of his crucifixion on his body and is pictured as the Lamb slain in the book of Revelation, is provided to the church throughout its entire history in the Eucharist.

I am stating in these words an unbreakable link between Bible and Eucharist, which, of course, applies only to the canonical unity of the Old and New Testaments. The Bible can be read, of course, without Christ and Christology with a reduced and limited level of meaning as it happens in the synagogue or any assembly of believers who do not pursue in principle the reference of the Old Testament to the New or who see the presence of Christ at the Eucharist in one or another reductionist way, a matter that has been and is under dispute on many levels.

But both historically and theologically the essential link between incarnation and revelation with its biblical expression on the one hand, and incarnation and Eucharist as extension of Christ' presence and availability on the other, must remain assured. Otherwise, the fullness of Christ's accessibility in the church is unduly restricted, theology becomes incomplete, the faithful are deprived of a fullness that had been divinely willed, the spiritual climate of church life becomes unhealthy and spirituality becomes lopsided.

Conclusion: Word Incarnate in Scripture and Sacrament

Christ in the world can be appropriated by all human beings by faith and grace. But faith is response to his word and grace is mediated through the incarnate Logos. "Heaven and Earth pass away, but my words do not pass away." The word of God remains forever not because of its human qualities or ultimate eloquence but on account of the risen Christ in whom all revelation and sanctification have reached their peak and are summarized. The celebration of the Eucharist is virtually one single continuous act constituted by divine will. The command "Do this unto my memory!" is not only a command by a man given to human beings to keep him alive as a subject of human memory. The command is carried out due to the divine empowerment which accompanied it. The Eucharist was willed as final testament to remain operational until the end of the aeon, the parousia.

Origen, when reflecting on what constitutes the dignity of God's scriptural word, compared it to the flesh of the Logos as well as the bread and wine of the eucharistic celebration. Before the ontological disputes broke out in the church about the Eucharist in much later centuries, there was such a teaching about a twofold analogy of the flesh taken up in the incarnation by the Logos, yet containing three dimensions of God's self-giving to mankind:

1. Humanity and divinity in Christ, mean not only, in a static sense, the assumption of a human nature by the Son, expressed through a human being of flesh and blood but the drama of his descent as *kenosis*, and his ascent in glory.

2. The bread and wine as food and drink in sensible signs provide Jesus' actual and effective presence to satisfy man's spiritual hunger and thirst, and transmit divine life to the soul at the present with immortality in the life to come.

3. The words of his prophets and apostles document and comment on the journey of the Logos into the realm of flesh but also operates as power and wisdom for the whole man, soul and body, by transmitting the grace of liberation from sin and a share in Christ's glorious everlasting life.

Henri de Lubac in his *Histoire et Esprit*[3] inserted a chapter under the title "The Incorporations of the Logos." He chose these words carefully so that the analogies of the Incarnation would not obscure the uniqueness of the Incarnation and that they (Bible and Eucharist) would be kept pointing not just to the *sarx*, the realm of sinful flesh but also to the *soma*, the glorified body of the risen Christ and the ecclesial body of Christ.

---

3. De Lubac, *Histoire et Esprit*, 336–63.

Much more could be said about this threefold analogy—Incarnate Christ, and his two modes of continued presence, Eucharist and Scripture.

There is a large array of patristic and medieval texts in which the Latin word *sacramentum* corresponding to the Greek *mysterion* is used in a variety of ways, often designating various facets of institutions, forms and manifestations of the life of grace in the church wherever the twofold structure, divine and human, of the Incarnate Logos manifests itself. Much of this was studied in Origen and Augustine, but starting with Tertullian and continuing in the Latin West, there is a widened semantic field giving rise to even more theological concepts. The different phases of scholasticism complicated this history, and the Protestant Reformation erupted into disagreements about the term "sacrament" and its meaning bringing about confusion and impoverishment on both sides of the Catholic/Protestant conflict. Since the issue has not been sufficiently studied, many ancient texts involving the term "sacrament" were unduly criticized, rejected or exalted. So the various uses of the term still remain obscure. Maybe it was helpful that Semmelroth and Schillebeckx began speaking about Christ as *Ursakrament* or primordial sacrament, reducing the concept to its Christological root. In fact, the Incarnate Son with his acts and words can be called the primordial sacrament and so each and every manifestation of Christ carries a certain "sacramental structure" of the human and divine elements. This would grant the church as a whole a sacramental character, implied in the image of the ecclesial body of Christ. In this sense the word "sacrament" may obtain a generalized meaning, but the history of the term becomes even less transparent.

Further and more detailed conclusions are potentially very numerous and broad. I will make only four and try to be concise.

1. At its birth scripture is incarnational. By this I should point to the role of the Holy Spirit by whom the Word became flesh and the analogous role of the same Spirit whose inspiration caused the word to become scripture. Hugo Rahner coined a German word which was taken up and used with some frequency by Hans Urs von Balthasar. The word is *Schriftwerdung*, coined to the analogy of *Fleischwerdung* (which translated the Latin *Incarnatio* into German) and meaning the process by which the verbal message becomes Scripture.[4] In those same years,

---

4. Hugo Rahner, "Das Menschenbild des Origenes" may be the first occurrence of the term *Schriftwerdung*, taken over by Hans Urs von Balthasar in his essay, "Schrift, Wort, Tradition."

Hugo's brother, Karl Rahner, also began writing about inspiration as a process, by which divine revelation, happening in words and deeds, *becomes scripture* as it is being carried and is spread by oral processes of preaching and tradition until it finally obtains the shape of an authoritative text. He also compares inspiration with Incarnation[5] but abstains—as far as I can guess, on purpose—from using the expression *Schriftwerdung*, probably because he sees in it a word-game dangerous to Christological precision. But as long as we see the validity of this analogy with its limits, the word is very useful since it has the power of summarizing a whole paragraph of an explanation.

2. But one may go on and say that Scripture is born from and for the Eucharist.

   a. That Scripture is born from the Eucharist is more obviously argued for in the case of the New Testament, because of the way we see history as a linear process and realize that both the Gospels and the apostolic letters reflect the ecclesial reality of the eucharistic assemblies in which the apostles and their co-workers transmit the apostolic preaching in both dealing with Jesus' words and deeds and reproducing or expanding the apostolic explanation and applications of the gospel received from the Lord. The cradle of the New Testament into which it was born is in fact the eucharistic assembly. But we learn time and again and increasingly accept something similar about the origins of the Old Testament. For also the books of the Hebrew Scriptures, at least in the way Jesus and the apostolic church read them, have come about in anticipation of the eucharistic assembly, namely the community life and constitutive experiences of the people of God, in both the *Torah* and the *Prophets*.

   b. Saying that Scripture came about *for* the Eucharist is equally valid. Scriptures' basic function in Christianity for which it was thought to have been ultimately written, copied, canonized and kept sacred was to form the mind and heart for the spiritual table fellowship with Jesus, for eating his body and drinking his blood under the sign of bread and wine:

    > For whatever was written in former days was written for our instruction, that by steadfastness and by the

---

5. Karl Rahner, *Über die Schriftinspiration*, 22 n. 5.

encouragement of the scriptures we might have hope. (Rom 15:4)

The report of Justin Martyr about the eucharistic assembly in the way it was celebrated around AD 150 is rather late and the reports of Acts about the breaking of the bread as a cultic event may be insufficiently explicit to convince those who want to disagree with their interpretation in the late second century. Rather than to lose myself in detailed arguing about Luke and Acts in this regard, I want to make some additional points.

3. Those who study the theology of the liturgy in its history are acquainted with the role of the *Epiclesis*, the invoking of the Holy Spirit upon the gifts of bread and wine before the words of the institutions are pronounced over them. While we often mention how the meaning and importance of the *Epiclesis* has faded in the West and has gone through a regrettable eclipse, the point can also be made how in the importance of the *Epiclesis* an awareness is expressed of a parallelism between the role of the Spirit in making the Eucharist happen and the role of inspiration by the same Spirit without which there can be no holy scripture. One should add—and I am quoting the document *Dei Verbum* of the Second Vatican Council—that, in fact, Scriptures "should be read in the same Spirit in which they have been composed."[6] A Spirit-filled Church celebrating its sacraments, and reading the scriptures in the same Spirit that moved the biblical authors and now moves the hearts of the faithful is a patristic model that has regrettably faded but is re-appearing in the church as an important priority in our times.

4. The relationship of scripture and Eucharist which I tried to outline could be developed on the basis of the gospel of John alone, mainly on chapter six, the eucharistic discourse about the "Bread descended from Heaven," which feeds by both the Lord's word proclaimed and his body and blood sacrificed, those who receive them in faith. One could make an exclusively Johannine presentation about the connections and parallelisms of incarnation, revelation and Eucharist, quoting mostly texts of the Fourth Gospel but in the light of their patristic

---

6. "Sacra Scriptura eodem Spiritu quo scripta est etiam legenda et interpretanda sit." This statement is found in no. 12 of the Apostolic Constitution *Dei Verbum* with a footnote referencing it to S. Jerome's *Commentary on Galatians* 5, 19–21: *Patrologia Latina* 26, 417 A.

exegesis. And we know from the Johannine use of "scripture" (*graphein* and *graphe*) how in the Johannine writings both law and the prophets and the Lord's teaching but also the Fourth Gospel itself are thought of as written texts.[7] This applies also to the first Johannine epistle, in which the teaching of the author as an eye- and ear-witness testifies to "what has been made manifest" (1:1–2) in a written document. This is the only book of scriptures in which the author emphasizes the importance of his testimony in written form by repeating nine times the phrase "I am writing to you" (*grapho/egrapsa* 1 John 2:1–13).

Bibliography

Balthasar, Hans Urs von. "Schrift, Wort, Tradition." In *Verbum Caro: Skizzen zur Theologie*, 1:11–24. Basel: Johannes, 1960.
Brown, Raymond E. *The Death of the Messiah : from Gethsemane to the Grave*. New York: Doubleday, 1994.
Lubac, Henri de. *Histoire et Esprit, L' intelligence de l'Ecriture d'après Origène*. Paris: Aubier, 1950.
Rahner, Hugo. "Das Menschenbild des Origenes." *EJ* 15 (1947) 197–248.
Rahner, Karl. *Über die Schriftinspiration*. Freiburg: Herder, 1958.

---

7. John 1:45; 2:17, 22; 5:39, 46; 6:31; 7:38, 42; 8:6–8; 10:35; 13:18; 17:12; 20:30–31; 21:24–25; 19:24, 28, 36–37.

3

Church and Eucharist in the Orthodox Tradition

—Paul Meyendorff

IT WOULD BE NO exaggeration to say that the Twentieth century, which concluded just a few years ago, was the age of eucharistic ecclesiology, not just for the Orthodox, but arguably for much of Christianity as well. This movement began with a revival in interest in the Eucharist, initially within Roman Catholicism and Orthodoxy, but then affecting mainline Protestantism as well, particularly after Vatican II.

The eucharistic revival simultaneously followed two main tracks. The first, particularly within Catholicism and Orthodoxy, led to an increase in the frequency of communion. The faithful, accustomed to partaking of communion only once or a few times a year, began receiving much more frequently, and often at every celebration of the Eucharist.[1] Second, but equally important, was an increased emphasis on the ecclesial dimension of the Eucharist. Orthodox theologians, building upon developments in biblical and patristic theology that began already in the nineteenth century,

---

1. It would be an exaggeration to say that the Eucharistic revival arose out of nothing in the twentieth century. Already in the nineteenth century, the Kollyvades in Greece, as well as St. John of Kronstadt in Russia, placed a strong emphasis on more frequent communion. Even earlier in the fourteenth and fifteenth centuries, the hesychast movement placed great stress on the Eucharist and on its reception—see especially the writings of Nicholas Cabasilas, *The Life in Christ* and the *Commentary on the Liturgy*.

twentieth-century theologians rediscovered the centrality of the Eucharist in the life of the church. Basing themselves on key scriptural passages, as well as the writings of Ignatius of Antioch, Maximus the Confessor, Nicholas Cabasilas, and others, leading modern Orthodox theologians—Nicholas Afanassiev, Alexander Schmemann, John Meyendorff, John Zizioulas, and their followers—focused on the Eucharist as the visible expression and manifestation of the church. Among Roman Catholics, in the decades leading up to Vatican II, leading scholars such as Jean Daniélou, Louis Bouyer, and Yves Congar, similarly discovered eucharistic ecclesiology through their reading of early Christian tradition and the Greek fathers, as well as their direct contacts with Orthodox theologians in France. This approach reached its apex in Vatican II's decree on the liturgy: "The liturgy ... most of all in the divine sacrifice of the Eucharist, is the outstanding means whereby the faithful may express in their lives and manifest to others the mystery of Christ and the real nature of the true church."[2] Subsequent to Vatican II, many Protestant churches similarly underwent eucharistic revivals of their own, and the language of "*koinonia*," with its strong eucharistic overtones, entered the ecumenical vocabulary.

It should be stated at the outset, however, that eucharistic ecclesiology—and, indeed, ecclesiology as a distinct discipline—is essentially a modern phenomenon. Take, for instance, the Nicene-Constantinopolitan creed, a statement of fundamental Christian faith shared by the vast majority of Christians across the world. After a concise affirmation about the Father follows a long and developed section about the Son, a rather brief but dense formulation about the Holy Spirit,[3] then only a few words about the church, defining it as "one, holy, catholic, and apostolic." The text then concludes with brief but important statements about baptism and the future resurrection, and there is not a single word about the Eucharist. It is remarkable that so little attention is paid to defining the Church, and this precisely at a time when it was racked by deep divisions and when the need to articulate clear boundaries was apparent. In fact, one has to wait until the modern era to find any significant reflection on the nature of the church, not to mention its connection to the Eucharist.

This lack of a clearly formulated eucharistic ecclesiology, however, does not imply its absence, but only its explicit articulation. In what follows,

2. *Constitution on the Sacred Liturgy*, Par. 2.

3. We need not here go into the later addition of the *filioque*, which was later to cause so much controversy between East and West.

then, I propose to reflect on my own, Eastern Orthodox tradition, to see what it offers. Though the initial articulation of eucharistic ecclesiology is found in the works of Nicolas Afanasiev, particularly his work *Trapeza Gospodnia* ("Table of the Lord"), published in 1952,[4] its clearest formulation is found in the writings of John Zizioulas, particularly chapter four of his *Being as Communion*, entitled "Eucharist and Catholicity," which I will follow here.[5]

The clearest expression in scripture of eucharistic ecclesiology is to be found in 1 Cor 10:16–17: "The cup of blessing which we bless, is it not a participation [κοινωνία] in the blood of Christ? The bread which we break, is it not a participation [κοινωνία] in the body of Christ? Because there is one bread, we who are many are one body, for we all partake of the one bread."[6] Thus it is precisely our participation in the Eucharist that unites the people into one corporate personality, the body of Christ—an idea drawn from the Old Testament notion of the corporate "servant of God." This notion of unity is further developed by St Paul in other passages, including Gal 3:28; 2 Cor 11:2, Eph 2:15; etc. In the Gospel of John, the theme of the Last Discourse is precisely the "unity of all in Christ," so that "they all may be one"; and in John 6, this unity is achieved precisely through the eating of the "Bread of Life."

Even more explicit is 1 Cor 11:17–22, particularly the subordinate clause in verse 18: "When you assemble as a church" (συνερχομένων ὑμῶν ἐν ἐκκλησίᾳ). Literally, Paul is saying that they gather together **to be** the church, and the context is clearly the Eucharist: they come together as the church to be gathered in the Eucharist. Paul then goes on to criticize them for failing to be united, and he warns the Corinthians, in the starkest possible language, that "it is not the Lord's Supper that you eat."

Others at the conference will be speaking about the Eucharist in the New Testament, so I will simply affirm the absolute importance of the Eucharist in the apostolic church. The church as ἐκκλησία ("the gathering") is central to St Paul's understanding of church, and Sunday, the first and eighth day came to be the privileged time for the eucharistic gathering. The expression, "the Lord's Day," very early on applied to Sunday, derives from the fact that this was the day on which the "Lord's Supper" was celebrated. Further evidence for the centrality of the Eucharist comes from the fact that

---

4. Afanasiev, *Trapeza gospodnia* (in Russian).
5. Zizioulas, *Being as Communion*:143–69.
6. Biblical quotations are from the RSV.

the theme of Jesus' expiatory suffering in the synoptic gospels and 1 Corinthians appears precisely in the institution narratives at the Last Supper.[7]

Thus, to summarize Zizioulas' argument, the "whole church" (Rom 16:23), "dwelling in a certain city" (1 Cor 1:2; 2 Cor 1:1; 1 Thess 1:1; Acts 11:22), would "come together" (1 Cor 11:20, 33, 34; Ignatius, *To the Ephesians*, 5:2–3), mainly on Sunday, to "break bread" (Acts 2:46; 20:7). This assembly, or *synaxis*, would be the only one in that place in the sense that it would include the whole church. Zizioulas then goes on to describe this eucharistic community as one that transcends all natural and social divisions, one in which there is neither Jew nor Greek, male or female, adult or child, rich or poor, slave or free.

Again basing himself on scriptural and early patristic texts, he goes on to describe the structure of the eucharistic community, which contains one altar, behind which stands the throne of the one bishop. Around the bishop stand the presbyters, next to him the deacons who assist him in the celebration, and in front stand all the "people of God" (λαὸς τοῦ θεοῦ), the order of baptized Christians. The bishop represents all the people to God: he presides over the assembly and brings their offering to God. He is the one in whom the many are united and become one. Zizioulas quotes texts such as Ignatius' *Letter to the Smyrneans* 8: "The sole Eucharist you should consider valid is one that is celebrated by the bishop himself, or by some person authorized by him. Where the bishop is to be seen, there let all the people be; just as wherever Jesus Christ is present, we have the catholic Church." Zizioulas thus concludes that the very idea of the episcopate develops out of the eucharistic community. It is no accident that, until the present day, ordinations always take place in the context of a eucharistic liturgy, because orders exist for and within the eucharistic community that is the church. In contemporary Orthodox practice, ordinations to the major orders (deacon, presbyter, bishop) take place at various points to the liturgy that reflect the particular liturgical role of each order.

Such an approach, which is found in the earliest available sources, clearly reflects a bottom-up ecclesiology, as it begins with the concrete, local eucharistic community, and not with a universal church that then finds its local expression. Thus, in the text from Ignatius just cited, the word "catholic" does not mean "universal," as it is sometimes translated, but

---

7. The differences that exist between the various accounts stem primarily from the different applications of suffering servant and covenant themes (Isa 53; Jer 31:31–34; Ex 24:8).

"full," or "complete." In other words, the fullness of the church is realized in the eucharistic assembly, presided over by its bishop, and is perforce an event situated in a particular time and place.

What, then, is the connection between the local and the universal? Certainly, the above approach could lead one to think that, since the local eucharistic community is already "catholic," then there is no need for anything more. An overly literal reading of Afanassiev could, indeed lead to such a conclusion; and our earliest sources do indicate that each local church did experience a high level of autonomy. Yet, from the very beginning, there was also a strong sense of connection among the local churches, so that St Paul, for example, urged the Corinthians, when they gathered each Sunday, to take up collections for the church in Jerusalem.[8] Both the initial apostles and their disciples traveled freely from church to church, and a council of apostles and elders in Jerusalem, described in Acts 15, resolved the thorny issue of whether the Jewish Law applied to Gentile converts. It is clear, therefore, that there is no mutual exclusion between local and universal. Very soon, this found a liturgical expression in the requirement that the ordination of bishops required the participation of at least two or three bishops from neighboring churches.[9] This same requirement also served as a factor in the development of church councils, which would meet not just for the ordination of bishops, but also to address common challenges, to settle differences, and, more importantly, to preserve the (eucharistic) communion between local churches. And ultimately, it led to the development of regional structures with their regional synods, and, by the fourth century, to the age of ecumenical councils.

The main point in all this is simply that the Eucharist has, from the very beginning, been the realization of the church and the visible sign of unity at all levels. Individual Christians become members of the church through baptism and live out their membership with the local eucharistic community, which gathers on the first day of the week to break bread. Eucharistic communion among local churches within dioceses, territorial churches, or at the global level is the primary visible sign and realization of church unity.

Allow me, then, to give two concrete example of the way in which this is understood and practiced in the Orthodox tradition.

---

8. 1 Cor 16:1–3.
9. Hippolytus, *Apostolic Tradition* 2, and in the later canonical tradition.

PART 1: PLENARY PRESENTATIONS

Diptychs

In contemporary Orthodox liturgical practice, when the primate of an Orthodox Church presides at the liturgy, the primates of all the other autocephalous and autonomous churches are commemorated on several occasions: just prior to the Trisagion, at the Great Entrance, and at the conclusion of the anaphora, or eucharistic prayer. These commemorations are an affirmation of the full communion among the local churches, and omitting any name therefore indicates a break in communion. This is what happened just a few years ago when the Patriarchate of Moscow removed the name of the Patriarch of Constantinople from the diptychs following a disagreement over the status of the Orthodox Church in Estonia. As a result, Russian Orthodox clergy were forbidden from concelebrating with clergy belonging to the Ecumenical Patriarchate. Fortunately, the rift was quickly resolved and the Ecumenical Patriarch's name was restored into the diptychs of the Russian Orthodox Church.

I will focus here on the commemorations at the conclusion of the anaphora, known as the diptychs, which developed by the fourth century. They are called diptychs because they consist of two lists of names, of the living and the dead, written on two tablets. The lists would typically include the succession of local bishops, the names of bishops of other neighboring or important churches, local saints, and important theologians. These names would be read aloud by a deacon and served as a vivid expression of the church as a communion that transcends both space and time. The subject has been studied at length by the preeminent historian of the Byzantine liturgy, Robert Taft, and it is largely on the basis of his work that I present this summary.[10]

The origin of the diptychs is not clear, and Taft argues that they developed out of two distinct traditions. The first was the custom of commemorating those who offered gifts in the Eucharist, and those for whom the gifts were offered. In this case, the commemorations were made not as part of the anaphora, but in connection with the pre-anaphoral offering (which later became the *proskomide* or *prothesis* rite) or the transfer of gifts (which later became the Great Entrance). These commemorations remain to this day, in various forms. The second tradition develops out of the ancient practice of commemorating the living and the dead during the

---

10. Taft, *A History of the Liturgy.*

anaphora, or eucharistic prayer. In the course of time, the two traditions were essentially merged.[11]

The content of the diptychs in the two traditions varied. In some areas, the diptychs were local and variable, frequently *ad hoc*. They contained the names of those who offered gifts and those in whose memory they were offered. Increasingly, though not exclusively, the lists became official, ecclesial, hierarchical, and fixed. The diptychs of the dead reflected the official apostolic succession of the local church, and increasingly contained the names of prominent deceased hierarchs from other churches. With the latter development, the diptychs became confessional. The diptychs of the living shift toward a listing of the hierarchical order of the regional communion, from the patriarch and metropolitans down through the local authorities, ecclesial and civil. The shift toward more official lists was no doubt inspired by the schisms and doctrinal debates during the fourth through sixth centuries.

It is in the disputes between the churches of Alexandria, Antioch, and Constantinople that this latter aspect becomes most evident. A good example is the case of John Chrysostom, bishop of Constantinople from February 398 until his deposition and exile in June 404 and his death in Pontus in September 407. Chrysostom's deposition at the Synod of the Oak was led by his archenemy Theophilus of Alexandria. With Chrysostom's deposition, Arsacius (404–405) and Atticus (406–425) succeeded him in Constantinople, but Chrysostom's supporters rejected his deposition and refused to accept his successors. Chrysostom's deposition meant that he was removed from the diptychs. The church of Antioch, from which Chrysostom had come, restored his name to the diptychs in response to popular demand. Soon, we learn from a letter dated in 418 of Atticus to Cyril of Alexandria (the nephew of Theophilus) that Atticus had restored Chrysostom's name to the diptychs of Constantinople, also as a result of public pressure, thus resolving the internal schism in Constantinople. Cyril, however, saw this as a provocation and responded that to restore a defrocked bishop to the diptychs was not acceptable, especially among the list of bishops. Theodoret of Cyrrhus subsequently reports in his *Church History* V that the western churches accepted communion with the eastern bishops only after the eastern bishops had restored Chrysostom's name in the diptychs

---

11. Ibid., 27–59

of dead bishops. This restoration was subsequently confirmed at the Fifth Ecumenical Council (Constantinople II) in 553.[12]

During the Monophysite controversies of the fifth and sixth centuries, the function of diptychs of both living and dead bishops to express confessional communion among the churches was solidified. If the commemorations of dead bishops in this era caused such controversies, the commemoration of living bishops did so to an even greater extent. A case in point is the Acacian Schism (484–519), the first major schism between East and West. We learn from Evagrius Scholasticus' *Church History* III, 20, that the monks of Constantinople reported to Pope Felix III (483–492) that under Patriarch Acacius of Constantinople (472–489) the name of Peter III Mongus, monophysite Patriarch of Alexandria, was commemorated in the sacred diptychs in Constantinople. As a result, Pope Felix convened a synod in 484 which deposed both Peter Mongus and Acacius. In October 485, these excommunications were reaffirmed by Felix, and Peter Fuller of Antioch was excommunicated as well. Acacius reacted by removing the Pope's name from the diptychs of Hagia Sophia (the "Great Church"), and this began the schism, which lasted for 35 years. Rome insisted on continuing the schism as long as the names of Peter Mongus (+490) and Acacius (+489) continued to be listed in the Constantinopolitan diptychs.[13]

In subsequent centuries, right up to the Union of Florence, communion diptychs remained an issue in the various controversies, from the condemnation of the "Three Chapters" in 553, to the debates over the Filioque in the eleventh century, to the troubles following the sack of Constantinople in 1204, and finally to the Council of Florence in 1438–39. Following the union of Florence, the Byzantine emperor ordered the Pope's name to be listed in the diptychs. As the union was rejected over the next few years, the Pope's name was dropped from the diptychs, and was not to reappear.

In summary, we can clearly see the central role played by diptychs during the first millennium and beyond. Developing out of lists of local bishops in the apostolic succession, during the period of Christological controversies, they became "communion diptychs" in the technical sense, expressing also confessional, and therefore eucharistic, communion with sister churches. With the developing structures of church life paralleling the structures of the Roman Empire in both East and West, diptychs gained

---

12. For a detailed description of this episode, see Taft, *History,* 97–100.
13. The details are recounted in Taft, *History,* 122–24.

in importance and became the official, visible expression of (eucharistic) unity between the churches.

We should briefly note, however, that communion diptychs were never as important in the West as in the East. Most of the theological disputes took place in the East, and as the pentarchy developed in the fourth and fifth centuries, four of the five sees were eastern. Diptychs thus remained important in the East, but, as Rome grew increasingly isolated from the eastern churches in later centuries, the diptychs had far less relevance for the church of the West. Indeed, as Taft points out, the diptychs in the West focused primarily on local church communion rather than relations with other churches, as in the Byzantine tradition.[14]

Ecumenical Worship and Intercommunion

Here we come to a very modern problem. A century ago, the very notion of the possibility of worship with other churches, much less intercommunion, would never cross anyone's mind. Divisions between churches were sharp, and there was little contact between them. Before Vatican II, Roman Catholic clergy and theologians were forbidden even to engage in discussion with non-Catholics. Orthodox, even those living in the West, lived in virtual isolation, and divisions among Protestant churches remained stark. I remember my father telling me about the situation in Paris in the nineteen forties and nineteen fifties when theologians from the Orthodox Theological Institute would meet secretly in private apartments with Roman Catholic scholars, including leading figures such as Danielou, Bouyer, Congar—the theologians who laid the groundwork for Vatican II!

In recent decades, however, as a result both of the conciliar ecumenical movement (WCC, NCCCUSA) and of numerous bilateral and multilateral dialogues and agreements, the situation has changed dramatically. The old hostilities have faded, boundaries between churches have faded, and, at least in America, people now frequently shift from one Christian denomination to another. In many Protestant churches, "eucharistic hospitality" has become the norm: any person (usually, but not always necessarily, baptized) is welcome to partake of communion in a church not his or her own. At WCC meetings, ecumenical worship has become established practice, and today one can even speak of a distinct ecumenical worship tradition.

14. Taft, *History*, 128.

Many Orthodox have reacted to these developments with dismay, particularly regarding eucharistic sharing. The issue came to a head in the years surrounding the 1998 Assembly of the World Council of Churches in Harare, when several Orthodox churches withdrew from the WCC. Following the assembly, a "Special Commission on Orthodox Participation in the WCC" was formed to address Orthodox concerns, among which the question of common worship and eucharistic sharing was paramount. I had the privilege of having a front-row seat in this debate by virtue of my membership in the Assembly Worship Committee, and subsequently in helping to draft the "Guidelines for Common Worship" that were prepared by the Special Commission and subsequently adopted by the Central Committee, the governing body of the WCC. I would like now to share some of that experience.

After the issuance by the WCC Faith and Order Commission of the text of "Baptism, Eucharist, Ministry" (BEM) in 1982, it became customary at WCC meetings to celebrate a eucharistic liturgy, typically the so-called "Lima Liturgy," actually an unofficial draft of a eucharistic liturgy prepared that same year by Faith and Order staff. Though no one was required to participate in these Eucharists, they became occasions for representatives from different churches to share eucharistic fellowship. The Orthodox, faithful to their principle that eucharistic communion is possible only once full union is achieved, always abstained, usually discreetly and quietly. In ensuing years, as eucharistic sharing grew increasingly common among churches issuing from the Reformation, the Orthodox grew increasingly uncomfortable, seeing in this a rejection of the 1950 Toronto Declaration, which had articulated the important principle that membership in the WCC did not imply the full recognition of other members as churches, and especially that the WCC is not itself a church or the "super-church." And since, in the Orthodox understanding, only the church can celebrate the Eucharist, how can the WCC, which is not a church, do so? In addition, the Orthodox were increasingly facing criticism from their ecumenical partners for their rejection of the possibility of eucharistic hospitality.

So it was that, at the initial meeting of the Assembly Worship Committee preparing for Harare, the question of the assembly Eucharist was raised. The Orthodox argued that there should be no eucharistic liturgy at all and described their concerns, not only about their personal discomfort in attending when they could not participate, but also about the ecclesiological principles that they saw as being violated—not only their own, but those articulated in the Toronto Declaration as well. The Protestant members of the committee saw this proposal as a step backward from the ecumenical progress that had been achieved in previous decades and argued that the assembly delegates would be greatly disappointed, and possibly scandalized in the absence of an assembly Eucharist.

Underlying these different positions, of course, lie different ecclesiological presuppositions. For the Orthodox, eucharistic communion is the visible sign of church unity. Sharing in the Eucharist implies full unity in faith, in structure, in decision-making, etc.—it can happen only once this hoped-for unity is achieved. To celebrate the Eucharist together in the absence of such unity would be dishonest, and it would violate the principle expressed by St. Paul in 1 Cor 11:17–22. The Protestant view does not place such a strong ecclesiological emphasis on the Eucharist, seeing it variously as the fulfillment of an ordinance, an act of personal piety, and a means toward the unity that we seek. While no agreement on the ecclesiological principles could be reached, the committee agreed to recommend that no Eucharist be celebrated at the assembly. A total fast from the Eucharist would, in a stark and painful way, express the fact that the full unity we seek has not been achieved.

This dramatic proposal, however, was not well received by the Assembly Planning Commission or the Central Committee of the WCC, who had not been involved in the extensive discussions that had led to the committee's recommendation, and it was sent back to us for reconsideration. After further deliberation by the Worship Committee, it was decided that, though there would be no official Eucharist as part of the official program, on the middle Sunday of the assembly local churches representing the four main ecclesial traditions (Protestant, Roman Catholic, Eastern Orthodox, and Oriental Orthodox) would hold simultaneous eucharistic liturgies in churches of each tradition in Harare. Delegates would then choose which to attend and would follow each tradition's eucharistic discipline. This decision was consistent with the understanding that the WCC is not itself a church, and that only a church can celebrate the Eucharist. In addition, on the eve of September 14 (the Feast of the Cross in the Orthodox tradition), an all-night penitential vigil was scheduled focusing on the fact that, because of the continuing divisions, no common Eucharist could be celebrated and all delegates were urged to observe a total eucharistic fast on that day, i.e., with no eucharistic celebration. The purpose was to encourage everyone to feel the pain of division.

In the years after the Harare assembly, the Special Commission did its work and, in its final report, made a number of recommendations which were then adopted by the Central Committee of the WCC. The section on "Common Prayer" basically affirmed the ecclesiological principles that lay behind the pattern of worship at Harare. The document made a distinction between liturgical worship properly speaking, which it called "confessional worship," and common prayer. Liturgical worship is the prayer of an ecclesial body and reflects the theology and practices of the specific church which is actualized in that prayer. Common prayer is described as the joint prayer conducted by persons from different churches, possibly using elements from different traditions, but lacking a properly ecclesial dimension. Liturgical worship is hosted by a particular church, while common prayer belongs to no particular church. I quote from the relevant paragraph in the report:

> . . . a clear distinction is proposed between "confessional" and "interconfessional" common prayer at WCC gatherings. "Confessional common prayer" is the prayer of a confession, a communion, or a denomination within a confession. Its ecclesial identity is clear. It is offered as a gift to the gathered community by a particular delegation of the participants, even as it invites all to enter into the spirit of prayer. It is conducted and presided over in accordance with its own understanding and practice. "Interconfessional common prayer" is usually prepared for specific ecumenical events. It is an opportunity to celebrate together drawing from the resources of a variety of traditions. Such prayer is rooted in the past experience of the ecumenical community as well as in the gifts of the member churches to each other. But it does not claim to be the worship of any given member church, or of any kind of a hybrid church or super-church. Properly understood and applied, this distinction can free the traditions to express themselves either in their own integrity or in combination, all the while being true to the fact that Christians do not yet experience full unity together, and that the ecumenical bodies in which they participate are not themselves churches.[15]

On the question of the Eucharist, the report indicates that eucharistic liturgies may be celebrated only in the context of confessional worship:

15. Final report of the Special Commission on Orthodox Participation in the WCC. Par. 42. http://www.oikoumene.org/en/resources/documents/assembly/porto-alegre-2006/3-preparatory-and-background-documents/final-report-of-the-special-commission-on-orthodox-participation-in-the-wcc.html.

> Eucharistic worship at ecumenical events has been a difficult issue for the fellowship of churches in the World Council of Churches. Not all can receive from the same table and there exists a range of views and disciplines among churches belonging to the fellowship of the World Council of Churches on the offering and receiving of the Eucharist. Whatever one's views on the Eucharist and how it may or may not be shared, the pain of not being able all to receive at the same table is felt by all. Following the pattern of distinguishing between confessional and interconfessional common prayer, confessional celebrations of the Eucharist at assemblies and other major events can be accommodated. The hosting church (or group of churches which are able to host together) should be clearly identified. While it should be very clear that the WCC is not "hosting" a Eucharist, these confessional Eucharistic services, though not part of the official programme, may be publicly announced, with an invitation to all to attend.[16]

Although these affirmations may at first glance seem unduly harsh, they are placed within a statement that looks very positively at ecumenical prayer as an essential dimension of the movement toward Christian unity. The text mentions the positive effect of churches getting know one another better through their exposure to one another's liturgical traditions, as well as the rich cross-fertilization that ensued from this, leading in recent years to full communion agreements among some (Western) churches. At the same time, it calls for a rigorous honesty, so as to avoid any confusion about the current state of disunity that still persists, while looking forward to the time when we will, indeed be one. Then, and only then, will we be able to celebrate that unity at a common eucharistic table.

Conclusion

The above reflections are, of course, only partial and only point to the greater reality that the Eucharist, as the manifestation and realization of the Church, is also an eschatological event. For if the Eucharist is a foretaste of the heavenly banquet, it is only because the church is itself also an experience, in the here and now, of the Kingdom of Heaven. This is certainly not unique to the Orthodox liturgical experience, though possibly it finds there its clearest expression.

---

16. Ibid., paragraph 44.

We will be hearing more about this eschatological dimension from others in this conference, but suffice it to say that it has remained a dominant feature in the Orthodox eucharistic liturgy. This is reflected in the Sanctus, common to many Christian traditions: in singing the song of the angels, "Holy, holy, holy," we join the choir of angels around the heavenly throne, in accordance with the vision of Isaiah.[17] We see it even more clearly in the central part of the eucharistic prayer of John Chrysostom: "Remembering therefore this our Saviour's command and all that has been done for us: the Cross, the Tomb, the resurrection on the third day, the Ascension into heaven, the Sitting at the right hand, the Second and glorious Coming again."[18]

In the liturgy, the church already remembers the second coming, for in the Eucharist, in the church, Christ does, indeed, come again. Like the disciples on the road to Emmaus, who recognize the Lord only when he takes the bread, blesses it, breaks it, and gives it to them—we can affirm that he is known to us in the breaking of bread. And when we share in that bread, together we become the Body of Christ, which is the church.

Bibliography

Afanasiev, Nicolas. *Trapeza gospodni*. Paris: Orthodox Theological Institute, 1952 (in Russian). Unpublished ET: "The Lord's Supper." Translated by M. Lewis. Crestwood, NY: St Vladimir's Orthodox Theological Seminary, 1988.

Cabasilas, Nicholas. *A Commentary on the Divine Liturgy*. Translated by J. M Hussey and P. A. McNulty. Creswood, NY: St. Vladimir's Seminary Press, 1977.

———. *The Life in Christ*. Translated by C.J. deCantazaro. Crestwood, NY: St. Vladimir's Seminary Press, 1974.

Constitution on the Liturgy, promulgated by Pope Paul VI at the closing of the Second Session of the Second Vatican Council, December 4, 1963. Washington, DC: National Catholic Welfare Conference, n.d..

Final report of the Special Commission on Orthodox Participation in the WCC. http://www.oikoumene.org/en/resources/documents/assembly/porto-alegre-2006/3-preparatory-and-background-documents/final-report-of-the-special-commission-on-orthodox-participation-in-the-wcc.html.

Hippolytus. *On the Apostolic Tradition*. Translated and introduction by A. Stewart-Sykes. Crestwood, NY: St. Vladimir's Seminary Press, 2001.

Taft, Robert F. *A History of the Liturgy of St. John Chrysostom*, Vol. IV, *The Diptychs*. OrChrAn 238; Rome: PIO, 1991.

17. Isaiah 6.

18. *The Divine Liturgy of our Father among the Saints John Chrysostom* (Oxford: Oxford University Press, 1995), 33.

Zizioulas, John. *Being as Communion.* Crestwood, NY: St. Vladimir's Seminary Press, 1993, 143–69. This chapter was published originally in French: "La communauté Eucharistique et la catholicité de l'Église." *Istina* 14 (1969) 66–88.

4

Eucharist and Church: Response

—Everett Ferguson

A Historical Prologue

THROUGH CHRISTIAN HISTORY THERE has often, although not always, been an important relationship between how the Eucharist was understood and other aspects of the Christian faith. Thus conflicts over the Eucharist have often reflected different teachings in regard to other doctrines. This has been especially true of Christology (see the comment below on Irenaeus and the incarnation). In a similar way the doctrine and practice of the Eucharist is often tied to an understanding of the nature of the church. The papers presented here give attention to the implications of the Eucharist for ecclesiology.

The interpretation of the Eucharist has been frequently a matter of controversy through Christian history, and these controversies not only involved different approaches to the interpretation of Scripture but also were sometimes tied to different emphases in regard to the nature of the church.

Different terminology in early Christian literature perhaps reflects different understandings of the Eucharist. Some authors made a straightforward identification of the bread and wine with the body and blood of Jesus.

Thus Justin Martyr said: "We receive these elements not as common bread and common drink . . . [W]e were taught that the food for which thanks have been given through the prayer of the word that is from him and from which our blood and flesh are nourished according to the bodily processes is the flesh and blood of that Jesus who was made flesh" (*1 Apology* 66).

Similarly Irenaeus used the material nature of bread and wine to argue against Gnostics that Jesus was the Son of the Creator of the world (*Against Heresies* 4.18.4–5). Jesus "acknowledged the created cup with which he moistens our blood as his own blood, and he confirmed the created bread from which our bodies grow as his own body" (*Against Heresies* 5.2.3).

Other authors used the Greek word *symbolon* (token, allegory) or the Latin word *figura* (form or shape, likeness) to express the relation of the bread and wine to the body and blood of Jesus. Clement of Alexandria stated, "The holy Scripture named wine a mystical symbol of the holy blood" (*Instructor* 2.2.32). He interpreted John 6:53–56 as spoken "through symbols" and "allegories" about partaking of faith, the Holy Spirit, and the divine Word (*Instructor* 1.6.38, 43, 47). Tertullian explained that Jesus' words, "This is my body" meant "a figure of my body" (*Against Marcion* 4.40.3–6). "The bread . . . represents [Jesus'] own proper body" (*Against Marcion* 1.14.3).

The contrast between a realist and a symbolic or figurative understanding of the eucharistic elements became explicit in the fourth/fifth centuries in Ambrose and Augustine and in the way they were read by later interpreters in the West. Ambrose expressed a literal change in the elements when the words of consecration were spoken: "This bread is bread before the words of the sacraments. When consecration has been added, from bread it becomes the body of Christ . . . Before the words of Christ the cup is full of wine and water. When the words of Christ have operated, then is made the blood which redeems the people." (*On the Sacraments* 4.4.14–4.5.23)

Augustine sometimes used ordinary realist language (*Sermon* 227); at other times he used the words "sign," "sacrament," or "figure" with reference to the eucharistic elements. He interpreted Jesus in John 6:54 and 63 as saying: "Understand spiritually what I have said; you are not to eat this body that you see; nor to drink that blood that they who will crucify me will pour forth. I have commended to you a certain mystery; spiritually understood, it will give life. Although it must be visibly celebrated, yet it must be spiritually understood" (*In Psalm* 99.8 [Latin, 98:8]).

It seems that Augustine believed in a symbolism of the visible sign but a realism of the supernatural invisible gift: "One thing is a sacrament [the sign]; another the virtue [power] of the sacrament" (*On the Gospel of John* 26.11).

The different emphases in the "Ambrosian" and "Augustinian" views resulted in theological debates in the ninth and eleventh centuries. In the "first eucharistic controversy" in the ninth century Radbertus, a monk at Corbie, championed the realist interpretation with the first treatise devoted to the Eucharist, *On the Body and Blood of the Lord*. He contended that there is a real presence of the body and blood of Christ in the elements and that the body and blood in the Eucharist are identical with the body and blood of the man on the cross. Ratramnus, a fellow monk at Cobie, responded with a treatise of the same name that emphasized the figurative interpretation of the Eucharist as an image of the body and blood. He wrote, "It has been most clearly shown that the bread which is called Christ's body, and the cup which is called Christ's blood, is a figure, because it is a mystery, and that there is no small difference between the body which exists through the mystery and that which suffered, was buried, and rose again."[1] As with Augustine, there is a spiritual presence of the body and blood that brings spiritual benefits.

The treatises of Radbertus and Ratramnus presented two different ways of looking at the Eucharist: a change in the elements from bread and wine to body and blood versus a change in their effects from the physical nourishment of ordinary food and drink to nourishment and sanctification of souls.

In the "second eucharistic controversy" in the eleventh century there were more viewpoints expressed and much more serious disagreements. The occasion of the dispute was a letter by Berengar of Angers and then Tours to Lanfrance of Bec and Canterbury. To abbreviate the discussion, Beregar advocated what may be termed a "dynamic symbolism." He drew on grammar and logic to contend that a change into a real bodily presence was impossible. Although repeatedly condemned by church officials and councils, Berengar made two positive contributions to further thought on the Eucharist: the standardization of the definition of a sacrament as "a visible form of invisible grace," and the use of the Aristotelian categories of substance and accidents in describing an object. Berengar was in part a victim of ecclesiastical politics, but his views failed because theological

---

1. Ratramnus, *On the Body and Blood of the Lord*, 97, p. 146.

thought as represented by Lanfranc and popular attitudes had become prevailingly realist without allowing the figurative option.

To condense the account of a flurry of writing and ecclesiastical political activity, the condemnation of Beregar led in the twelfth and thirteen centuries to the formulation of transubstantiation as the official Roman Catholic doctrine of the Eucharist. Transubstantiation provided what had earlier been lacking, a philosophical explanation of how the change in the elements is effected. As was more fully expounded by Thomas Aquinas, the distinction of substance and accidents provided the framework of interpretation. The substance of bread and wine, what the elements are in themselves, become the body and blood of Christ; the accidental qualities, what one sees and tastes, remain bread and wine.

In addition to different theologies, there were different practices in regard to the Eucharist. The Greek Orthodox churches' use of ordinary leavened bread and the Latin Catholic churches' use of unleavened bread was one of the items of debate in the break in communion between Constantinople and Rome in the eleventh century. Meyendorf recounts how other controversies between Catholics and Orthodox have continued into the modern ecumenical movement.

During the sixteenth and seventeenth centuries differences in regard to the Eucharist were central to the divisions between different branches of the Reformation. Although Martin Luther rejected transubstantiation, he remained closest of the major Reformers to the medieval view of the Eucharist. At the Marburg Colloquy in 1529 aimed at bringing unity to the German and Swiss Reformations, Luther famously wrote on the tablecloth *est*, the Latin word for "is" from Jesus' words at the Last Supper, in order to underscore his literal interpretation in contrast to Ulrich Zwingli's figurative interpretation. For Luther the real body and blood of Christ exists "in, under, and around" the elements of bread and wine: "[I]t is not necessary in the sacrament that the bread and wine be transubstantiated and Christ be contained under their accidents in order that the real body and real blood may be present. But both remain there at the same time."[2] This view has been called consubstantiation.

Ulrich Zwingli rejected Luther's view of the ubiquity of the body of Christ and insisted that it remained in heaven. He held to a metaphorical or spiritual understanding of the words "This is my body; this is my blood." He wrote: "[T]he very body of Christ is the body which is seated at the right

2. Luther, *Babylonian Captivity*, 151.

hand of God, and the sacrament of his body is the bread, and the sacrament of his blood is the wine of which we partake with thanksgiving. Now the sign and the thing signified cannot be one the same. Therefore the sacrament of the body of Christ cannot be the body itself."[3] Zwingli referred to many passages where the verb "is" meant "signifies."

Many factors were involved in the differences between Luther and Zwingli: the Scholastic education of Luther and the Humanist formation of Zwingli, different theological and ecclesiological views centered on their different understandings of predestination, personality differences and rivalry, and different temperaments, summed up in Luther's estimate that Zwingli and the Swiss were of a different spirit from him. The result of the differences was two different churches.

The Anabaptists picked up from Zwingli an emphasis on the memorial aspects of the Eucharist. The *Schleitheim Confession of Faith* in 1527 stated: "All those who wish to break one bread in remembrance of the broken body of Christ, and all who wish to drink of one drink as a remembrance of the shed blood of Christ, shall be united beforehand by baptism in one body of Christ."[4]

Along with the memorial aspect, there was a great emphasis on the Lord's Supper as an expression of unity and brotherly love. Conrad Grebel's "Letter to Thomas Müntzer" explained "Although it is simply bread, yet if faith and brotherly love precede it, it is to be received with joy, since, when it is used in the church, it is to show us that we are truly one bread and one body, and that we are and wish to be true brethren with one another . . . [F]or the Supper is an expression of fellowship, not a Mass and sacrament."[5] For the Anabaptists this view of the Lord's Supper, the preferred term among Reformed and Anabaptist churches, coincided with their view of the church as a company of committed disciples, a key difference from the magisterial Reformers (Luther, Zwingli, and Calvin) for whom the earlier territorial churches (although on a smaller scale) continued.

John Calvin took a mediating position between Luther and Zwingli. For him Christ by the Spirit was present in the assembly of believers, and the benefits of his body and blood were present in the Eucharist: "Thus, when bread is given as a symbol of Christ's body, we must at once grasp this comparison: as bread nourishes, sustains and keeps the life of our body,

---

3. Zwingli, *On the Lord's Supper*, 188
4. "Schleitheim Confession," 288–89.
5. Grebel, *Letter to Müntzer*, 76.

so Christ's body is the only food to invigorate and enliven our soul. When we see wine set forth as a symbol of blood, we must reflect on the benefits which wine imparts to the body, and so realize that the same are spiritually imparted to us by Christ's blood."[6] Calvin maintained the symbolism of bread and wine and the spiritual reality of the body and blood in the Eucharist.

Little of these historical differences surface in these theological presentations on the relation of Eucharist and church by three thinkers from the Russian Orthodox, Roman Catholic, and mainline Protestant churches. Given the historical background, it is remarkable the ways in which these papers converge and complement one another. To have members from three different ecclesiastical traditions offer so much from which all can learn about the relation of the Eucharist to the church is something to be celebrated.

I recall that in the 1950s Douglas Horton, then Dean of Harvard Divinity School, expressed impatience that the ecumenical movement was not making much progress on being able to share in the communion table. The situation is nearer achievement now, but it seems only to the extent that many no longer take seriously the issues in regard to the Eucharist and the church that separate different communions and only consider them pragmatically. The differences between the Orthodox and many in the ecumenical movement to which Meyendorff refers reflect different approaches. It is a matter for reflection how much is gained when participants no longer regard theological differences important enough to argue about them (not true of these three presenters). These papers will sharpen our thinking on some fundamental matters.

Paul Meyendorff

I first encountered the Orthodox definition of the church as the people who assemble on the first day of the week for the Eucharist in reading John Zizioulas, *Being as Communion*.[7] That definition resonated with my own understanding, which colors my paraphrase of Zizioulas. Meyendorf's presentation highlights the clash in the ecumenical movement of two viewpoints: the Eucharist as tied to the church and meaningful only in the context of ecclesiastical communion (the position of the Orthodox but also

6. Calvin, *Institutes*, 1363.
7. Zizioulas, *Being as Communion*.

others, among whom I would include some in the Free Churches) versus the Eucharist as a general religious act expressing mutual acceptance (the position reflected by most in the ecumenical movement). For the Orthodox to share the table would manifest a unity not yet achieved; many Protestants, however, thought sharing the Eucharist was a means to unity, and perhaps for some the only litmus test needed for unity.

The view that the Eucharist and church communion belong together is the premise behind the conference for which these three papers formed the plenary addresses. Meyendorf centers his discussion on the difficulties these conflicting views presented in regard to a Eucharist at a general assembly of the World Council of Churches. But he does so in the context of the search for unity. Nevertheless, his account calls attention to the problem that troubled Douglas Horton a half century ago.

Denis Farkasfalvy

Farkasfalvy begins his paper by noting that the slogan of Catholic Renewal that led to Vatican Council II was "Back to the Sources." That has often been the motto of renewal movements in Christian history, notably in the Renaissance and Reformation periods and in the Restoration Movement of which the host institution for this conference (Abilene Christian University) is a part. Farkasfalvy notes two contrasting pathways. One is "back to the sources," and the other reverses the direction by explaining the current state of affairs as a result of historical development. This two-way road emphasizes the importance of history, regardless of the current mood of impatience with the study of history.

The paper on "Bible and Eucharist in an Incarnational Model" offers a theological basis for the development, or unfolding, of doctrine and also a theological basis of the Eucharist. One does not have to be a Roman Catholic to appreciate Farkasfalvy's theology of the Eucharist, nor to be Orthodox to accept Meyendorf's association of the Eucharist with the gathered church.

Whereas Meyendorf speaks explicitly as an Orthodox, Farkasfalvy speaks as a theologian and historian, not as explicitly Roman Catholic, although his insights are shaped by that background.

An incarnational model is certainly congenial to Roman Catholic understanding of the Eucharist and the church. The parallels of the incarnation, revelation (Scripture), and the Eucharist are worth exploring further.

The Spirit who effected the incarnation and the inspiration of Scripture makes the bread and wine the body and blood of Jesus for believers. The language of incarnation is sometimes used by non-Catholics in reference to the church, particularly its mission if not for its nature. There are analogies, but the imagery needs to be carefully stated and nuanced. I have a concern that if one is not as careful as Farkasfalvy and not as theologically and historically informed as he is, the analogy of the incarnation may either say too little about Jesus or say too much about the church, Scripture, and the Eucharist. And here is where exploring these matters may surface fundamental theological disagreements, however fruitful the approach may potentially be.

Gary D. Badcock

Gary Badcock's treatment of Protestantism is more self-critical than the presentations by the Orthodox and Catholic representatives. (None of the three were authorized to speak for their traditions but only out of them.) Badcock correctly notes the significant change in the Protestant reality (if not in theology) of church—from magisterial churches where the theory was one church in one political jurisdiction to a situation where political jurisdictions contain multiple denominations. As a corollary, church membership is often determined by individual choice more than by birth or by society. The result of the secularization of public life and privatization of religion (Newbigin) is free choice of religion. "Denominational Protestantism is consumerism extended to the sphere of faith." The practice of intercommunion sanctifies this personal, individual freedom of choice in regard to the church. I concur that modern Protestantism needs a "more robust ecclesiology." This is even more true of Evangelical Protestantism than of mainline Protestantism.

Like Farkasfalvy, Badcock approaches ecclesiology through Christology and pneumatology. He sees the work of the Spirit in promoting diversity. Hence, he carries the Christological and pneumatological dimensions of ecclesiology in a direction Roman Catholics and many Protestants would not be comfortable with. The other movement of the Spirit is to unity. How these two impulses mesh is not clear. Is there reflected here the tendency to attribute whatever one is involved in to the work of the Spirit? He notes, "Much Protestant ecumenical engagement desires not unity, but only the affirmation of difference, and with it inter-communion as the acknowledgement of the principle of individuation." The movement of Christology is not only descending, whereby true God identifies with fallen humanity, but also ascending in raising the many to God.

Invoking the concept of the "invisible" church has been a common ploy when reality does not match theory, but it is problematic, for an invisible church is a theological abstraction, if not a contradiction in terms. The only church with which we have to do is the visible church, whatever its human failings that seem to contradict the theological affirmations, but so the situation has been with the people of God from Israel in the Hebrew Scriptures to those who have worn the Christian name through history.

Conclusion

The Eucharist sums up the mystery of the gospel. Thus it is a key practice for understanding the church and is central to what it is to be church.

Bibliography

Calvin, John. *Institutes of the Christian Religion* 4.17.3. Translated by Ford Lewis Battles. LCC 21. Philadelphia: Westminster, 1960.

Grebel, Conrad. "Letter to Thomas Müntzer." In *Spiritual and Anabaptist Writers*, edited by George Huntston Williams, 76–80. LCC 25. Philadelphia: Westminster, 1957.

Luther, Martin. *The Babylonian Captivity of the Church*. Translation in *Three Treatises: Martin Luther*. Philadelphia: Fortress, 1960.

Ratramnus. "On the Body and Blood of the Lord." In *Early Medieval Theology*, 118–47. Translated by George E. McCracken and Allen Cabaniss. LCC 9. Philadelphia: Westminster, 1957.

"Schleitheim Confession of the Faith." In *Great Voices of the Reformation: An Anthology*. Edited by Harry Emerson Fosdick. New York: Modern Library, 1952.

Zizioulas, John. *Being as Communion*. Crestwood, NY: St. Vladimir's Seminary Press, 1993.

Zwingli, Ulrich. "On the Lord's Supper." In *Zwingli and Bullinger*, edited by G. W. Bromiley, 176–238. LCC 24. Philadelphia: Westminster, 1953.

PART 2

Presented Essays

5

No One Has Ascended to Heaven but the One Who Has Descended from Heaven, the Son of Man Who Is in Heaven (John 3:13)

—*Roch Kereszty, O. Cist.*

The Dynamics of Augustine's Eucharistic Doctrine

TO EXPLORE THE DYNAMICS of Augustine's eucharistic doctrine, I will first describe the doctrinal context within which it becomes intelligible, then examine how Augustine describes the conjunction of the eucharistic mystery with the church and its sacrifice. This will illuminate Augustine's understanding of Christ's presence in the Eucharist.

Theological and Biographical Context

Reading Cicero's *Hortensius* as an adolescent instilled in Augustine a love of the quest for wisdom. The materialist metaphysics of the Manicheans derailed his quest for a time, but eventually he discovered Platonist philosophy and, in particular, Plato, Porphyry and Plotinos, whose writings made him realize the existence of spiritual reality (*mundus intelligibilis*) as well as its source, the Absolute, the One, the True and the Good.

Augustine yearned for union with the Absolute. Possessing wisdom fascinated him, but he felt entirely incapable of attaining it. The weight of his rebellious flesh and the chain of carnal pleasures made his ascent to wisdom seem an impossibility. However, in his conversion experience he encountered the incarnate Wisdom, the Second Person of the Trinity. Augustine realized that Christ is the Truth in the flesh of a real person. He had descended into our fleshly condition in order to make our ascent to the realm of Truth and Wisdom possible. This discovery intensified and also transformed Augustine's quest for wisdom. He knew that before his conversion he had taken the wrong path to wisdom, the way of proud knowledge. In contrast, Christ had descended to us by the way of humility. Augustine concluded that only by this way—the way of humility—can we ascend to him. In fact, by becoming man and taking on the form of a slave, Christ became the way to lead us to himself who is the Truth and the Life. "Descend so that you may ascend and ascend to God," Augustine heard God say to him.[1] Even though Augustine still expresses his goal in life with the vocabulary of Platonist philosophy—Life is blessed by ascending to contemplative union with Wisdom—he, as a Christian, understands that he can ascend only by descending by the way of humility and that he can reach God not through a lonely and solitary quest on his own, but only in union with the body of Christ in the church.

Within this Christian context, the Eucharist plays a central role. It is the bond which unites the church with Christ and, by doing so, enables the church to ascend with Christ to the Father. Moreover, the Eucharist inserts Augustine into the body of Christ so that he too may ascend in and with the One who alone can ascend to heaven. The same person, the eternal Son, who descended through the incarnation, ascends through his resurrection and ascension. In this upward movement, the risen Christ carries the church with him because his glorified humanity is inseparably linked to the church as head to its members, as the groom to his bride in one flesh.

The declaration of Christ in John combined with Ephesians 4:10a expresses this dynamic context of Augustine's eucharistic doctrine: "No one has ascended into heaven but the one who has descended from heaven, the

---

1. Augustine, *Confessiones*, 4, 12 All texts of Augustine quoted in this essay are my own translation. Various texts of his works were used, and given in the works cited, at the end of the paper.

Son of Man who is in heaven." And, "The one who descended is also the one who ascended" (Jn 3:13, Eph 4:10a) Christ, in his risen humanity, has already ascended, yet his ascension will not be complete until he has taken the last predestined member of the church with and in him. We will now focus on the Eucharist in this context of descent and ascent.

Christ Ascends with His Body, the Eucharist, and the Church

As mentioned above, Augustine's lifelong quest was his search for wisdom. He frequently described his longing for God in terms of reaching Wisdom and finding nourishment and delight in the food of angels. However, especially at the beginning of his conversion, he realized he is utterly incapable of tasting the food of wisdom:

> I heard your voice calling from on high saying: "I am the food of full-grown men. Grow and you shall feed on me. But you shall not change me into your substance, as you do with the food of your body. Instead you shall be changed into me."[2]

Here, God/Wisdom, the goal of Augustine's quest, speaks of eternal truth and true love. But already the eucharistic language indicates that at this point in his life Augustine knew that he could attain wisdom on high only if, by becoming humble, he embraced the humble Christ and that he could only do so in and through the sacrament of the Body and Blood of the Lord. He realized that by his incarnation, Christ had pulled us down from our haughty selves and drawn us to himself. Thus, seeing before our feet the God, who became weak by sharing the garment of our humanity, we might accept our weakness and, tiring of our futile efforts to ascend by the way of pride, we might prostrate ourselves upon him so that by the way of humility he might raise us up by his resurrection.[3] This and other similar texts clearly show that when he was writing the *Confessions*, Augustine was fully aware that one could participate in the eternal, loveable Wisdom only through the incarnate Jesus Christ, the mediator between God and men, in whom wisdom is mixed with flesh, and so becomes milk to nourish children.[4]

---

2. Ibid., 7,10:82.
3. Ibid., 7,9: 80.
4. Ibid., 7, 18: 85.

In this text he only insinuates that as weak and immature children of God our food is the sacrament of the flesh and blood of Jesus Christ through whom we share in Wisdom, *the* eternal truth and true love. In Sermon 132A, he is more explicit: since we could not ascend to the realm of Wisdom and eat the bread of angels, "the Son came into the flesh that he might be eaten."

In most of Augustine's eucharistic texts, he presents this dynamism of descent to the incarnate Christ by the way of humility that he might raise us up to enjoy his divinity. In focusing on the goal of Christ's presence, the fruition of Divine Wisdom, rather than on its mode, he continues the Alexandrian tradition. Just like the Alexandrians, Augustine also knows that it is through the flesh of the *risen* Christ that we can attain the realm of the spirit: "let Christ be eaten: he lives after he was eaten since he rose after he was murdered."[5]

In Augustine's thought, the vertical and horizontal dimensions of the Eucharist are inseparably linked. Just as the head cannot be separated from the body, Christ and the church cannot be separated from the sacrament of the Eucharist. Unlike later scholastic theology which considers the personal presence of Christ in the Eucharist the primary spiritual effect (*res et sacramentum*) of the eucharistic celebration and the unity of the mystical body its final effect (*res*), in Augustine these two appear as equally direct and simultaneous. The object of spiritual eating, the *manducatio spiritualis*, is Christ *and* the church. This is why Augustine says: "it is your mystery which is on the altar"; and, as he tells the communicant: "it is you yourself whom you receive."[6] On account of the unbreakable unity between Christ and the church, only those who are within the ecclesial body of Christ can spiritually eat his body. The excommunicated and heretics who attempt to receive sacramental communion cannot receive the *res*, the spiritual reality. Theirs is not a spiritual eating, but only the reception of a sacrament, which results in condemnation rather than life.[7]

The cause of this intimate union of Christ and the church is the charity of Christ. The Eucharist is the *vinculum unitatis* because it is the *vinculum caritatis*. Through the cross, Christ has purified the church, joining it to

---

5. *Sermo* 132, 1, 212. *Opere di Sant'Agostino*, All quotes from the Sermons are translated from the Latin texts of this edition.

6. *Sermo* 272: IV/2, 142.

7. So, for instance, *Johannis Evangelium Tractatus*, 26, 13, Ibid., 26,15:267, Ibid., 26,18:267–68, Ibid., 27,11: 275–76.

himself so that together Christ and church become *una caro,* one flesh with him, bridegroom and bride in the bond of perfect virginal *caritas*. At the same time, this *caritas* is inseparable from the Holy Spirit, whose gift is the grace of *caritas*. So for Augustine, *spiritualiter manducare* is not opposed to receive Christ in sacramental communion, but rather to receive him not only sacramentally, but also in reality. For Augustine, *eating Christ spiritually* is the culmination of the sacrament of Communion.[8] For modern man, "spiritual" connotes an attenuated reality in opposition to the material, but for Augustine it is the full reality of sacramental communion because Christ is always communicated in the Spirit and imparts the Spirit.[9]

As we have seen, the spiritual eating of the Body and Blood of Christ unites us with both Christ and the church. This union with Christ integrates us into his body/person and joins us to his ascent to heaven. Two texts serve as illustration:

> The Teacher of humility came not to do his own will, but the will of him who sent him. Let us come to him, let us enter into him, let us be incorporated into him so that we, too, might do not our will but that of the Father.[10]

The incorporation into Christ's body is so real that the church and Christ are truly one subject:

> The head is the body's savior, he who has already ascended to heaven; the body is the Church who is still laboring on earth. Had this body not adhered to its head by the bond of charity so much that one being (*unus*) has become from the head and the body, he would not have reprimanded a certain persecutor from heaven by saying: "Saul, Saul, why do you persecute me?"[11]

The same act of charity that unites us to Christ unites all the members together into one body; in fact, into one man: "we are one (*unus*) in Christ";

---

8. Augustine, however, also declares that one can obtain the goal of the spiritual eating of Christ even outside sacramental communion by faith: "*crede et manducasti:* believe and you have eaten." Ibid., 254–55.

9. Cf. for instance: *Non potest vivere corpus Christi nisi de spiritu Christi . . . carnem Christi et sanguinem Christi non edamus tantum in sacramento, quod et multi mali; sed usque ad spiritus participationem manducemus et bibamus, ut in Domini corpore tamquam membra maneamus, ut eius spiritu vegetemur . . .* (Ibid., 26 ,16 :268).

10. Ibid., 25,18:258.

11. *Enarrationes in Psalmos* 30:3: (ed. by Eligius Dekkers & Johannes Freipont, CCSL XXXVIII, 1956) 248.

"we are one in the one" (*unus in uno*). The unity of Christians is one (*unus*) man.¹² Thus, we are in some real sense one subject along with Christ; the two become one person in some sense, (*una quaedam persona*); namely, out of the head and body, out of the bridegroom and bride.¹³ Therefore, we speak with the same tongue and with the same words.¹⁴

As a result, Augustine can declare with Paul that the same person who has descended has also ascended to heaven:

> It is said about [Christ] that "no one has ascended but the one who descended even though he ascended along with that thing (*cum ea re*) with which he has not descended. Thus, no one but Christ ascended since no one but Christ has descended from heaven even though he descended without a body and ascended with a body. And we too will ascend, not by our own power but on account of our union with him.¹⁵

We should not think that our union with the glorified body of Christ takes place only after our death in heaven. It takes place in an initial but real way in every eucharistic communion, even though, as Augustine believes, the body of the risen Christ is in a certain place in heaven.¹⁶ Yet, since the Son of God is the same person as the Son of Man and God is present everywhere, we cannot be united with the person of the Word without being united also with his body. In every holy communion, this union is constantly intensified and perfected. In this way, Christ takes us up to heaven.¹⁷ Augustine explains this process in comments on Jesus' eucharistic discourse. He tells his audience that Jesus does the opposite of what the Jews assumed he would:

> It scandalizes you that I said: 'If you see the Son of Man ascending where he was before?' What is he doing? Did he [by these words] resolve their difficulty? Did he open up [the meaning of the words]

---

12. Ibid.,30, II, 4: II,5: 193–194.
13. Ibid., 30, II, 4: 193.
14. Ibid., 37,6:386–87.
15. *Sermo* 263A, 3: IV, 908.
16. Sermo 242, 4: IV, 656

17. Calvin's view, though close to Augustine's, is different. The Holy Spirit transports the communicant to heaven where the risen body of Christ is and unites the communicant with this body in heaven. In the case of Augustine, however, the Holy Spirit unites us primarily with the Person of Christ but through the Person also with his body which is inseparable from Him. That is why we become "one flesh" with the risen Christ here on earth. ("Confession of Faith concerning the Eucharist" Calvin, *Theological,* 168–169.)

> by which they were scandalized? Yes, he did, but would that they had understood [his words]. For they had thought that he would distribute his body while [in reality] he said that he would ascend to heaven and, of course, he would ascend with his integral self (*se ... integrum*). 'When you will see the Son of Man ascending where he was before,' then you will see that he distributes his body not in the way you think; then you will understand that his grace is not consumed by bites.[18]

Thus, all forms of cannibalism are excluded. Jesus speaks not about his earthly body but the risen spiritual one; and instead of offering bites of his earthly body, he is planning to take up his integral self (*se integrum*) that is the church to heaven through the Eucharist.

In this fundamental sense, then, while still on earth, we are already seated in the heavens, because we are one with the body of Christ, the head, and our head, who sits already at the right of God.[19] However, at the same time, our ascension is a process; in this life the members of Christ's body are on their way to heaven through spiritual communions with the flesh and blood of Christ and by turning their hearts to heaven. As Augustine said: We should lift up our hearts where Christ is seated at God's right hand; we should then seek and experience what is above not what is on the earth.[20]

The Eucharist as Sacrifice

Augustine writes about sacrifice in many of his works, but the main lines of his synthesis emerge only in one, the *City of God*. The synthesis is his own, but it draws on three different sources. The first is the classic Roman idea of sacrifice expressed in the terms: *sacrificare* or *sacrum facere*. Because it is offered by human beings, the sacrificial object must be made sacred in order to become a true sacrifice. In other words, it must be transferred from the human sphere to the divine. Therefore, a true sacrifice is always a divine reality (*res divina*).

The second ingredient can be traced back to Stoic and Platonic philosophies, which had by the time of Augustine developed the highly intellectual, yet spiritual concept of sacrifice as *thusia logike* or *pneumatike*. To varying degrees, these notions show contempt for material sacrifices and

18. Jo 27,3: 270–271.
19. *Enarrationes* 3,9:12, 55,3:679.
20. *Sermo* 362, 20: VI, 406

extoll the sacrifice of a virtuous mind and life whose goal is to achieve a blessed and happy life (*vita beata*). Porphyry, for instance, explained that we may offer material sacrifices to the lesser gods, but the Supreme God is above all. Silence alone is appropriate for him as well as a human being's seeking to be close to him, which is obtained by *apatheia* and *theoria*.[21]

The third and most decisive influence is the biblical notion of sacrifice. For Augustine the defining text is God's anti-cultic declaration in Hosea as quoted by Jesus against the Pharisees: "Learn what it means: I desire mercy, rather than whole-burnt offerings."[22] By using this text Augustine reconciles the prophetic critic with the external sacrifices in the temple of Israel. He shows that the Old Testament scriptures point the way to the internalization of sacrifice. His favorite quote is from Psalm 50:19: "Sacrifice to God is a contrite spirit; a contrite and humbled heart you will not spurn." By the conflation of this text with Hos 6:6 he explains that even in the Old Testament God did not require material sacrifices as ends in themselves, but rather that they expressed the inner attitude of the human being who consecrated himself to God. This inner attitude of consecration to God is expressed by having mercy on our soul and our neighbor, but in every case the act of mercy must be done for the sake of God. The material sacrifices of the Old Testament are only the sacrament; that is, the visible signs of the true interior sacrifice.[23]

In addition to the anthropological reference, the visible sacrifices of the Old Law refer also to Christ. In other words, they signify both an interior attitude of the offerer and an intrinsic ordering of the external rite to Christ's sacrifice. Thus, they are sacraments in a twofold sense: they are signs of interior sacrifice as well as signs of the "true and greatest sacrifice."[24]

---

21. See his work *On Abstinence*. Relying mainly on Stoic sources, Lactantius develops the Christian notion of sacrifice, a notion similar to certain aspects of Augustine's understanding, such as: the sacrifices of a true worshipper are "a kind heart, innocent life and good deeds . . . For God does not desire the offering of a mute animal, death or blood, but the offering which is man himself and his life" (*De divinis Institutis*, 6,24:intr, tr & ed Christiane Ingreman (Paris: Cerf, 2007) *Sources chrétiennes*, 509, 369. See also Minucius Felix, *Octavius* 32, 1–3: ed & tr Jean Beaujeu (Paris: Société d'éditions "Belles lettres," 1964) 54–55.

22. Mt 9:13 quoting Hos 6:6. All biblical quotations are from the New American Bible, Revised Old Testament, 2010.

23. *De civitate Dei* 10,5 : ed Bernardus Dombert & Alphonsus Kalb (Turnhout : Brepols, 1955) CC SL XLVII, 276–78.

24. Ibid., 17, 20,2. Augustine goes even farther by attributing a eucharistic meaning even to the simple commendation of the Ecclesiastes to eat your bread and drink your

All Old Testament sacrifices are signs and figures of Christ's one "true sacrifice," as if one and the same thing were expressed by a variety of words in order to emphasize it without causing annoyance by repetition.[25]

Although not made explicit by Augustine, the Old Testament rites have a twofold reference, both to the inner attitude of the sacrificer and to Christ. This must be so since the inner attitude of the sacrificer in the Old Testament, which is his invisible sacrifice, must in some sense share in the perfect sacrificial attitude of Christ. In fact, Christ himself is the full internalization of sacrifice, the human being consecrated and given over to God in the form of a slave about whom the many figures of the Old Law prophesy. Out of personal love for each of us, Christ has offered up his body as propitiation for our sins: "For he loved us and He gave himself over for us as an oblation and sacrifice in sweet fragrance." Therefore, Augustine claims with St. Paul that "him who had no sin God made sin" in the sense of making him a "sacrifice for sin."[26]

The reason why Christ's is the highest and truest sacrifice, which validates those of the Old Law and of Christians, lies not only in his sinless purity, but ultimately in the mystery of the incarnation, since he in one person is the sacrificial gift, the man who sacrifices, and the God who receives the sacrifice. Thus, because of his ontological unity with God, Christ joins together God and Man most perfectly by giving himself as man to God. He alone is the true mediator between God and man:

> [S]ince in the form of God the man Christ Jesus receives the sacrifice together with his Father with whom he is one, he has preferred to be sacrifice in the form of the servant rather than its recipient lest anyone might be misled to think that one must sacrifice to a creature. It is in this sense that he is high priest, he himself being the one who offers and the offering.[27]

Augustine does not dwell long on the sacrifice of Christ in any of his works. His main emphasis is on the sacrifice of the Christians, which has been made possible by the former. In fact, enabling the sacrifice of Christians has been the very goal of the sacrifice of our great High Priest "who offered himself in his passion for us so that we may become the body of such a great head." In a surprising way, since it is not expressed by Paul whose concept

---

wine.

25. Ibid., 10,20:294.
26. *Sermo* 155, 8: III/2, 545.
27. Ibid.

of the church as the body of Christ is the basis of Augustine's thought, the bishop of Hippo defines the sacrifice of Christians as *multi unum corpus in Christo*: "the many [being] one body in Christ."[28]

Becoming a member of the body of Christ is a dynamic process, which begins with baptism as we die to our old self and put on a new self, created again in Christ. But what we receive as totally undeserved gift, we must unfold and perfect in two mutually dependent ways: having mercy on our neighbor by our actions and on ourselves by acts of worship, primarily in the Eucharist.[29] To emphasize the sacrificial character of every part of a Christian life, Augustine joins Romans 12:12 to Hosea 6:6 as the scriptural foundation. Contrary to the Hellenistic understanding of the spiritual sacrifice, for Augustine our rational homage to God (*rationabile obsequium*) consists of that which the philosophers tend to despise, the offering of our bodies to God as a living and holy sacrifice. The Christian Augustine knows that love of neighbor is always exercised—and the surrender of the soul to God is completed—through the actions of the body. In this sense, we ourselves become the entire sacrifice: *totum sacrificium nos ipsi sumus*.[30]

Even though the sacrifice of our acts of mercy and the offering of our bodies always include the enabling power of the grace of Christ, the celebration of the Eucharist is the chief connection between the sacrifice of Christians and its source from which it receives the value and power and which result in a gradual identification with Christ's sacrifice in the Eucharist: [Christ] wanted the daily sacrament [of his sacrifice] to be the sacrifice of the Church which, being the body of himself as the head, learns to offer herself through him.[31]

Augustine articulates here both the intimate link and the distinction between the sacrifice of Christ and that of his church, the latter being the sacrament of the former. The two sacrifices are different, but the church is learning by her daily offering of the sacrifice of her head to close the gap, so to speak, between the two so that her sacrifice may become more closely identified with her head's sacrifice.

The church's sacrifice is the pattern and the source of grace for the members' moral sacrifice. On the one hand, a member of the body of Christ

---

28. *Civ* 10,20:294.

29. *Civ* 10,6: 278.

30. Ibid.

31. *Cuius rei sacramentum cotidianum esse voluit Ecclesiae sacrificium, quae cum ipsius capitis corpus sit, se ipsam per ipsum discit offerre* (Civ, 10, 20: 294).

receives in sacramental communion his own mystery; that is, the strengthening of his union with Christ and the other members of the church. The moral life of the Christian, on the other hand, derives from this union. His reception of the sacrament includes a pledge to live up to the mystery he receives; that is, to live and act as a member of Christ's body. Thus: If you are the body of Christ and its members, it is your own mystery that you receive. You respond "Amen" to what you are and ratify it by your response. Be, then, a member of Christ so that your Amen be true.[32]

The grace, which derives from the Eucharist and enables the living of a Christian life, is charity. In fact, Augustine sees a certain identity between charity and the Eucharist. As we saw above, the latter *is* that bond of charity which prevents the disintegration of the members and joins them as one body with the Head in a manner analogous to the union of Bride and Bridegroom who become one flesh.

The Presence of Christ in the Eucharist

There were many attempts in the past to answer the question whether or not, according to Augustine, Christ is really present in the Eucharist. Both those who affirm and those who deny find texts to support their position. The critics who dismiss any form of real presence in the Bishop's writings argue that Augustine himself ridicules a literal understanding of the Eucharistic texts and teaches a figurative interpretation in the modern sense, which would exclude a real presence. One of the texts allegedly supporting such an (externally) figurative interpretation is the following:

> "Unless you eat the flesh of the Son of Man and drink his blood, you will not have life in yourself." He appears to order a criminal or disgraceful act. In reality it is figurative speech: he commands that one should share in the Lord's passion and affectionately and fruitfully store up in his memory that for us his flesh was crucified and wounded.[33]

In a sermon to the newly baptized, he explains that the eucharistic bread and wine are called sacraments because "one sees one thing in them but understands something else."[34] "Here is the evidence—these critics

---

32. *Sermo* 272: IV/2 142.
33. *Jo* 26,15: 267.
34. *Sermo* 272: IV/2 142.

claim—that Augustine does not believe that the bread and wine are Christ's body and blood, but rather that these visible elements are only noetic signs, which remind viewers of the sacrificed body and blood of Christ.

Those who advocate for a form of real presence have also found texts to bolster their claim: He gave up his very flesh to eat for our salvation; no one, however, eats that flesh unless first he worshipped it.[35]

Augustine goes as far as to say that: Christ was carried in his own hands as he gave over his body and said, 'this is my body;' in fact he was carrying that body in his hands.[36]

To understand clearly, we should investigate the issue in light of Augustine's own philosophical and theological context.

The Body and Blood of the Lord for Augustine indeed belongs to the realm of sacraments, sacred signs and figures which are referred to in the words of Scripture. These words signify certain events, rites or persons which, beyond their primary meaning, have a hidden spiritual meaning concerning a particular detail or aspect of the mystery of Christ. In this sense, the biblical text is sacramental. To the extent that God's grace illumines our mind, we perceive a certain relationship of the biblical figure or event to the mystery of Christ and in this insight of faith we encounter Christ himself and are nourished by him. But this Christological reference of the Old Testament figure or event concerns only certain aspects, features or actions of the figures and events. Thus, the rock from which Moses made water gush forth is Christ insofar as Christ will be the source of the Holy Spirit for his people. Moses reveals certain features of Christ, but he is not Christ himself. Therefore, Augustine never tells us to worship the books of Scripture or Moses or Elijah or the Exodus or the rock in the desert, but— as we have seen—he does so regarding the bread and wine of the Blood of the Lord. Augustine knows that "our bread and wine . . . becomes, by a certain consecratory prayer, mysterious (*mysticus*)"[37] and tells his newly baptized people that in fact the Eucharist does not simply speak about the Son but it *is* the Son:

> You read and heard this in the Gospel [the words of the institution of the Eucharist]. But you did not know that this Eucharist is the Son. Now however, your hearts sprinkled in a good conscience

---

35. *Enarrationes*, SL XXXIX 98,9: 1385.

36. Ibid., 33: S I 10: Ibid. 281.

37. *Contra Faustum*, 20:13: *The Nicene and Post-Nicene Fathers v. IV* (Grand Rapids, MI: Eerdmans, repr. 1979) 258.

and your bodies bathed in clean water, approach him and be enlightened and your face will not blush with shame.[38]

Nor does Augustine warn that we are condemned if we read the Bible in the state of grave sin, as he warns those who eat the Body and Blood of the Lord unworthily.[39] If communion were only a psychological reminder of Christ and his sacrifice, it could not be condemnation for the sinner to participate in it. He might even be legitimately encouraged to do so because it could demonstrate his openness to repentance.

We must acknowledge, however, that Augustine has never clearly articulated the distinction between the sacramental nature of Scripture and the sacrament of Eucharist. Most likely the simple reason for this was that there was no heresy or doubt at that time, which would have called for further differentiation regarding the kinds of sacramental signification. These examples show that in the case of the Eucharist, Augustine maintains the traditional faith of the church. He asserts that Christ is not present transitionally, as He is when the Scripture is read or proclaimed and the inspiration of grace touches the hearer of the Word, but He is present independently in the Eucharist from the communicant's subjective disposition. The right disposition is only the condition for eating the real Blood of the Lord not only sacramentally but also in reality. Augustine's statement quoted above, where he applies to the Eucharist his definition of sign, does not deny the specific difference between the Eucharist and other signs, but rather states only what is common to all signs: "one sees one thing in them but understands something else." The Body and Blood of the Lord is in fact the ultimate truth (and therefore the ultimate reality) beyond the sense impressions of the Eucharistic bread and wine, impressions that our intellect can only understand in the light of faith.

In addition to explicit texts, the real presence of Christ in the sacrament is implied by its ecclesial and sacrificial aspects. How could Augustine insist that the church and Christ, Bride and Bridegroom, would become united in one flesh if the flesh of Christ were missing from the Eucharist?

---

38. *Sermo* 228B, 3: IV/1 400. He also explains that those Jews who converted in Jerusalem drank the blood they had shed (*Sermo* 97). In order to have the desired shock effect, "blood" must have been taken by Augustine in the same or an analogous sense in both members of the antithesis. So, if the blood they had shed was truly the blood of Christ, the sacrament also must be in a real sense his blood.

39. *Jo* 59,1: 476, *Enarrationes*, 142, 16: 2071; *Sermo* 132, 1: III/1 204.

In the following text Augustine takes for granted that the flesh of Christ is present in the Eucharist and argues that his congregation is one with Him:

> For you receive that flesh about which Life Itself says: "the bread that I shall give is my flesh for the life of the world ... Thus having life in him, you will be in one flesh with him. For [the apostle Paul] does not commend this sacrament as the body of Christ in such a way as to separate you from [that body]. For the apostle recalls that it has been foretold in the Sacred Scriptures: "the two will be in one flesh.[40]

Augustine's doctrine of sacrifice also presupposes the real presence. How could the church move closer every day to uniting herself with the sacrifice of Christ if He were not present?

Conclusions

Surveying the role of the Eucharist in Augustine's thought, we have seen how critical it is in fulfilling the dynamics of the descent and ascent of Christ.

1. In his conversion, Augustine realizes that he cannot ascend to God by his own intellectual efforts. He needs the food of the Eucharist that will gradually transform him into Christ and lead him on the way of humility to see Christ face to face in his divinity.
2. He cannot ascend to God alone, separately from the Church. The sacrifice of worship and adoration, the offering of his own body, is acceptable to God only if he is a member of the church, which is the Body of Christ united to Him as Bride to Groom in one flesh. We are joined with the church at baptism, but are constantly strengthened and perfected by participation in the Eucharist.
3. The Eucharist, being the sacrament of the sacrifice of Christ, which the church learns to offer as her own, reveals and intensifies the inseparable unity between love of God and love of neighbor, service of God and service of neighbor, cult and moral life.
4. The charity which springs from the Eucharist is the bond of unity which holds the church together as one body and the one Bride of Christ. Thus, Eucharistic charity is not simply a moral force, but,

---

40. *Sermo* 228B, 4: IV/1 400

because it comes from the Holy Spirit, it also has a creative power. It creates *una quaedam persona* out of the many and makes them ontologically united with Christ and through Christ with each other. Thus the one Christ cries to God with one voice from all the ends of the earth and praises him with a new song, with new hearts and deeds, so that his whole life becomes praise.[41]

5. This ontological unity does not abolish the differences among persons nor the infinite difference between human and divine nature. On the contrary, Eucharistic charity perfects each member of the body of Christ and enables each to become endowed with grace for his unique personal mission.

6. The *manducatio spiritualis,* "the eating of the Body and drinking of the Blood of Christ spiritually," means not what later Roman Catholic theology called "communion by desire," but rather spiritually fruitful sacramental communion. If we realize that "spiritual" in Augustine does not primarily refer to our spirit but to the Holy Spirit, we see the futility of the controversy about whether, according to Augustine, we receive the power of the Spirit *or* Christ himself in sacramental communion. In Augustine's thought these are not mutually exclusive alternatives—the risen Christ is always present in the Spirit within us and Christ's presence within us brings forth the fruits of the Spirit.

7. Our inquiry has also shown that Augustine does not analyze the mode of the real presence of Christ in the Eucharist. He simply affirms and presupposes it as the condition for the real unity of the Church and the Church's real participation in his sacrifice.

The Relevance of Augustine's Eucharistic Doctrine

Augustine's Eucharistic doctrine is quite relevant in our age for every Christian denomination. It offers us ground for furthering our ecumenical dialogue.

- It challenges the unilateral emphasis on community celebration versus God-centered worship and vice versa. For Augustine the ecclesial and theocentric aspects are inseparable.

---

41. See more on it, Cipriano Vagaggini, "La teologia della lode secondo S. Agostino."

- Not only are sacrifice and church unity mutual conditions of each other, but, in addition, Christian moral life and liturgy exist together. One should not expand the importance of one at the expense of the other.

- Augustine challenges both the materialistic and the mere noetic symbolist understanding of the real presence of Christ in the Eucharist. He makes us see that Catholics and Protestants cannot arrive at an ecclesiological convergence without first simultaneously discovering a common understanding of the Eucharistic mystery.

Bibliography

Augustine, *De civitate Dei*. Edited by Bernardus Dombert and Alphonsus Kalb. Corpus Christianorum Series Latina. Brepols: Turnhout, 1955.

———. *Confessions*. Edited and Introduction by James J. O'Donnell. Oxford: Clarendon, 1992.

———. *Contra Faustum*. In *The Nicene and Post-Nicene Fathers*. Reprinted, Grand Rapids: Eerdmans,1979

———. *Enarrationes in Psalmos*. Edited Eligius Dekkers and Johannes Freipont. Corpus Christianorum Series Latina 38. Brepols: Turnhout, 1956.

———. *Johannis Evangelium Tractatus*. Edited by Radbotus Willems. Corpus Christianorum Series Latina 36. Turnhout: Brepols, 1954.

———. *Opere di Sant'Agostino* III/1. Rome: Citta Nuova Editrice, 1965–89.

———. *La dottrina eucaristica di Sant' Agostino*. Bilingual ed. Translated by Gerardo di Nola. Rome: Libreria Ed. Vaticana, 1997.

Betz, Johannes. "Die Eucharistielehre der lateinischen Väter." In *Handbuch der Dogmengeschichte* IV/4a, edited by Michael Schmaus and Aloys Grillmeir, 142–59. Freiburg: Herder, 1979.

Calvin, John. *Theological Treatises*. Translated by. J. K. S Read. Philadelphia: Westminster, 1954.

Ferguson, Everett. "Eucharist." In *Encyclopedia of Early Christianity*, edited by Everett Ferguson, 1:393–98. 2nd ed. New York: Garland, 1997.

Jackson, Pamela. "Eucharist." In *Augustine through the Ages: An Encyclopedia*, edited by Allan D. Fitzgerald, 330–34. Grand Rapids: Eerdmans, 1999.

Kereszty, Roch. *The Wedding Feast of the Lamb: Eucharistic Theology from a Historical, Biblical and Systematic Perspective*. Chicago: Hillenbrand, 2004.

Kilmartin, Edward J. *The Eucharist in the West: History and Theology*. Edited by Robert Daly. Collegeville, MN: Liturgical, 1998.

Lactantius. *De divinis Institutis*. Translated and edited by Christiane Ingreman. Paris: Cerf, 2007.

Minucius Felix, *Octavius*. In *Sources chrétiennes*. Translated and edited by Jean Beaujeu. Paris: Société d'éditions "Belles lettres," 1964.

Vagaggini, Cipriano. "La teologia della lode secondo S. Agostino." In *La preghiera nella Biblia a nella tradizione patristica e monastica*, edited by C. Vagaggini, and G. Penco, 400–467. Rome: Paoline, 1964.

6

Eastern Orthodox Social Ethics and the Anaphora of St. Basil the Great

—Philip LeMasters

EASTERN ORTHODOX CHRISTIANITY IS often more readily associated with ancient and beautiful liturgies than with practical service to human beings. Despite the prophetic preaching and example of holy hierarchs such as St. Basil the Great, the church's liturgical entrance into the joy of the Kingdom has not always inspired a social witness to God's reign upon the earth. Likewise, the study of liturgy is typically separated from the daily work of the people in fulfilling the petition of Jesus Christ himself, "Thy will be done on earth as it is in heaven." In both the scholarly analysis and the popular piety of Eastern Christians, Eucharist and ecclesiology are topics that do not often intersect with moral theology or social ethics.[1]

Despite these notes of realism, the *anaphora* of the Divine Liturgy of St. Basil the Great provides substantial resources for displaying God's purposes for the collective life of humanity and how Christians should act in circumstances in which those purposes are not yet fulfilled. The point is not to reduce the Eucharist or the church to purely moral realities; neither is to

---

1. See LeMasters, "*Philanthropia*," 187–211, for further development of the themes introduced in this essay.

identify the church with a political agenda or school of thought. Instead, the goal is to heighten the awareness, especially of Eastern Christians, of the social implications of the church's liturgical practice.

This paper identifies selected implications for Orthodox social ethics of Basil's *anaphora*. These prayers, made in the context of the offering and reception of the Eucharist, call worshippers to embody the divine compassion and generosity for which they pray. In this way, the *anaphora* functions as a prophetic text the enactment of which calls the church and its members to live out in daily life what they celebrate liturgically. Otherwise, communicants risk eating and drinking their own condemnation as they fall into a spiritually unhealthy separation of liturgy and life.

"Very probably the work of Basil,"[2] the *anaphora* is the heart of a liturgy that provides "a springboard for social action and societal involvement."[3] Demetrios Constantelos notes that its "petitions and prayers are not meant to be rhetorical exclamations, poetic romanticism, or supplications for God alone to hear; they are meant to penetrate man's heart and mind and become an impetus for *agape* in *diakonia*—love in practice." Basil saw them as "an invitation to the metamorphosis of the congregation as well as of society . . . The prayers remind the faithful of the poor and the sick, of the weak and the powerless, of orphans and widows, of the aged and captives, of travelers, and of those in prison, in the mines, in hard labor."[4]

St. Nicholas Cabasilas commented that "The essential act in the celebration of the holy mysteries is the transformation of the elements into the Divine Body and Blood; its aim is the sanctification of the faithful . . ."[5] Prominent themes in Basil's *anaphora*, homilies, and ministry point to the social implications of communion in holy things, to a sanctified way of living in society for those nourished by Christ's Body and Blood. Paul Schroder comments that Basil "envisioned a new social order based upon simplicity and sharing rather than competition and private ownership."[6] For example, the communal life of the *Basiliad* integrated worship with philanthropic services for the sick, poor, and homeless in ways that displayed patterns of relationship and social order that manifested the "eschatological newness"

---

2. Hybrew, *Orthodox Liturgy*, 55–56.
3. Constantelos, "Basil the Great's Social Thought," 85.
4. Ibid., 85.
5. Cabasilas, *Commentary on the Divine Liturgy*, 25.
6. Schroeder, *Social Justice*, 21.

of the Kingdom of God.[7] Basil was the first bishop "who systematically organized philanthropic foundations—hospitals, hostels for poor travelers, homes for the aged, orphanages, and leprosaria; he was the first who made monasticism a redeeming social force."[8] As St. Gregory the Theologian said of the *Basiliad* in his eulogy for Basil,

> A noble thing is philanthropy, and the support of the poor, and the assistance of human weakness. Go forth a little way from the city, and behold the new city, the storehouse of piety, the common treasury of the wealthy, in which the superfluities of their wealth, aye, and even their necessities are stored, in consequence of his exhortations, freed from the power of the moth, no longer gladdening the eyes of the thief, and escaping both the emulation of envy, and the corruption of time: where disease is regarded in a religious light, and disaster is thought a blessing, and sympathy is put to the test.[9]

The integration of liturgy and life, which Basil proclaimed and exemplified, shines through the *anaphora* as the church prepares to enter mystically into the joy of the heavenly banquet. The prayers of petition following the *epiclesis* especially call for attention to the praxis of social ethics, as they include petitions for God to "remember . . . those who bear fruit and do good works in thy holy churches, and those who remember the poor" toward the end of eternal gifts for temporal offerings.[10] The celebrant prays for civil authorities and the armed forces for "peaceful times" so that "we in their tranquility may lead a calm and peaceful life in all godliness and sanctity." Prayers continue for "the people here present, and of those who are absent for reasonable cause," for "peace and concord" for their marriages and the well-being of infants, the young, and the aged. Petitions follow for vulnerable populations such as the demon-possessed, travelers, widows, orphans, captives, the sick, and those condemned to the mines, in exile, in harsh labor, and "in every tribulation, necessity, and danger." The celebrant beseeches God to "be mindful . . . of all thy people, and upon them all pour out thy rich mercy, granting to all their petitions which are unto salvation."[11]

---

7. Ibid., 38.
8. Constantelos, "Basil the Great's Social Thought," 81.
9. Gregory the Theologian, "Panegyric on St. Basil," 416.
10. *Service Book of the Holy Eastern Orthodox Catholic and Apostolic Church*, 140.
11. Ibid., 140–41.

The petitions invoke God's great compassion for "those who love us and those who hate us" and even those whose names we do not know or have forgotten to name in prayer. "For thou, O Lord, art the Helper of the helpless, the Hope of the hopeless, the Savior of the storm-tossed, the Haven of the voyager, the Healer of the sick. Be thou thyself all things to all men, O thou who knowest every man, his petition, his dwelling place, and his need. Deliver, O Lord, this city and countryside from famine, plague, earthquake, flood, fire, sword, invasion of enemies, and civil war." Appeals continue for God "to visit us with . . . longing-kindness . . . [and] manifest thyself unto us in thy rich divine compassions . . . [by] temperate and healthful seasons" and "gentle showers upon the earth unto fruitfulness." Requests for the healing of schisms, the pacification of "hostile nations," and the destruction of heresy anticipate a plea for God to "receive us all into thy Kingdom, making us children of the light and of the day; and grant unto us thy peace and love, O Lord our God, for all things hast thou given unto us."[12]

Cabasilas notes that Basil "unites thanksgiving and supplication . . . throughout the liturgy" in ways that "proclaim God as supreme benefactor of the human race."[13] In the larger context of giving thanks even as the celebrant and the people prepare to receive Communion, these petitions for God's blessing upon vulnerable and suffering people, as well as upon the civil order and the church, present a vision of the world fulfilled and transformed according to the purposes of God's Kingdom. Before the *epiclesis*, the celebrant proclaims "Thine own of Thine own, we offer unto Thee on behalf of all and for all," thus firmly grounding the church's liturgical offering in response to and participation in the divine compassion for human beings that led the Father to send the Son and the Son to offer himself for the salvation of the world.[14] The church's offering extends beyond the obvious, however, for as Alexander Schmemann observes, "this offering to God of bread and wine, of the food that we must eat in order to live, is our offering to Him of ourselves, of our life and of the whole world."[15]

It is fitting, then, that the *anaphora* places the eucharistic offering in the context of supplication for especially broken dimensions of life in the world to be healed. The compassion of the Father for corrupt humanity

---

12. Ibid., 141–42.
13. Cabasilas, *Commentary on the Divine Liturgy*, 84–85.
14. *Service Book of the Holy Eastern Orthodox Catholic and Apostolic Church*, 138.
15. Schmemann, *For the Life of the World*, 35

extends to those whose life circumstances fall short of the well-being appropriate to those created in the divine image and likeness. They are particularly in need of God's mercy and the prayers of the church. Those who mystically "ascend to heaven in Christ in order to become partakers of the world to come" do not abandon the world as we know it, but pray for the fulfillment of the world and all its inhabitants in the Kingdom.[16] Lawrence Farley agrees that these intercessory prayers manifest "the nature of the royal priesthood of the Church . . . As a kingdom of priests (Rev 1:6), we offer our broken world back to Him. He will receive it as an acceptable sacrifice through Christ and will heal it. The eucharistic sacrifice therefore establishes the world and gives it peace."[17]

As Schmemann notes, "The Eucharist is the sacrament of unity and the *moment of truth*: here we see the world in Christ, as it really is . . . Intercession begins here, in the glory of the messianic banquet, and this is the only true beginning for the Church's mission."[18] The '*prayer of intercession*" calls for "*the gathering of the Church*, the body of Christ, her manifestation in all fullness."[19] He refers to these petitions as being cosmic, ecclesiological, and eschatological in focus as they concern "All of God's creation, all salvation, all fulfillment."[20] It is within such a spiritually profound context that particular people prepare to commune in and with a body much larger than themselves in a fashion that should transform every dimension of their life in the world. As Christos Yannaras states, "The moral endeavor of the Christian is a personal extension of the Eucharist into every aspect of life. Work, economic life, the family, art, technology, politics and cultural life all become part of man's eucharistic relationship with God."[21]

The implications for Eastern Orthodox social ethics are profound and obvious. In order to pray such socially charged petitions with integrity, the members of the church must enact the very *philanthropia* and compassion for which they give thanks and pray. As the body of Christ in the power of the Holy Spirit, the church's very identity is to be an embodied social icon of God's salvation. The presence, witness, and ministry of the church may not be reduced to addressing poverty, disease, and other social problems.

16. Ibid., 42.
17. Farley, *Let Us Attend*, 79.
18. Schmemann, *For the Life of the World*, 44.
19. Schmemann, *Eucharist*, 235; italics original.
20. Ibid., 239.
21. Yannaras, *Freedom of Morality*, 93–94.

Nonetheless, the *anaphora* calls the members of the Orthodox church to live out practically what they enact liturgically in response to the needs of the human beings whom they encounter. To fail to do so is to fail to show love for Christ and to invite judgment: "In that you did not it to the least of these my brethren, you did not do it to me." (Matt 25: 45) Just as the Epistle of St. James condemns those who say "Depart in peace, be warmed and filled" without giving "the things which are needed for the body" of the hungry and naked (Jas 2: 15–16), those who separate liturgy from life are in a false position.

Even more is this the case due to the unique sacramental nature of participation in the Eucharist. As Cabasilas comments, "[W]hen He has led the initiate to the table and has given him His Body to eat He entirely changes him, and transforms him into His own state. The clay is no longer clay when it has received the royal likeness but is already the Body of the King. It is impossible to conceive of anything more blessed than this . . . After the Eucharist, then, there is nowhere further to go."[22] Those who receive into their own bodies the body and blood of Jesus Christ participate personally in the mystical supper of the heavenly kingdom. They "dare to partake of thy whole Body."[23] In the *anaphora*, the prayer before the Our Father, and prayers of preparation for communion, the sublimity and gravity of receiving the Eucharist are central themes. The celebrant prays "that no one of us may partake of the holy Body and Blood of thy Christ unto judgment or unto condemnation, but rather that we may find mercy and grace . . ."[24] Communicants pray for "salvation and sanctification of . . . soul and body . . . the expulsion of every evil imagination, sinful deed or work of the Devil." They beseech God that the "Holy Gifts" will cause them "to love thee always, to amend and keep firm my life; and to be ever in me to the increase of virtue, to the keeping of thy commandments, to the communion of the Holy Spirit, and as a good defense before they dread judgment seat, and for life eternal."[25] Those who commune do so for growth in holiness and union with the Lord that should be evident in their lives. They are to live out the implications of the great blessing they have received as "partakers of the divine nature." (2 Pet 1:4) Presumably, to refuse to do so would make one

---

22. Cabasilas, *Life in Christ*, 113–14.
23. *Service Book of the Holy Eastern Orthodox Catholic and Apostolic Church*, 208.
24. Ibid., 139.
25. Ibid., 206.

subject to the consequences of eating and drinking judgment upon oneself "through an unworthy partaking." (1 Cor 11: 27–30)

Among other dimensions of holiness, a life truly in communion with Jesus Christ will be characterized by generosity to the needy human beings in whom the Lord is present. Those whose lives do not become epiphanies of divine compassion to their desperate neighbors fall short of the social implications of communion with the Lord. If they refuse to show compassion after having received the Eucharist, they condemn themselves, rather like the wicked servant who refused to forgive a small debt after having been forgiven of a much larger debt by his master. (Matt 18: 23–35) They have received the divine compassion selfishly, refusing to extend the same generosity to others. "But whoever has this world's goods, and sees his brother in need, and shuts up his heart from him, how does the love of God abide in him?" (1 John 3:17)

Basil warned that such attitudes and action invite eternal judgment. As he proclaimed "To the Rich,"

> I know many who fast, pray, sigh, and demonstrate every manner of piety, so long as it costs them nothing, but would not part with a penny to help those in distress. Of what profit to them is the remainder of their virtue? The Kingdom of Heaven does not receive such people, for "it is easier for a camel to go through the eye of a needle than for someone who is rich to enter the Kingdom of God."[26]

To the rich who refused to share with the poor, Basil proclaims a hard truth: "You showed no mercy; it will not be shown to you. You opened not your house; you will be expelled from the Kingdom. You gave not your bread; you will not receive eternal life."[27] Because the fruits of the earth are to meet the needs common to all, greed amounts to theft:

> Who are the greedy? Those who are not satisfied with what suffices for their own needs. Who are the robbers? Those who take for themselves what rightfully belongs to everyone. And you, are you not greedy? Are you not a robber? The things you received in trust as a stewardship, have you not appropriated them for yourself? Is not the person who strips another of clothing called a thief? And those who do not clothe the naked when they have the power to do so, should they not be called the same? The bread you are

26. Basil the Great, *Social Justice*, 46.
27. Ibid., 49.

holding back is for the hungry, the clothes you keep put away are for the naked, the shoes that are rotting away with disuse are for those who have none, the silver you keep buried in the earth is for the needy. You are thus guilty of injustice toward as many as you ought to have aided, and did not.[28]

Citing the account of the last judgment in Matthew 25, Basil teaches that "those who are under accusation in this passage are not those who have stolen anything; these charges are rather leveled against those who have not shared with others."[29] "In Time of Famine and Drought," he insists that "whoever has the ability to remedy the suffering of others, but chooses rather to withhold aid out of selfish motives, may properly be judged the equivalent of a murderer."[30] Even as the consequences of disregarding the needy are grave, the rewards of showing compassion are sublime: "Give but a little, and you will gain much; undo the primal sin by sharing your food. Just as Adam transmitted sin by eating wrongfully, so we wipe away the treacherous food when we remedy the need and hunger of our brothers and sisters."[31]

Peter Brown describes the context of Basil's sermons during a time of famine as follows:

> The crisis appears to have been caused by a winter drought such as often afflicts Inner Anatolia. No snow or rain fell from an icy, empty sky. The result was not the collapse of the entire ecology of the region. It was, rather, a food shortage caused by the panic of the rich. Faced with the prospect of a famine of indefinite duration, they were unwilling to make available the grain already stored in their barns.[32]

Once the storehouses were opened, "Basil used his own wealth to found a soup kitchen, and could be seen in it, directing his servants as they laid tables for the poor. He even embraced lepers with the kiss of peace."[33] Raised in a family "clearly among the elite minority of the upper class," he "chose to sell some portion of the inheritance that fell to him after the death of his father, and distribute the proceeds to the poor, in keeping with the

---

28. Ibid., 69–70.
29. Ibid., 70.
30. Ibid., 85.
31. Ibid., 86.
32. Brown, *Poverty and Leadership*, 39.
33. Ibid., 40.

commandment of Jesus."[34] During the famine, "Basil sold and distributed much of what remained of his paternal inheritance in order to help provide for the starving people of Caesarea."[35] He called others to join in obedience to the example of Christ's *philanthropia* and kenotic self-emptying for the sake of others. (Phil 2:5–8) As the celebrant prays in the *anaphora*, "But albeit he was God before all the ages, yet he appeared upon earth and dwelt among men; and was incarnate of a holy Virgin, and did empty himself, taking on the form of a servant, and becoming conformed to the fashion of our lowliness, that he might make us conformable to the image of his glory."[36]

The Eucharist is a common meal in which people of all social classes and life circumstances partake of one loaf and one chalice. Communicants receive the body and blood of a savior who showed particular concern for the poor and described God's kingdom as a reign in which the needy would be especially blessed. In Orthodox Christianity, participation in the common Eucharist demands care for the weak and downtrodden; indeed, Christ Himself is present in them. For example, Brown notes that St. John Chrysostom's "sermons on the poor took place under the shadow of the Eucharist . . . Through the Eucharist, Christ gave his unique flesh and blood to every Christian. Chrysostom and many Eastern fathers believed that shared divinity, quite literally, ran in the veins of all who shared in the orthodox Eucharist."[37] Susan Holman makes the similar point that "As the Cappadocians use traditional New Testament images to identify the poor with Christ, the body of the poor—in its most literal, mutable sense—gains social meaning. The rhetorical expression of this body gains a language and voice of its own as it is viewed as the body of the Logos."[38] In Basil's preaching, "the poor enter the Christian consciousness as a body that is integral to God's creation. They enter the civic and religious liturgy through Basil's homiletical call to social change."[39] Service to the poor becomes an integral dimension of service to Christ. In this light, those who receive the Lord in the Eucharist have an obligation to care for him in the flesh and blood of the poor in whom He is present and with whom he has identified himself.

34. Schroeder, *Social Justice*, 16, 19.
35. Ibid., 33.
36. *Service Book of the Holy Eastern Orthodox Catholic and Apostolic Church*, 136.
37. Peter Brown, *Poverty and Leadership*, 96.
38. Holman, *Hungry Are Dying*, 22.
39. Ibid., 97.

All the more is this the case if the poor people in question are also members of the eucharistic assembly.

The Eucharist restores food to its original place of life-giving communion with God and neighbor. It is instructive that Basil refers to generosity with food as a way of setting right the paradigmatic sin of Adam. The same spirit of divine compassion that is present throughout the *anaphora*, and especially in the petitions following the *epiclesis*, entails an obligation for those who have received the Eucharist to live eucharistically. By offering their resources to others at risk of deprivation and death, they become living icons of the abundant mercy of God which they receive sacramentally. To refuse to do so is to refuse communion with the Lord and those who bear his image and likeness. The bold sacramental claims of Orthodoxy about the Eucharist imply equally bold claims about how those who commune should live their lives and treat others who bear the divine image and likeness. The church that enters mystically into the heavenly banquet has an obligation to become a practical embodiment of the very divine compassion for which it gives thanks in the Divine Liturgy.

This brief essay has identified a trajectory in Basil's *anaphora* that demands the integration of liturgy and life, which is an underdeveloped theme in the thought and practice of Eastern Christianity. Orthodox moral theology and social ethics will benefit from further exploration of this and other texts which call those who pray them to manifest the mercy for which they pray. How that mercy will be understood theoretically and applied practically in given settings will surely vary according to a host of factors. Nonetheless, it is incumbent upon those who celebrate the Divine Liturgy to make their life in the world an enacted icon of God's Kingdom in which the poor will be blessed.

Bibliography

Basil the Great. *On Social Justice: St. Basil the Great.* Translated with Introduction and Commentary by C. Paul Schroder. Crestwood, NY: St. Vladimir's Seminary Press, 2009.

Brown, Peter. *Poverty and Leadership in the Later Roman Empire.* Menahem Stern Jerusalem Lectures. Hanover, NH: University of New England Press, 2002.

Cabasilas, Nicholas. *A Commentary on the Divine Liturgy.* Crestwood, NY: St. Vladimir's Seminary Press, 2002.

———. *The Life in Christ.* Crestwood, NY: St. Vladimir's Seminary Press, 1998.

Constantelos, Demetrios J. "Basil the Great's Social Thought and Involvement." *GROT* 26.1–2 (1981) 81–86.

Farley. Lawrence. *Let Us Attend: A Journey through the Divine Liturgy*. Ben Lomond: Conciliar, 2007.

Gregory the Theologian. "The Panegyric on St. Basil." In *Nicene and Post-Nicene Fathers*, edited by Philip Schaff and Henry Wallace, 2/7:395–422. Peabody, MA: Hendrickson, 1994.

Holman, Susan R. *The Hungry Are Dying: Beggars and Bishops in Roman Cappadocia*. Oxford: Oxford University Press, 2001.

Hybrew, Hugh. T*he Orthodox Liturgy: The Development of the Eucharistic Liturgy in the Byzantine Rite*. Crestwood, NY: St. Vladimir's Seminary Press, 1990.

LeMasters, Philip. "*Philanthropia* in Liturgy and Life: The Anaphora of Basil the Great and Eastern Orthodox Social Ethics." *StVTQ* 59 (2015) 187–211.

Schmemann, Alexander. *For the Life of the World*. Crestwood, NY: St. Vladimir's Seminary Press, 1998.

———. *The Eucharist*. Crestwood, NY: St. Vladimir's Seminary Press, 1988.

Service Book of the Holy Eastern Orthodox Catholic and Apostolic Church. Englewood, NJ: Antiochian Orthodox Christian Archdiocese of North America, 1997.

Yannaras, Christos. *The Freedom of Morality*. Crestwood, NY: St. Vladimir's Seminary Press, 1996.

7

The Words of Institution
Their Function in the Earliest Biblical Traditions

—*Allan J. McNicol*

I HAVE ALWAYS BEEN impressed by something Leander Keck wrote years ago:

> . . . for the ancients in general, rites actually did something, the action had power.[1]

Keck wrote these words as part of a mild polemic against those who held that the earliest Christian rites of baptism and the Lord's Supper were "only symbols." For some it is reckoned that the importance of these rites rest almost entirely in realities that occurred earlier, separate and apart from the action of the rite itself.[2] Everett Ferguson, in whose honor this symposium is taking place, has raised similar concerns about such views.[3] Ferguson asserts that whether the meal on the last night before Jesus died was or was not a Passover meal it was infused with an atmosphere of *pesach*. There the guests are urged to engage in a process of identification, 're-actualizing' and participating in the benefits of the act of salvation at Exodus. This furnishes the background and functions as the model for

---

1. Keck, *Paul and His Letters*, 56.
2. Ibid., 56.
3. Ferguson, "The Lord's Supper," 22.

the use of ἀνάμνησις or "remembrance" that underscores early Christian understanding of the Lord's Supper.[4]

Given this background, anything that pertains to the whole area of historical study of the circumstances of the origin of Passover or the Lord's Supper is a matter of considerable importance for devout Jews and Christians. Nevertheless, the fragmentary nature of these ancient sources means that there remain many questions and points of dispute about what we know. These are not just matters that scholars can discuss intellectually in seminars. They impinge upon the beliefs and practices of people of faith.

With regard to the Last Supper, most of us regularly hear the words of institution spoken at a table in some liturgical context. The overwhelming number of people present, I suspect, consider these words to be the actual words (in translation) that Jesus said on the night before he died. But if we examine the accounts in the Synoptic Gospels and Paul, the wording is clearly not the same. Placing these accounts alongside one another in some sort of synoptic relationship we can observe there are significant differences that cannot be attributed merely to translation variants.[5] Literary analysis reveals quickly that what we have in these texts are the compositions of various authors based on received tradition. Still, allowing for this equivocation, it remains an important task to determine what these accounts have to say about these matters.[6] As Ferguson points out, so often important directions in later theology are determined by our assessment of the original sources.[7] Therefore, to have before us a coherent picture of what happened on the fateful evening before Jesus died is a matter of significance. This is especially true for those who wish to claim some continuity through the rite of the Lord's meal with the work and witness of the earthly Jesus.

---

4. Ibid., 21–22.

5. As Meier, "The Eucharist at the Last Supper," 348–349, notes the occasion of this being a unique meal raises special problems for a strict literalistic interpretation of the text. There are many instances in Jesus' ministry (healing incidents or feeding episodes) where the different biblical accounts can be attributed to their taking place on different occasions. In these instances we have different recollections because they took place at varied times. But not so with the Last Supper. This was Jesus' last evening before his death. It is hardly likely he could have repeated the words of institution four or five times.

6. Some scholars such as Fuller, "The Double Origin of the Eucharist," 72, would question the reliability of the tradition to the extent that it is denied that Jesus spoke "the interpretive words at the Last Supper." Thus it is an important issue to come to reasonable conclusions concerning the reliability of the traditions on which the compositional accounts are based.

7. Ferguson, "The Lord's Supper," 21.

Assessing the Biblical Traditions

There are four major accounts of the founding of the Lord's Supper (Matt 26:26–29; Mark 14:22–25; Lk 22:14–20; 1 Cor 11:23–25). In addition to these four accounts, the placing of John 6:48–58 at the end of the Bread of Life discourse so clearly echoes elements of these four accounts that, in some sense, it appears to be a reflective interpretation of the Supper. Finally, read in connection with 1 Cor 11, 1 Cor 10:14–22 also alludes to the Lord's Supper. Primarily it directs a warning to Christians against participating both in meals at the table of the Lord Jesus and meals in honor of pagan gods at their temples (the tables of demons). Thus, even setting aside other potential allusions and echoes of the Lord's Supper in the New Testament (viz., texts such as Acts 2:46, 20:7–11, Jude 12, 2 Pet 2:13 or Rev 3:20) there is a considerable body of material that appears to suggest the importance of this rite in early Christianity.[8]

At first appearance it would seem to be a relatively easy task to analyze the key core passages and accounts for their significant variations. Indeed, it is widely accepted that the four passages fall into two significant groupings: The passages in Matt/Mark and those in Luke/1 Cor. The passages in Matt/Mark are part of the narrative structure of their respective Passion accounts. They are clearly represented as historical. They have many similarities in wording and structure and both are immediately preceded and followed by pericopes on the same subject matter of imminent betrayal (Matt 26:20–25/Mark 14:17–21; Matt 26:30–35/Mark 14:26–31). On the other hand, 1 Cor 11:23–25 is widely recognized to be a body of tradition on liturgical practice of the observance of the Supper. Paul probably received it through his early connections with the church at Antioch.[9] Luke's account appears at a key transitional point in his Passion Account. It opens a lengthy farewell discourse to the disciples. It is especially noteworthy that the two concluding verses on the Lord's Supper (Luke 22:19–20) are close

---

8. *Contra* Caird, *New Testament Theology*, 225–32, who claims that its influence is marginal in the New Testament accounts. Space only allows for attention in this paper to be given to the synoptics and 1 Cor 11:23–25.

9. Or, perhaps, Damascus. See Stuhlmacher, *Jesus of Nazareth,* 81–82; Hofius, "The Lord's Supper and the Lord's Supper Tradition," 75, calls this form-critically a *cultic etiology*. It is widely recognized as having many literary features of tradition through the use of technical terminology such as παραλαμβάνειν and παραδιδόναι "to receive and to hand over."

linguistically to 1 Cor 11:23–25.[10] To complicate matters, with Luke's account there are some minor linguistic overlaps with Matthew or Mark as well as several apparent Lukan transpositions.[11]

These observations on source criticism and tradition-history are but the tip of the iceberg in noting difficulties that we encounter in any serious assessment of these units. In addition, key theological issues, for example, the source of the expiatory terminology in Jesus' instructions at the table, turn up all over the place. Nevertheless, in order to be of assistance in theological discussion about later developments in eucharistic theology within historic Christianity some weight should be placed on the shoulders of biblical scholars to bring a sense of coherence to the basic thrust of the biblical material. This is what I intend to do in this paper.

In this essay I wish to argue that the words and actions of Jesus at his last meal articulate the central concern of his ministry of preparing Israel for the Kingdom of God as he approached his arrest and crucifixion. Despite important formal and material developments after the resurrection in liturgical usage, the main contours of what Jesus was saying and doing at this meal can be known. At this meal Jesus offers his disciples a share of the benefits of his impending death and an offer of a place at the banquet of the Messiah in the fulfilled Kingdom of Heaven. What was spoken to the disciples was, in turn, heard to be applicable to later followers (including Gentiles) who come to his table in faith seeking, through participation, a share in these benefits.

Procedurally, I will construct the foundation of my argument by giving a brief summary of how I conceive Jesus' ministry had developed by the time of the Last Supper. Second, by analyzing what is widely recognized as the two most solid bodies of the earliest traditions of the meal (Matt/Mark and 1 Cor 11:23–26) the argument will be developed in the direction of determining the import of what took place on that fateful night.[12] Special at-

10. Stuhlmacher, *Jesus of Nazareth*, 82, thinks that the Lukan account is based on a similar version of tradition from which Paul also drew. This seems to be a reasonable conclusion.

11. Examples of linguistic overlaps would be ὑπέρ in Luke 22:20/Mk 14:24 but not in Matthew and ἔδωκεν αὐτοῖς "he gave to them" with respect to the bread and the cup (Mark 14:22, 23) and Luke 22:19 (bread). Matthew 26:27 has this terminology only on the cup.

12. Special attention will be given to how expiatory motifs are embedded in this tradition. Given the tenuous nature of our sources it will be inevitable that a number of assertions put forward about the text may be contested. However, I would contend that the main points of my argument rest on solid ground. Unfortunately, space will not

tention will be given to "the words of institution." Luke's account of the Last Supper raises a number of special issues. Before the conclusion I will give a brief overview of how I believe Luke's contribution fits into this discussion.

Jesus' Mission to Restore Israel: The Prolegomenon to Jesus' Last Meal

What took place at Jesus' last meal before his arrest was no accidental occurrence. It must be examined within the spectrum of his total ministry. If there is one thing gospel scholars agree upon it is that central to everything with Jesus was his conviction that the emergence of the realm of God's end-time salvation (the Kingdom of Heaven/God) was taking place. Above all this implied that the ancient promises of the restoration of Zion in association with an end-time banquet when the faithful of all ages would participate in a triumphant meal was soon to be fulfilled. From beginning to end this eschatological perspective was a major accent point of his ministry.

The outset of Jesus' preaching in Galilee is marked by his baptism. The words attributed to the divine voice tell us much (Matt 3:17; Mark 1:11; Luke 3:22). They not only echo Psalm 2:7 (the promise of a new Davidite) but also echo Isa 42:1–4. The latter text asserts that God's servant "the well pleased one" will initiate salvation for Israel by leading his people through the travail of suffering. If we follow the Matthean account this journey started with Jesus' designation as "Yeshua" the one designated to save his people from their sins (Matt 1:21).[13] Matt 26:26–29 represents a critical closing marker in this journey. In between, after his baptism, Jesus' announcement of the kingdom fans out across Galilee and impacts Judea. Thousands gather on the hillsides. They are attracted by the prospects of massive changes with these announcements of a new era. They are fed in meals of anticipation of the coming banquet of the new age (Matt 14:13–21; 15:32–39).

---

allow for an extensive response to the widely discussed view that the Lord's Supper first emerged in Christian communities as a parallel to the meetings of other Greco-Roman associations.

13. As has often been noted the Greek word for people ὁ λαός in this context is a reference to servant-Israel. Especially in the latter chapters of Isaiah this is the community where God has "anointed him." (Isa 61:1) to be the agent to restore righteousness and bring the restoration of divine power to the nations (Isa 42:6; 49:6–8; 61:8; 62:1–3). Cf. Leske, "The Influence of Isaiah," 243.

But the initial excitement quickly changes into icy reservations: especially among Israel's leaders. How could someone from such an insignificant place as Nazareth be God's special envoy for initiating the coming of the new world? It was all too preposterous to accept. And thus, in response, Jesus begins to chart a new course.

Viewing himself as the representative of God's servant-people, the "anointed son," Jesus openly confronted the leaders of Israel and began to confront the cost of passing through the time of travail of suffering on their behalf. As Ben Meyer has pointed out, the acceptance or rejection of his announcement was not a trivial matter. Israel needed to be prepared for the new day. Everything turned on its acceptance or rejection: "Like John, Jesus confronted the nation with a message in no way optional, which called for a response in no way optional. Hence an enormous risk. A mission geared to acquittal and life for Israel ran the risk of ending in condemnation and death for Israel. How were the refusers to be saved from themselves? Jesus' answer was the offer of his life, i.e., the will to go to his death in the service of forgiveness."[14]

In effect, Meyer argues that Jesus in his last days was prepared to deal with Israel's rejection. He prepared himself to suffer in place of Israel for her sins. This decision is paired with the necessary corollary; this sacrifice which precipitates the ordeal of the end only makes sense if the benefits of his death are expiatory and made available to Israel.[15]

In many diverse and significant ways the combined witness of the Synoptics affirms this portrayal of Jesus. Yet it is interesting to observe that it is Matthew who underscores most closely the connection at the Last Supper between the mission of Jesus and its culmination in the shedding of his blood for the forgiveness of sins.[16]

This direction may be seen already in Matt 8:17 in Jesus' healings and exorcisms. Here the connection with the servant of Isa 53 taking upon himself the infirmities and sins of others is transparent. Even more, there is a direct correlation with the phraseology "the forgiveness of sins" and "the shedding of blood" between Matt 26:28 and 23:33–36. Matthew 23:33–36

---

14. Meyer, '"Phases" in Jesus' Mission,' 14. A portion of Meyer's argument is attributed to Pesch, *Das Abendmahl*, 103–9.

15. Ibid., 14. Meyer makes the obvious step that this conclusion provides the basis for the continuity of the mission to Israel after the death of Jesus.

16. Matt 26:28. The concept of the shedding of (innocent) blood emerges multiple times in the latter chapters of Matthew (Matt 23:30, 35; 27:4, 6, 8, 24, and 49 in some texts).

has been called "the counterpoint" to Matt 26:28.[17] Earlier Jesus had told the leaders of his generation that "the kingdom of God will be taken from you and given to a nation producing fruits" (Matt 21:43). Then in Matt 23:33–36 Jesus adds that these leaders of 'this generation' are now standing at the apex of a long history of shedding innocent blood. The unjust death of the righteous ones of the past calls out for God to exercise stern judgment. But there is the counterpoint in Matt 26:28. There Jesus, on the eve of his arrest, expresses his intent to offer his life for 'the many' (Matt 26:28). In a real sense this is a climactic announcement that shines light on what would take place a few hours later at the cross. No valid analysis of the words of institution can be isolated from the context. With this in mind, we will now give attention to what takes place at the Last Supper.

The Words of Institution: In the Earliest Traditions

As previously noted, what appears to be the two earliest traditions on the Lord's Supper are the ones embedded in Matt/Mark and 1 Cor 11:23–25.[18] They are similar enough to discuss jointly.[19] Recent research on emergence

17. Kereszty, "Eucharist in the New Testament," 221.

18. It is generally acknowledged that Matthew was composed about a generation after the martyrdom of Jesus in the Roman province of Greater Syria. Whether it was written in the Decapolis, Galilee or Antioch itself is unclear. Thematically, it differs some from Mark in that it seems comfortable with presenting Jesus as teaching strong obedience to Torah and viewing his mission as primarily focused toward Israel. Also, it presents Jesus' kin and his disciples as more accommodative to his mission than Mark. In sum, it is far more likely, in my estimation, that Jesus' earthly family and the early pillars of the church in Jerusalem would view more favorable Matthew's account of Jesus' life than Mark. Thus, regardless of our view of the order of composition of the gospels, both the sources themselves and Matthew's use of the traditions of Jesus' life that he utilized in his gospel should be taken with utmost seriousness. I would understand 1 Cor 11:23b–25 as having close affinities with this tradition which may have been taken at an early date to the churches in the trans-Jordan and possibly picked up there by Paul or later in Antioch. A question still remains about the composition of Mark (Galilee or Rome?). In the particular instance of Mark 14:26–29, its close affinity in wording with Matthew does not make the time and circumstances of Mark's composition a crucial issue.

19. Most of the scholarship on Mark 14:26–29 has been built on the presupposition that Matthew expanded Mark with the general intent of making it more applicable for liturgical usage. One of the strongest arguments for Markan priority was made by my teacher Dahl, "The Passion Narrative," 39–41. Dahl's major argument was a literary one. Dahl argued that Matthew recast narrative sentences from Mark in the form of direct address. He listed Matt 26:27/Mark 14:23 as a major example. He concludes this is decisive proof of Markan dependence. On the other hand, in instances where two texts, in brief

of observance of the Lord's meal in the earliest Christian communities seem to point increasingly to a wide diversity of liturgical practices.[20] Yet, conceding this diversity, Peter Stuhlmacher points out something that is often forgotten. We know that from the earliest days after the resurrection believers in Jesus gathered together around a table of some sort for a meal; but it was not to celebrate the continuity of fellowship with tax collectors or sinners or other aspects of Jesus' ministry but to focus on "his symbolic action during the farewell meal."[21] In short, on the grounds of encounter with the risen Jesus they were ineluctably drawn back to the legacy of his death for them, a death most crucially explained at the Last Supper.[22] These traditions and the theology that informed them constitute the critical links to that fateful evening.

The structural pattern of the words of explanation (institution) can be condensed into four elements.[23] We will examine them in the order they are listed:

1. The Saying over the Bread
2. The Saying over the Cup

---

literary contexts, are very similar, arguments (as with Dahl) based on literary style are notoriously difficult to convince. For example, it can just as well be argued that analogous to such passages as Matt 13:1–15/Mark 4:1–34 or Matt 15:1–20/Mark 7:1–23, Mark's eucharistic pericope is a fragmentary preservation of Matthew's more technical intertextual pattern of exegesis. This is on display as a feature throughout his gospel. cf. Peabody with Cope and McNicol, *One Gospel From Two*, 284–88. No doubt the arguments will continue. Dahl himself in the same article (38) concedes that "some weighty arguments support Matthean priority." This is because Matthew stands closer to the original Palestinian milieu than Mark.

20. The secondary literature is immense. Especially significant is Andrew B. McGowan, "Is There a Liturgical Text in the Gospel," 73–87; McGowan, *Ancient Christian Worship*; Paul F. Bradshaw, *Eucharistic Origins* (New York: Oxford University, 2004) 1–23; Smith and Taussig, *Many Tables*. The recent book by Alikin, *The Earliest History*, 103–46, gives a succinct defense of this perspective that is dependent on a presupposition that there was an intermingling of observance of the Lord's meal with practices of various Greco-Roman associations in other places. Alikin, *passim*, 118–21, claims that the Last Supper tradition in the Gospels is very old (probably early thirties of the first century) but not historical. It functions as an aetiology. It arose to explain the existence and meaning of the early Christian group meal held in their assemblies. In this paper I have attempted to make the case for the alternative position that the Gospel account of this meal fits well into the life and ministry of Jesus and thus does have a historical foundation.

21. Stuhlmacher, *Jesus of Nazareth*, 77.

22. Hengel, *The Atonement*, 65–75.

23. Higgins, *The Lord's Supper*, 24–44.

3. The Command to Continue Observance
4. The Eschatological Saying[24]

The Saying over the Bread

In keeping with the narrative flow of the tradition behind Matthew/Mark the 'bread saying' is introduced while Jesus and the disciples are engaged in the course of a meal. The precise nature of this meal is a strongly contested point. Clearly the tradition utilized by Matthew and Mark does not carry a full description of what took place during the meal. Only Jesus' special actions and expressions that extend beyond what it takes to constitute a significant holy meal are noted.[25] Here the focus on these actions and expressions are strongly directed toward Jesus' impending death.[26]

Jesus takes bread and expresses a prayer of thanksgiving. Here we do have a difference between our two major traditions. Matt/Mark both have, εὐλογήσας while Paul has εὐχαριστήσας (cf. Luke 22:19a).[27] Whether one uses "to bless" or "to give thanks" inherent in the offering of the prayer is the element of consecration. In either case, the point is that the material

---

24. This list differs somewhat from the reconstruction of the "fourfold primitive Eucharist" of Dix, *The Shape of the Liturgy*, 78–82. That reconstruction is a classic in the history of liturgy. But, by general consent, it tends to read generously back later developments in eucharistic practices into the earliest times.

25. Stuhlmacher, *Jesus of Nazareth*, 67, makes a strong case that Jesus' actions and expressions that are highlighted are consistent with what can be constructed concerning the order of a normal Passover seder at this time. Thus the saying over the bread would come at the time of the prayer of Thanksgiving at the beginning of the main festal meal. The saying on the cup would come at the time of the third (Passover) cup at the end of the main course (cf. μετὰ τὸ δειπνῆσαι in 1 Cor 11:25 and Luke 22:20). The earlier references to eating (Matt 26:21/Mark 14:18) presumably refer to the preliminary course. The whole issue of the chronology and debate over whether the Last Supper was a Passover meal cannot be discussed here in detail. Since it was Passover week and those themes were deeply in the air, I am happy to adopt a term from current technology and call it a "virtual Passover meal."

26. In one sense this is understandable given the focus of the narrative in Matt and Mark: Jesus' Passion. But note also the introduction to the tradition in 1 Cor 11:23 (ἐν τῇ νυκτὶ ᾗ παρεδίδετο) concentrates on the death of Jesus.

27. Bradshaw, "The Eucharistic Sayings of Jesus," 3–4, traces the different Greek words back to different Jewish liturgical usage, "to bless God" and "to give thanks." However, there are a number of steps in this argumentation that constitutes arguments from silence including whether Paul, in particular, accepted this distinction.

food about to be consumed is consecrated to be received for spiritual nourishment as a result of divine beneficence.

Following the prayer of thanksgiving a specific action takes place. Record of this action occurs uniformly in both the traditions used by Matt/Mark and Paul. Jesus breaks the bread. This marks the recapitulation of an action that commonly took place at a Jewish meal after the prayer of thanksgiving. Thereupon the bread was broken and given to those present. Jesus gives the bread to the disciples accompanied by the word 'Take' followed by the distribution.[28] Then comes the momentous words appearing with considerable uniformity in the two traditions: τοῦτό ἐστιν τὸ σῶμά μου "This is my body."[29] This phraseology, which came to be called the words of institution, originally, of course was spoken in some Semitic form. Reflecting on the amount of effort invested in reconstructing the original Semitic phrasing, N. T. Wright playfully refers to this as "a Greek translation of a dense Aramaic original."[30] However, the literary context of this short oblique phrase must be the determinative factor in interpreting its meaning. If one takes τοῦτο "this" as referring to the bread, and as the subject of the sentence, Jesus is saying that *this* bread is his body: in the sense that it "signifies" his body.[31]

This gathering at the table was the last recorded meal of the earthly Jesus before his death. Given our understanding of the context, the burden of proof is on others to show that these words spoken there were not connected directly with the implications of his impending arrest and death. Indeed the additional references of Paul (and Luke) τὸ ὑπὲρ ὑμῶν "on behalf

---

28. Matthew has also the imperative, "eat."

29. In 1 Cor 11:24 Paul has, in addition, τὸ ὑπὲρ ὑμῶν "on behalf of you." Cf. Luke 22:19b which has the participle "given." Adhering to the principle that the earliest traditions omit details of the meal unless they are essential to the theological message, I would conclude that the breaking of the bread (what later came to be the fraction) seems to have had some special significance, perhaps in its original setting. The clue may be found in Matthew's special reference to naming Jesus as the host (cf. 1 Cor 11:23, "The Lord Jesus"). For Matthew, ever since 1:21, Jesus is the one who will save his people from their sins. The means of salvation will, of course, be his death. The broken bread thus evokes Jesus' death for our sins (cf. Matt 26:28).

30. Wright, *Jesus and the Victory of God*, 559.

31. As Marshall, *Last Supper and Lord's Supper*, 85–86, points out, those present at the table could see that the earthly Jesus and the bread were separate entities. Marshall uses the illustration of someone showing a friend a photograph of himself in a special situation. Here Jesus is comparing the broken bread to the special situation of his death; in a similar way Old Testament prophets used different images to speak of Israel in some particular situation—usually in crisis.

of you," (1 Cor 11:24; Luke 22:19–20) clearly evoke the terminology of sacrificial offering. Ben Meyer has identified fifteen passages in the New Testament in which he thinks ὑπέρ + gen. carries a sense defined by reference to Isa 53 as expiatory."[32] Both Matt and Mark anchor this tradition firmly in a Passover context. The Passover observance was replete with echoes of sacrifice, covenant and expectations of the restoration of Israel.[33] In the action of referring to his life (i.e. body) as broken and given for his people Jesus was bringing his ministry to Israel to its climactic point. He was about to give his life as a sacrificial ransom (Matt 20:28). As N. T. Wright notes:

> Jesus' actions . . . must be seen in the same way as the symbolic actions of certain prophets in the Hebrew scriptures. Jeremiah smashes a pot; Ezekiel makes a model of Jerusalem under siege. The actions carry prophetic power, affecting the events (mostly acts of judgment) which are then to occur . . . Jesus' central actions during the meal seem to have been designed to reinforce the point of the whole meal: the kingdom agenda to which he had

---

32. Meyer, "The Expiation Motif in the Eucharistic Words," 20. They are Mark 14:24; Luke 22:20; John 6:51; 1 Cor 15:3; Gal 2:20; Eph 5:2, 25; Gal 1:4; 1 Tim 2:6; Titus 2:14; Rom 5:6–8; 2 Cor 5:14–15; 1 Pet 2:21, 3:18; 2 Cor 5:21. Even if some of these references may be regarded only as distant echoes of Isa 53, together they constitute a considerable body of material that connects ὑπέρ + gen. with a sin offering. To be sure, there are many others uses of ὑπέρ in the New Testament which are not connected with expiation or sacrifice such as expressing a request in prayer. Thus it has been argued often that the Pauline and Lukan use of ὑπέρ at the Last Supper came into the tradition sometime later, perhaps as early as it was Hellenized in its transfer to Antioch (cf. Fuller, "The Double Origin of the Eucharist," 60–72). However, also in light of Matt 26:28 and the general argument of Matthew, there seems to be little doubt that Matthew understands the bread saying as connecting Jesus' death with the Old Testament tradition of a sacrificial offering. In light of the fact that Mark also connects the ὑπὲρ saying with the cup it is highly questionable as some claim whether Mark omitted it in the bread saying because of a concern that it would be misunderstood as expiatory.

33. As we have noted the conversation at the meal in Matthew and Mark is massively abridged. Luke extends it somewhat (Luke 22:21–38). Joachim Jeremias, *The Eucharistic Words of Jesus*, 220–25, has made a strong case that at the meal Jesus also spoke of his sacrifice as that of the eschatological pascal lamb. This could have taken place during the main course. It is possible; but it is very difficult to substantiate from the very brief words of 1 Cor 5:7. Certainly the latter text drew such a conclusion along with the Johannine account of the crucifixion. But the early church drew many things from Jesus' life that cannot be traced to the earthly Jesus. Normally, in the Judaism of the first century, it is claimed Passover offerings were not thought to be expiatory. However, there are instances where Rabbis could be quoted as saying that the blood of the original Passover lambs along with circumcision did have redemptive benefits. Smith, *Jesus' Last Passover Meal*, 43–6.

been obedient throughout his ministry was now at last reaching its ultimate destination . . . the meal, focused on Jesus' actions with the bread and the cup, told the Passover story and Jesus' own story and wove these two into one.[34]

The literary context of the Last Supper is not just the Passion Story but Jesus' whole life. And that ultimately revolves around the destiny of the kingdom.

The Saying Over the Cup

As I have noted, the precise time of the taking of the cup during the course of the meal has raised some questions. Matthew and Mark do not, on the surface, suggest there is an interval of any magnitude. But if the Supper was based on the traditions of a formal Jewish meal, widely known to Jewish people, this may well be presumed. On the other hand, in Paul (1 Cor 11:25) and the remarkably parallel text in the longer ending of Luke (Lk 22:20), the cup saying is introduced by the terminology ὡσαύτως μετὰ τὸ δειπνῆσαι "likewise after the meal." The simplest reason for this addition is that it's an explanation to readers in the Diaspora and Gentile churches of the earliest remembrance of what took place at Jesus' last meal.[35] All indicators show that this was a formal Jewish meal if not more likely a celebration of some version of *pesah*. During these meals the host would offer a prayer of thanksgiving over the bread at the beginning of the main course, and at the end of the meal conclude with a similar prayer over a cup of wine.

In both Matthew and Mark, after Jesus gives thanks, the disciples all drink from the cup. Jesus requests them to become full participants in what is taking place. The gravity of this invitation is underscored by the words spoken over the cup: τοῦτο "this" (i.e. by metonymy the content of the cup) is my blood of the (new) covenant."[36] Jesus is alluding to his impending

---

34. Wright, *Jesus and the Victory of God*, 558–59.

35. Hofius, "The Lord's Supper," 80–88. Hofius discusses at length what may or may not have been the practice at Corinth with respect to the observance of the Lord's Meal as well as its relationship to a Hellenistic *Symposium*. I regard as special pleading by all those commentators who state strongly 'that there is not even an echo of Passover terminology in Paul's version of 1 Cor 11.'

36. A strong case can be made for the acceptance of καινῆς"new" as the qualifying adjective of covenant in Matthew. It appears in the Paul/Luke tradition (1 Cor 11:25; cf. Luke 22:20). Its omission in some manuscripts of Matthew is found mainly in the Egyptian witnesses and P37 which is of uncertain provenance. It certainly cements the

death. As with the Pauline tradition, although the wording is different, the cup saying is coupled with the bread saying in focusing directly on Jesus' death. Blood was utilized in the sealing of the Mosaic covenant (Exod 24:6–8). Jer 31:31–34 is clearly being echoed as well in that the benefits of the new era are being inaugurated by coming events. But there is also another strong scriptural echo. It is affirmed in Zech 9:9–12 (LXX) that by the αἵματι διαθήκης "blood of the covenant" the new era will be celebrated in a great feast as a result of the messianic victory of Israel's king.[37] Stuhlmacher points to a rabbinic expectation that all Israel at the banquet of the messiah will drink jointly from one enormous cup of salvation (Ps 116:13).[38] By requesting the disciples to participate from this one cup Jesus is inviting them, in an anticipatory sense, to prepare themselves to share in the festival of salvation that will come as a result of the sin offering given in his martyrdom. In both the tradition behind Matthew and Mark and Paul the latter is underscored with the terminology "my blood."

The tradition behind Matthew and Mark adds one additional note to this cup saying (cf. Luke 22:20). The allusion to the giving of Jesus' life which inaugurates the new covenant is supplemented with the statement that Jesus' life is ἐκχυννόμενον "about to be poured out" for the many (ὑπὲρ ὑμῶν in Luke 22:20).

The reference to the life poured out for the many is clearly an attempt to connect with the expiatory life of the servant in Isa 53:11–12. In the Greek Bible the servant makes himself an offering περὶ ἁμαρτίας "for sin" and his life is poured out for the many. The use of the preposition περί by Matthew ties it closer to Isa 53:11–12; but Mark's inclusion of ὑπέρ as we have shown, is also used regularly in constructions to express the theme of expiation.[39] The Pauline version of the cup saying is more abbreviated. It does stress the covenantal aspect of Jesus' death; although it does have τὸ ὑπὲρ ὑμῶν "on behalf of you" after the bread saying and then introduces the cup saying with ὡσαύτως "likewise" there is no further expiatory reference.

This brings us to the reference to πολλῶν "the many" in Matt 26:28/ Mark 14:24. This reference has stimulated a debate as to whether this direct connection with Isa 53:12 (cf. 52:14–15) which Jesus echoes is meant to refer to Israel only or whether it embodies the nations as well. Rudolf

---

connection with Jer 31:31 (LXX Jer 38:31).

37. Wright, *Jesus and the Victory of God*, 560–61.
38. Stuhlmacher, *Jesus of Nazareth*, 71.
39. Meyer, "The Expiation Motif," 18–9.

Pesch argued for the former.[40] However, Ben Meyer, mainly following his teacher, Jeremias, understood it in a more inclusive sense to already embody the nations (at least those who were responsive to the mission described in Matt 28:19–20).[41] This seems to be the most appropriate reading of the function of the "many" in Isaiah and is definitely congruent with the theology of Matthew and especially Mark. The early church clearly read it this way and since we are not able to intuit the mind of the earthly Jesus we will simply have to rely on their judgment. Nevertheless, given the fact that the Twelve, the future pillars of the renewed people of God were the first to drink from the cup, the eschatological theme of the restoration of Israel should not be discounted as the major emphasis. The death of Jesus for Israel was the presupposition for the inclusion of Gentiles because Israel would not be complete without the universality of Israel's God being recognized by faithful Gentiles.

Finally, it is striking to notice that the Matthean version of the cup saying concludes with the comment that the pouring out of Jesus' life is "for the forgiveness of sins" (Matt 26:28). This not only makes an interesting inclusio for the Matthean account of the table episode but connects with the wider story that Matthew is telling.[42] As Wright points out, this is not a reference to "some abstract spiritual transaction" as in the various later well-traveled theories of atonement, but a preliminary announcement of the offer of forgiveness for Israel.[43] As we have earlier noted, Matt 26:28 is the counterpoint to Matt 23:33–36. In the latter the sins of the previous generations were enumerated. Now, by stubborn rejection of God's present messenger, the entire history of the righteous blood poured out in the past lay at the door of 'this generation.' But in Matt 26:28 Jesus makes the momentous announcement that his death will initiate a renewed offer of forgiveness. By drinking the cup, in a preliminary sense, the disciples would be the first to share in these benefits.

---

40. Pesch, *Das Abendmahl*, 105–22.

41. Meyer, "The Expiation Motif," 25–6.

42. Jesus is described in Matt 1:21 as the one "who will save his people from their sins." A kind of inclusio comes first with the reference to Jesus in Matt 26:26 and the ending of the description of his expiatory work in 26:28 as being "for the forgiveness of sins."

43. Wright, *Jesus and the Victory of God*, 561. As with many others I do not follow Wright's unwarranted overemphasis on the theme of exile. The focus on Israel, at least as far as Matthew is concerned, is much more on the consequences of the rejection of 'this generation' to Jesus' announcement of the kingdom.

The Command to Continue Observance

In 1 Cor 11:24, immediately after the bread saying, Paul records Jesus giving the injunction, "Do this in remembrance of me." A similar charge is found after the cup saying in 1 Cor 11:25, "Do this as often as you drink (it) with a view toward my remembrance." There is little question that liturgical influence has intruded into the transmission of the tradition at this point. This conclusion is substantiated by the fact that Matthew and Mark do not have these words. Most likely it found its way into the tradition that Paul used and which he passed on to his churches in his ministry.

Joachim Jeremias has argued that the phrase εἰς τὴν ἐμὴν ἀνάμνησιν, literally "into my remembrance" is meant for a call for the church to observe the Lord's meal in the sense of offering a prayer.[44] The prayer is that God may remember Jesus and his words of anticipation of the kingdom by bringing the parousia quickly. His argument is still worth reading but ultimately is not convincing. This is not a proclamation to God but, as 1 Cor 11:25 makes clear, it is a word from Jesus for believers to give to one another.[45] Likewise, the idea sometimes suggested that the concept of remembrance emerged in the tradition as a version of meals in memory of the deceased, although widespread in the Greco-Roman world, does not commend itself either. A central presupposition of the meal in the first place is the Lord was alive and present with them.

Elsewhere I have argued that more careful attention should be given to the injunction "Do this!"[46] The injunction is not meant to be read as a manual on correct liturgical procedure. Rather, the "this" is to be connected with the proclamation (καταγγέλλετε) made at the table. When one receives the bread and the cup one remembers by viewing these words and actions in the context of a proclamation of the central deeds that brought about salvation.[47] This injunction brings to mind the Passover celebration and the attention given to the drama of the Seder. In "re-actualizing" the return

---

44. Jeremias, *The Eucharistic Words of Jesus*, 237–55.
45. Marshall, *Last Supper and Lord's Supper*, 90.
46. McNicol, "In Remembrance of Jesus," 20–23.
47. Hofius, "The Lord's Supper," cites passages such as Pss 77:12; 105:1–5; and 114:4 as instances of a similar process among the Hebrews. There a strong connection is made between remembrance and proclamation. Procedurally, for the earliest Christians, this proclamation took place in recital of the Passion narrative at the table and in prayers. This may well be the genesis of later developments where the eucharistic prayer focusing on the acts of salvation becomes central in what takes place at the table.

to Exodus and receiving the benefits of this great act of Yahweh's deliverance early believers in Jesus found an anticipation of the understanding of Christian anamnesis set forth in this command. But observance is not something that only resides in the past. The whole argument of 1 Cor 11 is for the Christians at Corinth to reframe their *present* religious and ethical activity in light of the story proclaimed at the meal in their assembly.[48]

The Eschatological Saying

The Matthean/Markan account of the meal in the upper room concludes with another saying of Jesus. "Under no circumstances," Jesus states, "will he drink of the fruit of the vine until the coming of the kingdom" (Matt 26:29/Mark 14:25). Aside from several minor stylistic and linguistic differences the saying is essentially the same in both Matthew and Mark. It is generally reckoned that Paul's extended enumeration of the tradition (1 Cor 11:23–26) does not have this saying; the echo "until he comes" in 1 Cor 11:26 may or may not reflect an awareness of it in the tradition he received. The matter is complicated because the Lukan account (discussed below) has a version of this saying toward the beginning of the meal where it appears to be integrated into a vow of abstinence by Jesus (Luke 22:17–18). Also, in the background, there is a stream of interpretation that considers this saying may be the only clearly genuine expression of Jesus that remains from the Last Supper. This view is championed by those who think that Jesus' central purpose at the meal was to articulate to the disciples the restoration of his life in the kingdom.[49]

The question of the placement of the saying in the tradition should not be confused with the issue of whether this is a genuine saying of Jesus. Although there are questions about the former, the latter seems to be very plausible in this context. Moreover, in its present form in Matthew and Mark, it is fully compatible with Jesus' announcement at the table that, as the mediator of eschatological salvation, he anticipates his expiatory death

---

48. Stern, "Remembering and Redemption," 7, has some interesting things to say on this matter in connection with Jewish observance of the Passover seder. "The ultimate goal of the seder, it seems to me, for all of its drama of identification, is not to make the Exodus contemporaneous to the participant . . . the goal is to remember the reality of redemption: to reassemble our own world view . . ." Presumably this is done in light of reflection upon the sacred events of the past.

49. Sanders, *Jesus and Judaism*, 332, seems to lean in this direction.

and future testing of the disciples would spill over into "the hour of crisis" only to be resolved by the arrival of the kingdom of God.

Pierre Benoit once told me that due to its particular geographical location, Jerusalem was usually bathed in a kind of eerie light. Perhaps this contributed toward its connection with so many eschatological movements over the centuries. In any case, for early Christianity, this climactic saying fits well into the pattern of crucial anticipatory events in the march toward the eschaton.[50] With this reading the placement of the saying in Matthew and Mark is fully understandable.

Luke's Creative Use of Tradition in His Farewell Discourse

Our analysis of the earliest traditions behind the biblical accounts of the words of institution would not be complete without discussion of Luke 22:14–20. This pericope functions as the opening section of a lengthy farewell speech in Luke 22:14–38. Jesus addresses his disciples (here named apostles) in anticipation of an impending arrest. The speech is replete with instructions of how they are to conduct themselves after this coming crisis that will befall their leader. In some sense this address represents the transition to the longer farewell discourse given in the Gospel of John.

Luke is following the custom of a Hellenistic historical biographer who portrays his hero, on the eve of the most important situation of his life, giving a speech to his followers expressing his thoughts and intentions about the future.[51] Luke 22:14–20 bristles with massive literary and textual issues.[52] Our focus will be to comment briefly on the source traditions utilized by Luke and how they were used compositionally.

---

50. Of course, the difficulty finally, is not the placement of the saying, in the meal, but what later believers are to make of it. Although brief, Goppelt, *Theology of the New Testament 1*, 206–17, gives some suggestions how the church can sustain herself in view of the delay of the parousia and arrival of the kingdom. He places the emphasis on the need for a communication of salvation as being available to all.

51. McNicol, et al., *Beyond the Q Impasse*, 276–79. The authors give examples from the description of the gathering and the choice of subject matter that is based on the model of a *Symposium*.

52. Not the least, of course, is the question whether the text of Luke 22:19b–20 (the longer ending) is part of Luke's original composition. Actually the issue is even more complicated with a number of ancient texts having various omissions and transpositions of different verses in this pericope. A comprehensive summary and fair analysis is that of Evans, *Saint Luke*, 786–91. Only a lengthy article on the issue itself could address competently these complicated textual and literary issues.

The "longer text" of 22:19b–20 remains the best attested in the manuscripts. Assuming the authenticity of this text the pericope seems to be composed by welding together two source traditions. Luke 22:19–20 has very close affinities with 1 Cor 11:24–25. Based on the common linguistic evidence (e.g., "This cup is the new covenant in my blood," vis-à-vis Matt/Mark) between Luke and Paul it is widely accepted that these two texts come from a common tradition.[53]

The major difficulty arises in accounting for the appearance and compositional arrangement of Luke 22:14–18 as well as the way it is connected with Luke 22:19–20. First, it is worthy of notice that it is in 22:14 Luke's account of the Passion Narrative begins to show major differences with Matt/Mark. At this point Luke may have begun to incorporate another source tradition that he will utilize for the rest of the Gospel (Luke 22:1–24:53).[54] This has recently, somewhat in a neutral sense, been labeled Luke's "non-Matthean material."[55] Research has not come to any clear conclusions about its origin. Compositionally, in Luke 22:14–15, in the beginning of the discourse, Luke is primarily concerned to give a fitting description as to why the apostles are present at this meal! An appropriate verb for seating at a *symposium* ἀνέπεσεν "reclined" is used along with the announcement that it is a Passover meal. These descriptions provide an appropriate setting for what is about to take place. The aura of the impending crisis begins to emerge (Luke 22:15b). There are hints that there are deeper reasons for the gathering.

But, with the exception of the hinted delay of the coming of the kingdom, Luke has no major interest in the meaning of the Passover meal itself. Jesus will not eat it again until the kingdom (Luke 22:16). Rather, he takes a cup from the table and announces a vow of abstinence until the coming of the kingdom (Luke 22:17–18). The vow of abstinence heightens the theme of crisis. It creates the idea that something ominous is about to take place and provides the basis for the reader to take seriously the later instructions given to the apostles about their future conduct. The emphasis is not on the cup but on the eschatological saying (cf. Matt 26:29; Mark 14:29) which in

---

53. Stuhlmacher, *Jesus of Nazareth*, 75, assumes it is some version of a tradition on the Last Supper held by the churches in Antioch. It should not be ruled out that Luke had some acquaintance with the letters of Paul. McNicol, et al., *Beyond the Q Impasse*, 284. That is not my argument in this case. I prefer Stuhlmacher's conclusion that both Paul and Luke are utilizing some version of the Antiochene tradition.

54. Jeremias, *New Testament Theology 1*, 38–41.

55. McNicol, et al., *Beyond the Q Impasse*, 25–29.

Luke precedes the words of institution. Word of the coming crisis is balanced out with the promise of future vindication in the kingdom of God.[56] Then Jesus will eat and drink with his apostles when the kingdom comes (Luke 22:16b, 18b). Vindication in the coming kingdom is an important theme throughout Luke-Acts.

Editorially, Luke has laid the theological groundwork for the farewell discourse. The real concern is to prepare the disciples for the impending crisis and a delay in the coming of the eschatological kingdom. The rest of the discourse will be concerned with instructions about how the disciples are to conduct themselves in this interval (Luke 22:17–19a, cf. 1 Cor 10:16–17). This may well represent the tradition of observance of the Supper that was also known by Paul. In Luke 22:19b–20 there is inserted into the account the standing historical record of what originally took place as told by Matthew and Mark (cf. 1 Cor 11:23–25). Thus, based on a very early tradition Matthew/Mark give us an historical account of what happened at the Last Supper. The Pauline (1 Cor 10) and Lukan (Luke 22:17–19a) accounts perhaps supplements this record with a tradition of how these events were celebrated liturgically in some Gentile churches of the Greco-Roman world.[57]

Conclusion

We commenced with Keck's observation that, for the ancients, rites did something. In Paul and the Gospels certain words and actions of Jesus at his last meal on the night before his death inaugurated a rite that has stood at the center of the life of the people of God ever since. In the case of the Lord's Supper what did it do and wherein was its power?

In this essay I have attempted to show that what happened on that fateful evening was no accident. Throughout his ministry signified by a series of special acts Jesus had announced the arrival of the Kingdom of God. This announcement involved considerable risk. If Israel did not accept this word it faced destruction. It could not stand on the fence. As Ben Meyer has stated, after the resistance of Israel to Jesus' message, "How were the refusers to be saved from themselves?"[58] The answer can be stated succinctly. Israel's salvation could only come through acceptance of the benefits of forgiveness

---

56. Neyrey, *The Passion According to Luke*, 15.
57. Cf. Marshall, *Last Supper and Lord's Supper*, 34–35.
58. Ben Meyer, "Phases," 14.

of sins brought about by Jesus' expiatory death! This pre-understanding informed the structuring of the core of words and actions of Jesus when he gathered with the disciples in the upper room.

Various traditions and interpretations are involved in processing what happened on that night—even within the New Testament. I have focused on what I regard as the two most substantive traditions: (1) a tradition now embodied in Matthew and Mark and 1 Cor 11:23–25; (2) a tradition (emerging in the Diaspora churches) and perhaps echoed by Paul in 1 Corinthians 10:16–17, and to some degree, by Luke in Luke 22:17–19a. The latter tradition already shows the effect of early Christian liturgical use.

Nurtured within the context of centuries of Passover observance, both the Twelve and later Jewish followers could readily understand the typology of what Jesus was doing with the bread and the cup. The disciples (apostles in Luke), in an anticipatory sense, would become the first to participate in the benefits of the expiatory accomplishments of Jesus' martyrdom with its initiation of the new covenant. Through anamnesis, the benefits of this death (the reception of forgiveness of sins and anticipation of having a place at the messianic banquet) continued to be claimed by later believers including Gentiles. These claims were grounded by faith in his expiatory death as believers met together around the table after the resurrection. Above all, the Lord's meal, like a hand within a glove, linked formal participation in physically partaking of the bread and cup with the reality of a claim on the spiritual benefits of the once-and-for-all sacrifice of the death of Jesus. That accounts for its continuing power among the people of God until this day.

Bibliography

Alikin, Valeriy A. *The Earliest History of the Christian Gathering: Origin, Development and Content of the Christian Gathering in the First to Third Centuries*. VCSup 102. Leiden: Brill, 2010.

Bradshaw, Paul F. *Eucharistic Origins*. New York: Oxford University, 2004.

———. "The Eucharistic Sayings of Jesus." *Studia Liturgica* 35 (2005) 1–11.

Caird, G. B. *New Testament Theology*. Edited by L. D. Hurst. Oxford: Clarendon, 1994.

Dahl, Nils A. "The Passion Narrative in Matthew." In *Jesus in the Memory of the Early Church: Essays by Nils Alstrup Dahl*, 37–51. Minneapolis: Augsburg, 1976.

Dix, Dom Gregory. *The Shape of the Liturgy*. San Francisco: Harper & Row, 1945.

Evans, C. F. *Saint Luke*. Philadelphia: Trinity, 1990.

Ferguson, Everett. "The Lord's Supper in Church History: The Early Church through the Medieval Period." In *The Lord's Supper: Believers Church Perspective*, edited by Dale R. Stoffer, 1–45. Scottsdale, PA: Herald, 1997.

Fuller, Reginald H. "The Double Origin of the Eucharist." *BR* 8 (1963) 60–72.

Goppelt, Leonhard. *Theology of the New Testament*. Vol. 1. Translated by John Alsup. Edited by Jürgen Roloff. Grand Rapids: Eerdmans, 1981.
Hengel, Martin. *The Atonement: The Origins of the Doctrine in the New Testament*. Translated by John Bowden. Philadelphia: Fortress, 1981.
Higgins, A. J. B. *The Lord's Supper in the New Testament*. SBT 1/ 6. London: SCM, 1956.
Hofius, Otfried. "The Lord's Supper and the Lord's Supper Tradition: Reflections on 1 Corinthians 11:23b-25." In *One Loaf, One Cup: Ecumenical Studies of 1 Cor 11 and Other Eucharistic Texts*, edited by Ben F. Meyer, 75-115. New Gospel Studies 6. Macon, GA: Mercer University Press, 1993.
Jeremias, Joachim. *The Eucharistic Words of Jesus*. Translated by Norman Perrin from the 3rd German edition with the author's revisions. Philadelphia: Fortress, 1966.
———. *New Testament Theology*. Vol. 1, *The Proclamation of Jesus*. Translated by John Bowden. New York: Scribner, 1977.
Keck, Leander E. *Paul and His Letters*. Proclamation Commentaries. Philadelphia: Fortress, 1979.
Kereszty, Roch. "The Eucharist in the New Testament." In *The International Bible Commentary*, edited by William R. Farmer, 215-38. Collegeville, MN: Liturgical, 1998.
Leske, Adrian M. "The Influence of Isaiah on Christology in Matthew and Luke." In *Crisis in Christology: Essays in Quest of Resolution*, edited by William R. Farmer, 241-69. Livonia, MI: Dove, 1995.
Marshall, I. Howard. *Last Supper and Lord's Supper*. Grand Rapids: Eerdmans, 1980.
McGowan, Andrew B. *Ancient Christian Worship: Early Church Practices in Social, Historical and Theological Perspective*. Grand Rapids: Baker, 2014.
———. "Is There a Liturgical Text in the Gospel? The Institution Narratives and Their Early Interpretive Communities." *JBL* 118 (1999) 73-87.
McNicol, Allan, David Dungan, et al. *Beyond the Q Impasse: Luke's Use of Matthew*. Valley Forge, PA: Trinity, 1996.
———. "In Remembrance of Jesus." *CS* 18 (2000/2001) 15-28.
Meier, John. "The Eucharist at the Last Supper: Did It Happen?" *TD* 42 (1995) 335-51.
Meyer, Ben F. "The Expiation Motif in the Eucharistic Words: A Key to the History of Jesus?" In *One Loaf, One Cup: Ecumenical Studies of I Cor 11 and Other Eucharistic Texts*, edited by Ben F. Meyer, 11-33. New Gospel Studies 6. Macon, GA: Mercer University, 1993.
———. "'Phases' in Jesus' Mission." *Greg* 73 (1992) 5-17.
Neyrey, Jerome H. *The Passion according to Luke: A Redaction Study of Luke's Soteriology*. 1985. Reprinted, Eugene, OR: Wipf & Stock, 2007.
Peabody, David B., with Lamar Cope, and Allan J. McNicol, eds. *One Gospel from Two: Mark's Use of Matthew and Luke*. Harrisburg, PA: Trinity International, 2002.
Pesch, Rudolf. *Das Abendmahl und Jesu Todesverständis*. QD 80. Freiburg: Herder, 1978.
Sanders, E. P. *Jesus and Judaism*. Philadelphia: Fortress, 1985.
Smith, Barry D. *Jesus' Last Passover Meal*. Lewiston, NY: Mellen Biblical, 1993.
Smith, Dennis E., and Hal F. Taussig. *Many Tables: The Eucharist in the New Testament and Liturgy Today*. Philadelphia: Trinity, 1990.
Stern, David. "Remembering and Redemption" in *Rediscovering the Eucharist: Ecumenical Conversations*, edited by Roch A. Kereszty, 1-15. New York: Paulist, 2003.
Stuhlmacher, Peter. *Jesus of Nazareth: Christ of Faith*. Translated by Siegfried Schatzmann. Peabody, MA: Hendrickson, 1993.
Wright, N. T. *Jesus and the Victory of God*. Christian Origins and the Question of Go. 2. Minneapolis: Fortress, 1996.

8

Toward Locating Eucharistic Theology in the Fourth Gospel[1]

—*Curt Niccum*

THE FOURTH GOSPEL (FG) omits the very foundation of the Christian Eucharist—the Passover meal Jesus shared with his disciples "on the night he was betrayed" (1 Cor 11:23). Despite narrating events at a dinner immediately preceding Jesus's arrest, the Fourth Evangelist (FE) removes virtually all vestiges of the Seder and has Jesus's life end before Passover begins.[2] Christianity's most cherished symbols are gone: There is no chalice. There are no words of institution.[3] There is only one small morsel of bread, and *that* Jesus hands to Judas (13:26).[4]

---

1. It is an honor to participate in this colloquy celebrating the life and work of Everett Ferguson, my teacher, mentor, colleague, and friend.

2. "Fourth Evangelist" refers to the person(s) who gave final form to the Fourth Gospel. As to clues that potentially point to a Passover meal in John 13–17, see Jeremias, *Eucharistic Words*, 41–84.

3. Lindars overreacts to this lacuna, claiming, "The whole question hinges on the eucharistic words of Jesus. If John contains no reference to them, it cannot be claimed that he knows and approves the Christian practice of the Eucharist," "Word and Sacrament," 59.

4. Craig Koester uses this event to argue against a sacramental reading of chapter 6,

Undaunted by the FE's efforts to obliterate every trace of the "Last Supper," theologians have continued the quest for the Holy Grail, often scouring the sixth chapter because of its flesh and blood language.[5] However, that chapter only sounds eucharistic because of the Synoptic accounts, which perhaps should not be conversation partners when exegeting the passage.[6] Tensions in the text have also led some to suspect that the most pertinent section (vv. 51c–58) is a later interpolation.[7] On the surface, the evidence for the Eucharist in the FG appears very weak.[8]

There are, on the other hand, no a priori reasons for doubting that a Johannine eucharistic theology exists. But if it is to be established, it must be based on more solid evidence. For this reason I seriously doubt another study of John 6 or chapters 13–17 would move scholarship forward. However, perhaps we have missed the forest for the trees. Taking in the panorama of the FG might provide a better perspective from which to judge the presence or absence of eucharistic theology in the book.

Macrostructures of the FG

Whatever the earlier transmission history, seven signs and seven "I am" statements undergird the final form of the book. The former may have belonged to a pre-Johannine "Signs Gospel," but the FE has significantly reworked the material, including the designation of or limitation to exactly seven signs. In contrast, most if not all of the seven sayings are redactional, so they, too, and perhaps more clearly, betray the theological interests of the FE. They certainly add another layer of depth to the overall message

Symbolism, 301–9. See also Culpepper, *Anatomy*, 195–97.

5. For a survey of positions see Menken, "Eucharist or Christology?" 184–87; and Kobel, *Dining*, 183–86. In this essay "Last Supper" will designate the Synoptic and Pauline accounts while "Last Meal" will refer to the Johannine tradition.

6. There are parallels, though, with later Christian literature. See Ignatius, Smy 7.1; Rom 7.2; and Phil 4.1.

7. Most notably Bultmann, *John*, 218–20. More recent scholarship has tended to regard these verses as integral to the discourse (Dunn, "John vi," 328–38; Rensberger, *Johannine Faith*, 70–81) or a later reworking by the original author or his community (Lincoln, *John*, 50–55; Richter, "Formgeschichte," 39–48; Wilkens, "Abendmahlszeugnis," 354–70).

8. Although identifying echoes of the Synoptic tradition in John, especially in chapter 6, Kobel states, "Despite the amount of scholarly attention to this problem, it remains an unsolved, indeed, unsolvable, issue," *Dining*, 180.

and balance the seven deeds with seven words. If one seeks a Johannine eucharistic theology, this pair of septets is a place to start.

The Seven Signs

The traditional enumeration of the signs is as follows:[9]

1. Turning water into wine (chapter 2)
2. Healing the ruler's son (chapter 4)
3. Healing the lame man (chapter 5)
4. Feeding the five thousand (chapter 6)
5. Walking on water (chapter 6)
6. Healing the blind man (chapter 9)
7. Raising Lazarus from the dead (chapter 11)

There are problems, though, with this configuration. In particular, it is difficult to understand how walking on the water works as a sign. Whether or not the FE was aware of any Synoptic version or independent miracle tradition, the story seems muted in comparison to the other signs in the FG and in fact is never identified as a sign.[10] To account for this anomaly, some have suggested the transversing of the Tiberian Sea and the feeding miracle constitute one literary whole that presents Jesus as the coming Prophet.[11] Working from Jewish messianic speculations inspired by Deut 18, Jesus, like Moses, feeds Jews in the wilderness and miraculously crosses water. It is more likely that the aquatic tale serves a completely different purpose; the scene on the lake is an epiphany or a theophany. Jesus thus rewards the few disciples who did not abandon him (6:66) with yet another revelation of his glory.[12] In general, though, scholars continue to count it among the seven.

---

9. Additional signs have been identified (see, for example, Brown, "Creation's Renewal," 275–90; and Smalley, "Sign," 275–88) and other enumerations of six or seven signs have been proposed. For overviews, see Köstenberger, "Seventh Johannine Sign," 87–103, especially 87–90. Concerning the "Signs Gospel" as a potential source for the FG, see the seminal work of Robert Fortna in *Gospel of Signs* and *Fourth Gospel*. For a summary of scholarly inquiry, see Belle, *Signs Source*.

10. See Köstenberger, *The Mission of Jesus*, 54–74; and Meye Thompson, "Thinking about God," 242–43.

11. See Clark, "Signs," 205; and Köstenberger, *Mission*, 64–67.

12. O'Day, "John 6:15–21," 149–59. See also Anderson, "John and Mark," 175–88.

Köstenberger argues instead that the FE denotes the cleansing of the Temple as a sign.[13] Here, though, he misses the point, for John does not describe the Temple cleansing itself as a sign; rather it is the event in which Jesus most clearly articulates what will be the seventh and ultimate sign. After clearing the Temple courts, "the Jews" confront him and demand validation for his actions (2:18). To their request for a corresponding "sign," he responds, "Destroy this temple, and in three days I will raise it" (2:19). The seventh sign, then, is the death, burial, and resurrection of Jesus. The resulting tabulation is:

1. Turning water into wine (chapter 2; see 2:11)
2. Healing of the ruler's son (chapter 4; see 4:54)
3. Healing of the lame man (chapter 5; see 6:2; 7:21, and 31)
4. Feeding the five thousand (chapter 6; see 6:14)
5. Healing the blind man (chapter 9; see 9:16)
6. Raising Lazarus from the dead (chapter 11; see 12:18)
7. Death, burial, and resurrection of Jesus (chapters 18–20; see 2:18–19)

This arrangement better fits the Gospel's emphasis on the Passion narrative. First, it eases the tension in the FG between the express purpose statement that "these [signs] are written that you might believe" (20:31) and the apparent inability of those who "believe" because of the signs to remain believers in Jesus.[14] For example, in the first half of the gospel, Nicodemus (chapter 2) and the sated crowds (chapter 6) abandon Jesus despite seeing the signs and "believing," but those who did not actually observe signs, like the official with the mortally ill child (chapter 4), the Samaritan woman (chapter 4), and the blind man (chapter 9) come to have true faith.[15] Not surprisingly, the summary after the first six signs reads: "Even though he performed signs such as these in their presence, *they did not believe* in him" (12:37; emphasis added). Results dramatically differ with the seventh sign. Upon seeing the identifying wounds of the resurrected Jesus, Thomas

---

13. Köstenberger, *The Mission of Jesus*, 54–74.

14. von Wahlde, on the other hand, is convinced that only attention to the different editorial layers can render these contradictions understandable, *Gospel and Letters*, 2:132. All translations are mine.

15. Jesus's own disciples interestingly bridge the gap. Those observing the first and last signs believe (2:11 and 20:27–29). Compare the injunction at 14:11. See also the discussion by Nicol, *Semeia*, 106–13.

responds with a radical application of the Shema, "My Lord and my God" (20:28). It is the seventh sign which engenders faith, both in those who see and those who do not (20:29). It is the ultimate sign, and a summary likewise follows: "Indeed Jesus performed many other signs in the disciples' presence, . . . but these are written that *you might believe*" (20:30–31; emphasis added).

Second, the other six signs point toward the ultimate sign. The prime example is the story of Jesus changing water into wine (2:11). The story opens with "on the third day" (v. 1) and then goes on to mention Jesus's mother (v. 1), his "hour" (v. 4), the revealing of his glory (v. 11), and the faith of his disciples (v. 11). All of these resurface in the Passion Narrative. Also, as already mentioned, the cleansing of the Temple immediately follows this story and directly connects this sign with Jesus's prediction of *the* sign: "Destroy this temple and in three days I will raise it" (v. 19).[16]

This enumeration of the seven signs also more closely ties the Gospel to the Exodus story, especially the Passover. In Exod 2–12 God reveals himself in a particularly personal way to his people, including performing by himself or through his agent ten "signs" so that they might believe he is YHWH. Clearly the first signs in Exodus and the FG overlap: water to blood and water to wine. But the same is true of the last. The Passover is the tenth sign in Exodus, the death of the firstborn (πρωτότοκος). Likewise Passover is the last sign in the FG, the death and resurrection of the firstborn (μονογενής). Might the failure to believe after the first six signs in the Gospel mirror the lack of faith displayed after the first nine signs in Exodus?

Discovering additional parallels with the other ten signs in Exodus is unnecessary.[17] Elsewhere John does not push strict parallelism. The focus is on the superiority of Christ as God's agent.[18] By making the first and last signs in Exodus and the FG correspond, he establishes the analog, which he further explicates in various ways throughout the book. The other signs

---

16. See Koester, *Symbolism*, 82–89. For a brief survey of positions and an argument for regarding "third day" as an inclusio, see Palmer, "Repetition," 403–17.

17. Smith observes how scholars have gone on flights of fancy in pursuit of parallels, a problem that he himself does not completely avoid even though establishing some methodological controls, "Exodus Typology," 293–300.

18. This is not to dismiss any further parallels with the Exodus story. The feeding of the five thousand, for example, is explicitly connected to Israel's flight from Egypt, but only the first and last signs need to align with the "ten signs" to make the point. On agency in the FG, see Borgen, "God's Agent," 137–48.

primarily serve to establish the relevance and meaning of the Christ and his Passion.

As for the numerical discrepancy, both Ps 105 and Wis 11–19 reduce the number of signs performed in Exodus to seven. Thus a truncated tradition already existed which John could employ. Nevertheless, the more likely motivation for selecting seven is the FE's equally important emphasis on Jesus as agent in creation (cf. 1:1–5 and 20:22).[19]

The "I Am" Statements

Seven times in the FG Jesus collocates "I am" with a theologically rich predicate. The so-called "I am" statements are:

1. I am the bread of life (6:35 and 48)
2. I am the light of the world (8:12 and 9:5)
3. I am the gate of the sheep (10:7)
4. I am the good shepherd (10:11 and 14)
5. I am the resurrection and the life (11:25)
6. I am the way, the truth, and the life (14:6)
7. I am the true vine (15:1 and 5)

The aporia at the end of chapter 14 highlights the significance of this order; the FE has intentionally repositioned material in order to have the vinocultural reference appear last.

Thus, as with the seven signs, the FE emphasizes the first and last elements, Jesus as bread and vine.[20] Obviously from a Christian vantage point, this smacks of the Eucharist. On the other hand, given the Old Testament influences found with the first and last signs, the Passover must be the primary referent.[21]

---

19. See, for example, Rae, "Testimony," 295–310.

20. Paranomasia may tie the last statement to the first: κλάσματα - κλήματα. Brown notes that Sir 24:17–21 may also bond these two sayings, *New Testament Essays*, 84–85. The form of the "I am" statements also points to Jesus as God's agent, so Bühner, "Exegesis," 166–80.

21. Léon-Dufour aptly recognizes the importance of placing the FG "in the Jewish context of the first century. If we end up failing to recognize all this, it is because we allow ourselves to be dazzled by the light of Easter," "Symbolic Reading," 445–46.

PART 2: PRESENTED ESSAYS

In Tandem

Separately the two Johannine structural patterns draw the reader into the Passover. The signs reframe those performed in Egypt that culminated with the Passover, and the "I am" statements reimagine the Passover Seder.[22] That is sufficient to warrant interpreting individual passages in the Gospel through these lenses. However, it is worth briefly pursuing how the two structures might further illuminate one another.

Without a doubt the Passover indelibly shapes the FG's depiction of the seventh sign. The evangelist uniquely has Jesus crucified during the time when the Passover lambs were slaughtered, giving flesh to the proclamation first made by John the Baptist, "Behold the lamb of God that takes away the sin of the world" (1:29).[23] Other distinctive contributions of the FE include references to hyssop (19:29) and the skeletal integrity of the sacrificed Jesus (19:36), a requirement for the lamb that was slain.

Although some have attempted to connect the first sign to the Eucharist, the arguments are not persuasive.[24] Even if the mixing of water and wine was a component of the paschal meal by the time of the FG's composition, in this miracle the two liquids are distinct rather than mixed. If any Old Testament parallel is envisioned beyond turning water to blood, it is Moses drawing drink from rock (Exod 17:6 and Num 20:7–11). Indeed, the thematic development of water in the FG streams toward the moment in the Festival of Booths when the High Priest pours water and wine over the altar (John 7:37–39), which is actualized when water and blood pour forth

---

22. Historically it is unclear whether any Jews had a detailed liturgy for the Passover Seder before the destruction of the Temple in 70 CE. Although in many ways the celebration probably differed little from a symposium, there is sufficient evidence to conclude that at least some recognizable framework was in place. (See especially Marcus, "Passover," 303–24, for New Testament evidence; Schlund, *Kein Knochen*, for Second Temple Period evidence, and Filsch, *Feste*, for rabbinic evidence.) Chilton thus draws a false dichotomy between symposium and Eucharist, *Feast*, 137; cf. Bahr, "The Seder," 181–202. On the Passover see the following essays in *Passover and Easter*: Leyerle, "Meal Customs," 29–61; Tabory, "Paschal Meal," 62–80; and Yuval, "Easter and Passover," 98–124. See also Bokser, *Origins*. Because the FG was composed decades after the temple's destruction, a more elaborate ritual may have already developed from which the FE could have worked for his literary purposes.

23. A more detailed examination of the Lamb of God theme would support the conclusions of this study, but it remains outside the scope of the paper. For soundings in that direction, see Nielsen, "Lamb," 243–56.

24. See Nielsen, "Lamb," 253. McGowan suggests that the story may oppose the use of water rather than wine in the Eucharist of some Christian groups, *Eucharists*, 236–37.

from Jesus's side (19:34).²⁵ The most that can be safely concluded is that the first sign anchors the Gospel's seven signs to the ten signs Moses performed in Egypt, of which the Passover is the climax.

In view of the influence of the Seder on the seven sayings, the concentration of sheep language in the middle is interesting. As with the signs, one should eschew parallelomania, but the inclusion of ovine metaphors between the bread and the vine is suggestive. Furthermore, there is no recognizable need for their inclusion. "I am the good shepherd" seems reasonable enough (10:11), but identifying oneself as "the door of the sheepfold" (10:7) seems odd even within an ancient pastoral setting. Although Jesus is not a sheep in either the third or fourth "I am" statements, ideationally the sequence of bread, sheep, and wine points to Passover.

With a bit of imagination, we can discover ovine traces in the third and fourth signs as well. In 5:2 we find an unusually full description of the Pool of Bethesda (cf. that of the Pool of Siloam, 9:7). As if the five porticoes were not specific enough, we learn that it is near the προβατική, the "sheep" (gate?). As is well known, this historical reference is supported by archeological excavations in the Holy City, but this could also be a theological clue. The two need not be mutually exclusive, especially since προβατική is hardly requisite for the story. If "gate" is understood from either Nehemiah (see 3:1) or local knowledge, this third sign intersects nicely with Jesus's equally enigmatic third statement, "I am the gate of the sheep."

Finding sheep in the fourth sign, the feeding of the five thousand, is more difficult. We know the FE plays with well known scripture as he composes and redacts. Almost certainly the primary passage in the background of the fourth sign and attending discourse is Deut 8:3: "A person will live not just by bread, but by every word that proceeds from the mouth of God."²⁶ Are there other texts underneath the surface? One could argue that the scene, clearly dependent upon the Exodus, implies Israel is again "like sheep without a shepherd" (Num 27:17), but this is so obscure as not even to qualify as an echo, even though that passage probably informs the discourse surrounding the fourth "I am" statement (chapter 10). Perhaps the reference to "much grass" (6:10) echoes Ps 23, implying that "the Lord is my shepherd." The resulting parallel with "I am the good shepherd" is attractive, but borders on circular reasoning.

---

25. See Koester, *Symbolism*, 200–203.
26. Borgen, *Bread*, and Brant, *John*, 128–29.

To conclude this section, the FE's emphasis on Passover is impressive.[27] The seven signs connect the story of Jesus to the rescue of Israel from Egypt, beginning with water turned to blood/wine and ending with the death of the firstborn. The seven sayings sharpen the focus to specific components of the Seder, beginning with bread and ending with the vine. The third and fourth members of each group may offer reminiscences of the Passover lamb, but this is far from certain, especially with regard to the series of signs.

Specific Passages in the FG

Because the macrostructures of the Gospel indicate the FE's interest in paschal theology, those Johannine passages often read as eucharistic may be re-examined.[28] Here only summary overviews are offered.

John 6

The fourth sign, the feeding of the five thousand, serves as the backdrop to the discourse about the Bread of Life/Jesus's words (6:35, 48, 51, 60, 63, and 68). "The Jews" mistakenly focus on the initial bread and then fixate on the messianic hope of renewed manna. To advance the discussion the FE has Jesus introduce new concepts: eating flesh and drinking blood (vv. 51–58). As commentators have noticed, these elements are foreign to the context: "Flesh" does not immediately conjure up the idea of bread, and drink lacks an antecedent in the immediately preceding narrative.

Many have naturally gravitated to the eucharistic words of institution as the catalyst for this turn in the story, seen as proof by some of a later interpolation. In light of the larger gospel framework, though, a Passover reference is more probable. Decisive in this matter is the temporal marker introducing the entire scene: "the Passover, the Feast of the Jews, was near" (v. 4).[29]

---

27. For a brief thematic study, see Howard, "Passover and Eucharist," 329–37.

28. Additional passages have been interpreted eucharistically and perhaps should be revisited in light of the Gospel's macrostructures. See the extensive and sometimes overreaching study of Hodges, "Synecdoche"; cf. Kobel, *Dining*, 205–14.

29. Chilton suggests that the Mosaic typology is central in John 6 and the Passover reference is subservient to it, *Feast*, 133. The key note of the discourse, "I am the bread of life," suggests otherwise. For more possible Passover parallels, see Gärtner, *John 6*, who

If the FE constructed the discourse around paschal elements, then the "flesh" would most naturally be taken with the lamb and the "blood" with the wine.[30] We immediately run into a problem, though, because Jesus unequivocally states, "The bread that I will give is my flesh on behalf of the life of the world" (v. 51). Such a tension should not surprise in the FG. Whether or not the confusion is attributed to a single author or a series of editors, Jesus's speech in John 6 is awash with varied referents: Jesus is both the bread (v. 35) and the giver of bread (v. 51).[31] His words are both flesh and bread (vv. 63 and 68). He is also the source of the heretofore unmentioned beverage, whether it be water, wine, or blood.

However one tries to disentangle the mess, the progression from bread to flesh to drink found in the final form of the Gospel is clear. This sequence parallels that found in the seven "I am" statements: bread and wine (certainly) or bread, sheep, and wine (possibly).[32]

John 13–17

The seven words and deeds of Jesus must also inform the interpretation of chapters 13–17. Here we encounter another paradox. The meal recounted in the FG cannot (historically) be the Seder because the Passover lambs have not yet been slaughtered, yet the FE (literarily) specifies the nearness of the Passover as he did in the sixth chapter (13:1). As a result, the FE must wish readers to interpret this meal as paschal in some sense.

As expected, the meal begins with bread. In a fascinating twist to the story Jesus "gives bread," which is life, only to his betrayer, who brings death (13:18 and 26).[33] The verbal parallels with the "Bread of Life" discourse

---

argues too much. At a minimum the use of later Jewish sources skews his results, but not all is thereby compromised. Cf. Brown, *New Testament Essays*, 77–82. Daise identifies this scene as a "Second Passover," *Feasts*, 104–52.

30. The "subordination" of the fish in the Gospel accounts may further point toward a bread-wine Eucharist, especially in the FG, according to Hiers, "Bread and Fish," 21–48.

31. See Schnackenburg, *John*, 2:65–69.

32. Anderson disagrees with paschal readings of John 6, primarily because scholars base them on comparisons with the Synoptics, "Gradations," 163. Establishing the paschal theology on the FE's own macrostructures counters that objection. Note also the possible connection with the seven signs if they are to be read chiastically as Rae suggests, "Testimony," 295–310, building off of Girard, "Composition," 315–24.

33. Kobel argues that remarks about Judas's betrayal form a strong literary connection between John 6 and 13, *Dining*, 271–94. She further presents the foot washing scene

(ἄρτον and τρώγων) are particularly striking and further contribute to the paschal theme. "I am the true vine" closes the meal (15:1–8), in a section clearly dislocated for this purpose. Despite the presence of bread and the vine, no "flesh" is mentioned. However, the Bread of Life discourse (6) and the Farewell discourse (13–17) make it evident that Jesus and his words are the main course.[34]

John 21

There is also a meal mentioned in the epilogue. Only here and in chapter 6 do we find reference to prepared fish (ὀψάριον) and to the Sea of Tiberias indicating some intended interplay between the two stories. The specific reference to the charcoal fire (ἀνθρακιά) also ties the story to the seventh sign (chapter 18).[35] Sheep, too, play a role when Peter thrice receives a commission from the Great Shepherd (vv. 15–17). A direct connection to the Passover is elusive, but this omission may be due to the shift of attention away from Christ to Peter, who himself will become a good shepherd and a slain lamb.

Johannine Eucharistic Theology

The victual reality of John is first and foremost paschal. Just because the FG roots its theology in the Passover, however, does not exclude it from also being eucharistic. The other Evangelists, for example, connect Eucharist with Passover as perhaps does Paul (1 Cor 5:8 and 11:23–26). But how does one discern eucharistic overtones, especially in a gospel with a nondescript Last Meal that lacks the words of institution?

Although we might assume that every Christian reading this Gospel in the late first century could not avoid missing the eucharistic language of John 6, it is far from certain that all Christians participated in a celebratory meal.[36] Even if a universal practice existed, there is no need to presume churches shared a common liturgy.[37] For the Gospel of John, we need to

---

in John 13 as the replacement for the Eucharist, 192–205.

34. Others offer quite different interpretations. For a summary and challenges, see Schnackenburg, *John*, 3:33–47.

35. Other parallels have been identified. See, for example, Spencer, "Echoes," 57–64.

36. Note that the Eucharist is not among the "seven ones" in Eph 4:4–6.

37. The prescriptions in the *Didache*, for example, present a fundamentally different

identify elements foreign to the Jewish Passover that appear consistent with distinct early Christian practices.

If the FE were interested in merely paschal theology, then we would expect to find additional parallels to the Passover ritual in the seven signs and seven "I am" statements. Although clear details of Second Temple period Seders are lacking, there is reason to believe that partaking of bitter herbs and eating lamb constituted highlighted elements of the celebration. In contrast, the FE accentuates only bread and wine. He only obliquely refers to sheep or shepherds and omits any counterpart to bitter herbs. Currently there is only one known paschal setting where bread and wine were instilled with special significance—the Lord's Supper.[38]

More importantly, the closest Johannine parallels to the words of institution are the first and seventh "I AM" sayings, "I am the bread of life" and "I am the true vine," not John 6:51–58 as supposed by Bultmann and others.[39] Rather, the "Bread of Life" discourse exegetes these claims. As already noted, contrary to expectations, the flesh is identified as bread rather than lamb in John 6. (Alternately, if the manna tradition is primary, the heavenly food is unexpectedly equated with flesh rather than bread.)[40] Additionally, there is no immediate cause in the narrative for Jesus's sudden interest in drinking, let alone his beverage of choice. Instead the reader must rely on previous references to water, wine, blood, and Spirit. Only at the Lord's Supper do we find a paschal meal in which bread is equated with flesh and drink with blood. Significantly, the very idea of anthropophagy would have been repulsive to Jews.[41]

The presence of these words of institution is remarkable. That they only remotely resemble the Synoptic and Pauline traditions is not, since early Christian meal practices and their theologies differed. Nonetheless, the FE pushes paschal symbolism beyond biblical antecedents and contemporary practices. At these edges we find parallels solely with early Jesus traditions about a shared meal imbued with salvific significance.

---

picture. See also McGowan, *Eucharists*.

38. This observation about elements of the meal is quite distinct from Felsch's observation that bread and blood played essential roles in the Passover, *Feste*, 252–55.

39. Bultmann, *John*, 218–19.

40. For the latter, see Borgen, *Bread*.

41. Cahill, "Drinking Blood," 168–81. Harrill draws attention to Roman responses, "Cannibalistic Language," 133–58.

Future Directions

Given that the FG concerns itself with the Eucharist, where do we go from here? That in itself would be another paper, but some observations might be appropriate for the colloquy. In terms of practice, bread and drink provided the pivotal anchors for the rite. It is unclear whether the community used wine or water, leavened or unleavened bread, or also included a full meal with lamb or fish. Frequency of celebration is also unknown, although the imprint of Creation theology on Johannine time combined with the resurrected Jesus's uncanny knack for revealing himself only on Sundays might suggest weekly observances (20:1, 11, and 26). More than likely such issues would have been relegated among the adiaphora. The FE's interests are far more Christological and incarnational than cultic.

More important to the Johannine circle would be the meal's function as a boundary marker and means of community formation.[42] Like the Passover, this communion was closed.[43] Only Jesus's friends could partake, although occasionally betrayers lurked among them.[44] The common meal unites the community, and it reminds them they are in the world but not of the world. For some the meal signifies membership in the true Israel (1:47), their false kinsmen, "the Jews," have missed the messianic banquet, the "true" food and drink (6:41 and 66). The believers recline at the table in the presence of their enemies; their cups overflow (6:35 vs. Sir 24:19–21). Yet even though the meal was exclusive, it contained important reminders of inclusivity. The command to love and the washing of feet, likely a component of subsequent celebrations, impelled a witness to the world through which the world would recognize true discipleship.[45]

Presumably there would also be meditation upon Jesus's words and Scripture (5:39).[46] The Spirit-filled community does this in his memory

---

42. Wheaton fortifies and expands Schlund's observations about the role of Passover as a boundary marker, *Role*, 83–126. See also Kobel, *Dining*, 37–107.

43. Cf. Brant, *John*, 227–29.

44. See Kobel, *Dining*, 92–95 and 271–93, and Matsunaga, "New Solution," 516–24.

45. See Moody Smith, *John*, 254–56, and Kobel, *Dining*, 99–104. But cf. Gundry, *Jesus*, 51–70.

46. The FE often offers contrasting responses to Jesus. One response is incorrect and the other is, although not necessarily embodying the entire truth, more correct. Also, one frequently results from a literal and, therefore, superficial hearing of Jesus and the other from a deeper, spiritual perception of Jesus's message. Clearly the cannibalistic response of "the Jews" to Jesus's challenge to consume his flesh is the incorrect response; Peter's "you have the words of life" is FE's summation of the truth, affirmed in the narrative by

(14:26).⁴⁷ Although not examined in this paper, the Bread of Life discourse has strong ties with Jewish wisdom.⁴⁸ The Last Meal in the FG is modeled after Greco-Roman symposia; here philosophers meet over supper to pursue life and truth. The Johannine churches eat the flesh and drink the blood of Jesus; they ingest the word(s) of life.⁴⁹

Thus the Johannine communities not only celebrated the Lord's Supper, for them Eucharist was ecclesiology. It was, as Dwight Moody Smith states, "the hallmark of discipleship."⁵⁰ Within the common supper the Word became flesh, and there they beheld his glory.

Bibliography

Anderson, Paul N. "John and Mark: the Bi-Optic Gospels." In *Jesus in Johannine Tradition*, edited by Robert T. Fortna and Tom Thatcher, 175–88. Louisville: Westminster John Knox, 2001.

Bahr, Gordon. "The Seder of Passover and the Eucharistic Words." *NovT* 12 (1970) 181–202.

---

the immediately following theophany.

47. Bornkamm and others unfortunately read later Christian sacramentalism into the FG, especially through Ignatius, "Eucharistische Rede," 161–69. Such an approach precludes identifying Jesus's flesh and blood with his words and prevents any reimagining about how the bread and wine might be interpreted differently, say, for example, in terms of wisdom as found in the *Didache*'s feast(s) and Philo's description of the meal shared by the Therapeutae (*de Vita Contemp.* 75–79).

48. See Thompson, "Thinking," 221–46; Brown, *Essays*, 82–92, and *John I—XII*, 272–75. Note that the FE associates baptism with Jesus's word too (15:3; compare also Eph 5:26).

49. This view is markedly different than the roughly contemporary apotropaic and purificatory interpretations of Passover identified by Schlund, although she finds some Johannine parallels, *Kein Knochen*, 98–181. This view also differs from Philo's allegorical interpretation. For a summary, see Nielsen, "Lamb," 235–39. Although not the particular topic of the paper, this suggests that the FG's theology is sacramental, but not as sometimes imagined. Entrance into the kingdom is not predicated on participation, per se, as the feeding of the morsel to Judas makes clear. Jesus, both in and outside of the meal setting, must be engaged at a deeper level. In John, superficial/literal readings lead only to darkness (3:2 and 13:30). On sacramentality see Brown, *Essays*, 51–76; Cullmann, *Early Christian Worship*; Guyette, "Sacramentality," 235–50; and Schnelle, *Antidocetic Christology*, 176–210.

50. Moody Smith, *John*, 165. On the connection of Eucharist to Johannine ecclesiology, see also Cosgrove, "Allusions," 522–39, and Beutler, "John 6," 126. Without a doubt the Johannine Eucharist also embodies Christology and pneumatology, but these are not the subject of the colloquy.

PART 2: PRESENTED ESSAYS

Beutler, Johannes. "The Structure of John 6." In *Critical Readings of John 6*, edited by R. Alan Culpepper, 115–28. BibIntSer 22. Atlanta: Society of Biblical Literature, 1997.

Boismard, Marie-Émile, and Arnaud Lamouille. *Synopse des quatre évangiles en français*. Vol. 3: *L'Evangile de Jean*. Paris: Cerf, 1977.

Bokser, Baruch. *The Origins of the Seder: The Passover Rite and Early Rabbinic Judaism*. Berkeley: University of California Press, 1984.

Borgen, Peder. *Bread from Heaven: Exegetical Study of the Concept of Manna in the Gospel of John and the Writings of Philo*. NovTSup 10. Leiden: Brill, 1981.

———. "God's Agent in the Fourth Gospel." In *Religions in Antiquity: Essays in Memory of Erwin Ramsdell Goodenough*, edited by Jacob Neusner, 137–48. Studies in the History of Religions 14. Leiden: Brill, 1968.

Bornkamm, Günther. "Die eucharistische Rede im Johannes-Evangelium." ZNW 47 (1956) 161–69.

Brant, Jo-Ann. *John*. Paideia. Grand Rapids: Baker, 2011.

Brooks, Oscar. "The Johannine Eucharist: Another Interpretation." *JBL* 82 (1963) 293–300.

Brown, Jeannine. "Creation's Renewal in the Gospel of John." *CBQ* 72 (2010) 275–90.

Brown, Raymond E. *The Gospel according to John I–XII*. AB 29. Garden City, NY: Doubleday, 1966.

———. *New Testament Essays*. New York: Paulist, 1965.

Bühner, Jan-A. "The Exegesis of the Johannine 'I-Am' Sayings." In *Der Gesandte und sein Weg im vierten Evangelium*, 166–80. WUNT 2/2. Tübingen: Mohr/Siebeck, 1977.

Bultmann, Rudolf. *The Gospel of John: A Commentary*. Translated by G. R. Beasley Murray. 1971. Reprinted, with a new foreword by Paul N. Anderson. Johannine Monograph Series. Eugene, OR: Wipf & Stock, 2014.

Cahill, Michael. "Drinking Blood at a Kosher Eucharist? The Sound of Scholarly Silence." *BTB* 32 (2002) 168–81.

Chilton, Bruce. *A Feast of Meanings: Eucharistic Theologies from Jesus through Johannine Circles*. NovTSup 72. Leiden: Brill, 1997.

Clark, Douglas. "Signs in Wisdom and John." *CBQ* 45 (1983) 201–209.

Cosgrove, Charles. "The Place Where Jesus Is: Allusions to Baptism and the Eucharist in the Fourth Gospel." *NTS* 35 (1989) 522–39.

Cullmann, Oscar. *Early Christian Worship*. SBT 1/10. London: SCM, 1953.

Culpepper, R. Alan. *Anatomy of the Fourth Gospel: A Study in Literary Design*. Foundations and Facets: New Testament. Philadelphia: Fortress, 1983.

Daise, Michael. *Feasts in John: Jewish Festivals and Jesus' "Hour" in the Fourth Gospel*. WUNT 2/229. Tübingen: Mohr/Siebeck, 2007.

Dunn, James D. G. "John vi—A Eucharistic Discourse?" *NTS* 17 (1971) 328–38.

Felsch, Dorit. *Die Feste im Johannesevangelium: Jüdische Tradition und christliche Deutung*. WUNT 2/308. Tübingen: Mohr/Siebeck, 2011.

Fortna, Robert T. *The Fourth Gospel and Its Predecessor*. Philadelphia: Fortress, 1988.

———. *The Gospel of Signs: A Reconstruction of the Narrative Source Underlying the Fourth Gospel*. SNTSMS 11. Cambridge: Cambridge University Press, 1970.

Gärtner, Bertil. *John 6 and the Jewish Passover*. Coniectanea Neotestamentica 17. Lund: Gleerup, 1959.

Girard, Marc. "La composition structurelle des sept signes dans le quatrième évangile." *SR* 9 (1980) 315–24.

Gundry, Robert. *Jesus the Word according to John the Sectarian*. Grand Rapids: Eerdmans, 2002.
Guyette, Frederick. "Sacramentality and the Fourth Gospel: Conflicting Interpretations." *Ecc* 3 (2002) 235–50.
Harrill, J. Albert. "Cannibalistic Language in the Fourth Gospel and Greco-Roman Polemics of Factionalism (John 6:52–66)." *JBL* 127 (2008) 133–58.
Hiers, Richard. "The Bread and Fish Eucharist." *PRSt* 3 (1976) 21–48.
Hodges, Horace. "Food as Synecdoche in John's Gospel and Gnostic Texts." PhD diss., University of California, Berkeley, 1996–97.
Howard, J. K. "Passover and Eucharist in the Fourth Gospel." *SJT* 20 (1967) 329–37.
Jeremias, Joachim. *The Eucharistic Words of Jesus*. Translated by Norman Perrin. New Testament Library. London: SCM, 1966.
Kobel, Esther. *Dining with John: Communal Meals and Identity Formation in the Fourth Gospel and Its Historical and Cultural Context*. BibIntSer 109. Leiden: Brill, 2011.
Köstenberger, Andreas. *The Mission of Jesus according to the Fourth Gospel*. Grand Rapids: Eerdmans, 1998.
Koester, Craig. *Symbolism in the Fourth Gospel*. 2nd ed. Minneapolis: Fortress, 2003.
Léon-Dufour, Xavier. "Towards a Symbolic Reading of the Fourth Gospel." *NTS* 27 (1981) 439–56.
Leyerle, Blake. "Meal Customs in the Greco-Roman World." In *Passover and Easter: Origin and History to Modern Times*, edited by Paul F. Bradshaw and Lawrence A. Hoffmann, 29–61. Two Liturgical Traditions 5. Notre Dame: University of Notre Dame, 1999.
Lincoln, Andrew. *The Gospel according to Saint John*. BNTC. London: Continuum, 2005.
Lindars, Barnabas. "Word and Sacrament in the Fourth Gospel." *SJT* 29 (1976) 49–63.
McGowan, Andrew. *Ascetic Eucharists*. Oxford: Clarendon, 1999.
Marcus, Joel. "Passover and Last Supper Revisited." *NTS* 53 (2013) 303–324.
Matsunaga, Kikuo. "Is John's Gospel Anti-Sacramental?—A New Solution in the Light of the Evangelist's Milieu." *NTS* 27 (1981) 516–24.
Menken, Maarten. "John 6:51c–58: Eucharist or Christology?" In *Critical Readings of John 6*, edited by R. Alan Culpepper, 184–87. BibIntSer 22. Atlanta: Society of Biblical Literature, 1997.
Meye Thompson, Marianne. "Thinking about God: Wisdom and Theology in John 6." In *Critical Readings of John 6*, edited by R. Alan Culpepper, 242–43. BibIntSer 22. Atlanta: Society of Biblical Literature, 1997.
Nicol, Willem. *The Semeia in the Fourth Gospel: Tradition and Redaction*. NovTSup 32. Leiden: Brill, 1972.
Nielsen, Jesper. "The Lamb of God: The Cognitive Structure of a Johannine Metaphor." In *Imagery in the Gospel of John*, edited by J. Frey, 217–56. WUNT 200. Tübingen: Mohr/Siebeck, 1996.
O'Day, Gail. "John 6:15–21: Jesus Walking on the Water as Narrative Embodiment of Johannine Christology." In *Critical Readings of John 6*, edited by R. Alan Culpepper, 149–59. BibIntSer 22. Atlanta: Society of Biblical Literature, 1997.
Palmer, Syd. "Repetition and the Art of Reading: KAI TH HMEPA TH TPITH, 'On the Third Day' in John's Gospel." In *Repetitions and Variations in the Fourth Gospel*, edited by G. van Belle, et al., 403–17 BETL 233. Leuven: Peeters, 2009.

Rae, Murray. "The Testimony of Works in the Christology of John's Gospel." In *The Gospel of John and Christian Theology*, edited by Richard Bauckham and Carl Mosser, 295–310. Grand Rapids: Eerdmans, 2008.

Rensberger, David. *Johannine Faith and Liberating Community*. Louisville: Westminster John Knox, 1996.

Richter, Georg. "Zur Formgeschichte und literarischen Einheit von Joh 6,31–58." *ZNW* 60 (1969) 39–48.

Schlund, Christine. *"Kein Knochen soll gebrochen werden": Studien zu Bedeutung und Funktion des Pesachfests in Texten des frühen Judentums und im Johannesevangelium*. Wissenschaftliche Monographien zum Alten und Neuen Testament 107. Neukirchen-Vluyn: Neukirchener, 2005.

Schnackenburg, Rudolf. *The Gospel according to St John*. 3 vols. Translated by Cecily Hastings et al. HTCNT. New York: Crossroad, 1987.

Schnelle, Udo. *Antidocetic Christology in the Gospel of John*. Minneapolis: Fortress, 1992.

Smalley, Stephen. "The Sign in John xxi." *NTS* 20 (1964) 275–88.

Smith, D. Moody. *John*. ANTC. Nashville: Abingdon, 1999.

Smith, Robert H. "Exodus Typology in the Fourth Gospel." *JBL* 81 (1962) 329–42.

Spencer, Patrick. "Narrative Echoes in John 21: Intertextual Interpretation and Intratextual Connection." *JSNT* 75 (1999) 49–68.

Tabory, Joseph. "Towards a History of the Paschal Meal." In *Passover and Easter: Origin and History to Modern Times*, edited by Paul F. Bradshaw and Lawrence A. Hoffmann, 62–80. Notre Dame: University of Notre Dame, 1999.

van Belle, Gilbert. *The Signs Source in the Fourth Gospel*. BETL 116. Leuven: Peeters, 1994.

von Wahlde, Urban C. *The Gospel and Letters of John*. ECC. 3 vols. Grand Rapids: Eerdmans, 2010.

Wheaton, Gerry. *The Role of Jewish Feasts in John's Gospel*. SNTSMS 162. New York: Cambridge University Press, 2015.

Wilkens, Wilhelm. "Das Abendmahlszeugnis im vierten Evangelium." *ET* 18 (1958) 354–70.

Yuval, Israel. "Easter and Passover as Early Jewish-Christian Dialogue." In *Passover and Easter: Origin and History to Modern Times*, edited by Paul F. Bradshaw and Lawrence A. Hoffman, 98–124. Notre Dame: University of Notre Dame, 1999.

9

From Passover to Eucharist
The *Didache* and Early Eucharistic Observance

—*Jeffrey Peterson*

SINCE THE PUBLICATION OF the *Didache* in 1883, differences between the instructions for eucharistic observance included in this early church order (chaps. 9–10, 14) and the eucharistic traditions preserved in New Testament sources have often been noted. Prominent among these are the *Didache*'s introduction of cup and bread in that order (although cf. Luke 22:17–19; 1 Cor 10:16), the lack of an institution narrative or interpretation of the meal's elements as betokening Christ's blood and body, and the absence of any explicit reference to the eucharistic observance as a memorial of Jesus' death. Scholars have offered a variety of proposals to account for the text's apparent singularities.[1]

Paul Bradshaw has suggested that the problems posed by the text are reduced (if not eliminated) if its eucharistic prescriptions are regarded as "one of a number of different patterns that existed side-by-side in early Christianity, each being the practice belonging to a particular community or group of communities."[2] John Dominic Crossan similarly takes *Didache*

---

1. Bradshaw, *Eucharistic Origins*, 25–32.

2. Ibid., 32. Bradshaw's advocacy of this "new paradigm" appears to stand in some tension with his apparent endorsement of the critique of various theories of a twofold origin of the Eucharist as "based on extremely tenuous evidence" and "making the improbable assumption of a radical dichotomy between the thinking and practice of the

9–10 and 1 Corinthians 10–11 as evidence of two distinct eucharistic traditions: the Pauline evidence is representative of "the Jerusalem tradition" of "a ritual meal institutionalized by Jesus himself and connected with his own execution," the elements of this meal "symboliz[ing] . . . Jesus' own body and blood," while the *Didache* preserves "the Q Gospel tradition," which has "none of these connections" and in which the "prayers are extremely similar to standard Jewish prayers."[3] Bradshaw and Crossan agree in their reticence to credit a formative role in the shaping of the Eucharist to memories of the "Last Supper," the final evening meal that Jesus shared with his disciples, as recounted in 1 Cor 11:23–25 and in Mark 14:12–26 and parallels.[4]

Crossan does regard the Pauline evidence and the *Didache* as witnesses to a "Common Meal Tradition," which developed in different directions. In this essay, I suggest that this is a step in the right direction, but that on closer inspection of the evidence, a greater degree of commonality can be discerned between the *Didache* and the NT texts than Crossan and other interpreters recognize. In outline, I propose that the Pauline evidence preserves catechetical instruction concerning the rationale for the observance of the meal, while the *Didache* represents properly liturgical instruction, including representative wording of the blessings to be employed in the meal's observance, but that the two sources reflect the same general form of eucharistic observance.[5]

Pauline Evidence

The starting point for the study of eucharistic origins is Paul's first letter to the Corinthians (ca. AD 55). In this letter, Paul likely alludes to the Corinthians' annual observance of Passover in his exhortation to purge immorality from the community (1 Cor 5:7–8), and also, in his typological

---

primitive Jerusalem church and the Pauline communities" (28). His proposal seems predicated on precisely this assumption.

3. Crossan, *Birth of Christianity*, 434.

4. The question how accurate or inaccurate such memories may have been is distinct from the question whether early eucharistic observance proceeded under the conscious remembrance of a formative event. For the sense of "memory" employed here, see especially Dahl, *Jesus in the Memory of the Early Church*.

5. I can only aspire here to the clarity of Everett Ferguson's survey of the evidence in his essay, "Lord's Supper and Love Feast," 27–38. It is a privilege and a pleasure to contribute to this volume in honor of a teacher whose careful scholarship, patient instruction, good counsel, and Christian example have benefitted me for more than three decades.

rendering of the Exodus narrative, to the weekly supper the Corinthians shared in memory of Christ (1 Cor 10:1–4). He refers explicitly to the material elements of the more frequent meal in his plea to avoid idolatry (10:16–17, 21) and he instructs the Corinthians on proper observance of the supper early in his discussion of the Corinthian assemblies (11:17–34).[6]

In this latter passage, Paul rehearses a narrative from his prior oral instruction of the community recounting Jesus' institution of this meal as a memorial to his death "on the night in which he was handed over" (11:23–25).[7] In its immediate literary context, this institution narrative serves to remind the Corinthians that they observe this supper as a memorial of the death of their risen Lord, whose very body and blood are present in the meal's material elements, according to Jesus' own words (cf. 10:16). Thus, to conduct the meal in a divisive fashion unworthy of Christ, "not discerning the body" in the communal fellowship, is to commit sacrilege against "the body and blood of the Lord" and invite divine judgment (11:27–29). When Paul had originally inculcated this narrative as part of the catechesis in which the community was formed, it doubtless served other, more fundamental purposes, before the problem that he uses it to address in 1 Cor 11:17–34 had appeared.[8] In its present context, the emphasis rests on the kind of conduct that will serve to fulfill Jesus' command to observe the supper "toward my commemoration" (εἰς τὴν ἐμὴν ἀνάμνησιν); the earlier catechetical instruction presumably emphasized the importance of the supper's very observance (τοῦτο ποιεῖτε) as a regular occasion for gathering as a community.

The clearest point of similarity between the Last Supper described in the institution narrative and the Corinthian observance that Paul now corrects is that each is described as a δεῖπνον, the main daily meal taken in the afternoon or evening. This is reinforced for Jesus' "supper" by the mention that it occurred "at night" (11:23) and that the cup was shared "after the

---

6. Overall, the evidence of the letter commends Austin Farrer's judgment: "Of the yearly Jewish feasts the primitive Christians kept Passover alone; they kept it yearly, and they commemorated it every Sunday" (*Study in St Mark*, 217). For the annual "Christian Passover" celebration presupposed by 1 Cor 5:7–8, see Peterson, "Redeeming the Time," 37–39.

7. Translations of the New Testament and the *Didache* are the author's.

8. On 1 Cor 11:23–25 as a reminder of catechesis (i.e., instruction inculcated in the Corinthians' formation as a Christian community and now recalled to address a deficiency in communal practice) rather than liturgy (i.e., tradition regularly rehearsed in the Corinthian assemblies), see McGowan, "Is There a Liturgical Text," 77–80.

supping" (μετὰ τὸ δειπνῆσαι, 11:25). Paul indicates that the Corinthians observed a meal on occasions when they would "come together" (11:18, 20) by offering the critique that each of them "proceeds with eating his own supper" (τὸ ἴδιον δεῖπνον προλαμβάνει ἐν τῷ φαγεῖν), so that in the end "one goes hungry and another is drunk" (11:21). He advises those solicitous of their appetites to "eat at home" (11:34), even if the references to drunkenness and hunger involve hyperbole, they suggest a meal setting in which appetites for food and drink could be indulged if one were so inclined. Paul contrasts this boorish behavior with the considerate, hospitable practice of "awaiting one another" (11:33), and he calls for the gathering to be conducted in such a way that it could truly be described as "a dominical supper" (κυριακὸν δεῖπνον, 11:20), i.e., one hosted by the Lord or (perhaps more likely) pertaining to him, specifically through commemoration of his death.

Dennis Smith has contextualized this passage among others within ancient Mediterranean dining practices and made an impressive case that "the banquet as a social institution . . . [,] practiced in similar ways and with similar symbols or codes by Greeks, Romans, Jews, Egyptians," and other Mediterranean peoples provided the formative matrix for the early development of eucharistic practice, and indeed of earliest Christian worship generally.[9] From Paul's apparently synonymous use of the expressions "when you come together in assembly" (συνερχομένων ὑμῶν ἐν ἐκκλησίᾳ, 11:18; cf. ὅταν συνέρχησθε, 14:26), "when you come together . . . to eat the Lord's supper" (συνερχομένων οὖν ὑμῶν ἐπὶ τὸ αὐτό . . . κυριακὸν δεῖπνον φαγεῖν, 1 Cor 11:20), and "if then the whole church comes together" (ἐὰν οὖν συνέλθῃ ἡ ἐκκλησία ὅλη ἐπὶ τὸ αὐτό, 14:23), Smith concludes that chaps. 11 and 14 describe different phases of the same assembly context; the early Christian assembly followed the culturally ubiquitous pattern of a *deipnon* preceding a *symposion*, the latter the occasion for a "program" accompanying the drinking of wine, in this case consisting of instruction and edification.[10]

---

9. Smith, *From Symposium to Eucharist,* esp. 173–217. Against the clear distinction between sacral Eucharist and banquet ("love feast") perceived by many scholars (including Ferguson, "Lord's Supper and Love Feast," 34–35), see McGowan, "Naming the Feast," 314–18.

10. Among other passages, Smith's proposal helps to account for the close association and contrast between drunkenness with wine and the influence of the Spirit in Eph 5:18–21, the latter manifest in the well-ordered relationships of mutual regard existing between those gathered for the eucharistic assembly (5:22—6:9; note the ESV of 5:21 for

Smith further argues from the Pauline evidence that such a banquet as the mode of Christian assembly was by no means limited to Corinth, but is rather presupposed by Paul throughout the churches that he founded.[11] When he recounts his controversy with Cephas and other Jews at Antioch (Gal 2:11–14), Paul presupposes that the Galatians will appreciate the sacral significance of the communal meal and the scandal involved in the refusal of fellowship. Moreover, the banquet was not limited to communities that Paul founded; the anecdote he relates to the Galatians attests sacral meals observed by Christians in Antioch, as one such was the occasion for the controversy. The story also attests the observance of such meals in Jerusalem, for "otherwise the issue when the guests from Jerusalem arrived would not have been which table but why have a community table at all."[12] Finally, in the letter to the Roman communities, not founded by Paul, Smith notes that when Paul comes to focus on specific communal issues in Rom 14:1–15:13, "differences over diet . . . get the most attention and . . . seem to be the focus for the problems" in Rome. He concludes it was "likely, therefore, that such ideological divisions came to the fore at the community meal."[13] Significantly, in regard to the tradition recounting Jesus' last supper, Smith argues that "[s]ince Paul presents this tradition as one that was passed on to him, he seems to assume its practice for all of the churches with which he was familiar."[14]

Between Paul and the Synoptics

Implausibly, Smith argues that the meal recalled in 1 Cor 11:23–25 does not refer to an event in the career of the earthly Jesus but "takes place on a mythological level . . . in the heavenly sphere"; the expression "the Lord

---

the connection between the two passages).

11. This is perhaps already intimated in Paul's discussion of the Supper in the context of the Corinthians' fidelity to the "traditions" that Paul had delivered to them (1 Cor 11:2), which in context refer not only to doctrines but also to the practices discussed in 11:2–16; these relate specifically to the adornment appropriate to men and women engaged in prophetic activity (11:4–5) and presumed to be concerned to do so in a manner consistent with the practice in "the assemblies of God" (11:16). This in turn builds on Paul's earlier commendation of Timothy as able to remind the Corinthians of Paul's "ways in Christ" which he teaches "everywhere in every church" (1 Cor 4:17).

12. Smith, *From Symposium to Eucharist*, 176.

13. Ibid., 177.

14. Ibid., 176–77.

Jesus," he argues, is inappropriate to describe an episode in the life of an earthly figure and "removes the text from any historical imagining," placing the Last Supper tradition in a mythological context.[15] This interpretation neglects the common and unexceptional use of presently held titles in retrospective discourse, a usage evident in the same letter in Paul's ascription of Jesus' earthly teaching to "the Lord" (ὁ κύριος, 1 Cor 7:10–11; 9:14).[16]

More broadly, and in agreement with many Pauline scholars, Smith contrasts the Gospels, which present the Last Supper within a narrative of Jesus' life, with Paul, whose letters do not recount the story of Jesus' earthly life. Yet while Paul's letters offer no connected *bios* of Jesus, much less a modern critical biography, they do include a number of references to events in Jesus' earthly career, and these references are so casual and incidental as to suggest that Paul presupposes his audience's familiarity with at least an outline of Jesus' earthly life. Although the biographical material about Jesus in Paul's letters would not be adequate to construct a narrative Gospel, it certainly amounts to a respectable entry in a biographical dictionary. Thus, Paul reports Jesus' birth as a Jew subject to Torah and of specifically Davidic lineage (Gal 4:4; Rom 1:3), his work among his fellow Jews as "a minister of the circumcision" (Rom 15:8), and his teaching, addressing topics including marriage (1 Cor 7:10–11) and the conduct of a mission to promulgate "the gospel," over which he presumably presided (1 Cor 9:14).[17] Against Smith's contention that the "phrase 'Christ crucified' virtually summarizes the entire plot" of Paul's "Christ story," which "represented a negotiation between Jesus and God" and omitted mention of "any human actors in this drama,"[18] Paul's references to Jesus' death on the supreme instrument

---

15. Ibid., 189.

16. In the 2004 American presidential election, there was considerable discussion of "the President's National Guard service" and "the Senator's tour of duty in Vietnam," but the median voter was not led to imagine the President reporting for Guard duty to the strains of "Hail to the Chief," or a sitting senator captaining a swift boat through Cambodian waters. Paul's references to the Lord's being handed over and crucified are readily intelligible as exhibiting a parallel logical structure, and once that is recognized, there is no difficulty in the use of such language in reference to the earthly Jesus.

17. His coming return in glory may be regarded as more difficult to credit to the earthly Jesus on the basis of Paul's appeal to a "word of the Lord," but the verbal parallels between the teaching Paul summarizes in 1 Thess 4:15–17 and the Synoptic apocalyptic discourse (esp. Matt 24:30–31) commend this interpretation. The crucial question for Pauline interpretation is whether Paul understood Jesus to have taught this, not whether he was correct in doing so.

18. Smith, 189.

of Roman torture and terror imply human agency, and in this connection Paul mentions both "the rulers of this age" (1 Cor 2:8), which may include human rulers as well as demonic, and the initiative of his fellow Jews (1 Thess 2:15).[19] In the aftermath of his death, the risen Christ appeared "to *Cephas*, then to the Twelve" (1 Cor 15:5), evidently a recognized group of Aramaic-speaking (and so presumably Palestinian) associates. This group seems to have been in existence prior to Jesus' death (so that the risen Lord could appear to them shortly thereafter), and the group's name suggests the eschatological tribal symbolism made explicit in the Synoptic tradition (Matt 19:28//Luke 22:29–30). Though Paul's lack of interest in the earthly career of Jesus is frequently asserted, it is difficult to maintain in view of this evidence.

Smith further seeks to dissociate the Pauline institution tradition from the Synoptic Last Supper narratives by arguing that the use of παραδιδόναι (1 Cor 11:23) is a reference not to Judas' action against Jesus as recounted in the Gospel narrative, but to divine action, to God's having handed Jesus over to death (cf. Rom 8:32)—"hardly a historical detail, but a richly mythological/theological one."[20] Yet the action of a divine agent need not be understood as confined to "the heavenly sphere" in the understanding of early Judaism; for example, God's "handing over" (παραδιδόναι) of his people's enemies into their hand, or vice versa, is presented as playing out in earthly events (e.g., Gen 14:20 LXX; Exod 23:32 LXX; Lev 26:25 LXX). Further, so confident an exclusion of a possible allusion to Judas, while another commonplace of recent Pauline scholarship, may not be warranted. Paul explicitly presents the narrative in 1 Cor 11:23 as tradition that he received from others. What he recalls is thus not originally his own composition, and it is clearly parallel in content to the Synoptic accounts of the Last Supper. This seems reason enough to question whether παραδιδόναι in 1 Cor 11:23 was originally chosen to suit Paul's diction or whether it may originally have alluded to the story of Jesus' being "handed over" by his apostle. This possibility is strengthened by the observation that παραδιδόναι is prominent in the Marcan passion narrative, with seven

---

19. In endorsing Charles B. Cousar's judgment that in the Pauline corpus "we do not even find speculation about the events leading to the death of Jesus, or who killed Jesus" (*From Symposium to Eucharist*, 189), Smith neglects 1 Thess 2:14–16 and presumably regards it as a secondary interpolation; but its integrity within 1 Thessalonians is commended by a number of studies, most notably Schleuter, *Filling Up the Measure*.

20. Smith, *From Symposium to Eucharist*, 190.

uses having Judas as the expressed or implied subject (Mark 14:10, 11, 18, 21, 41, 42, 44; cf. 3:19).

In view of its multiple attestation in Paul and the Gospels (the strongest attestation possible for any element of the Jesus tradition, since Paul is our earliest witness), E. P. Sanders and Margaret Davies conclude that the substance of the institution narrative is "authentic beyond reasonable doubt."[21] There are broadly historical, not narrowly theological, grounds for concluding that the memory of this event, witnessed by the Twelve and other disciples of Jesus and widely retold in early Christian communities, as 1 Cor 11:23–25 attests, exerted a continuing influence over the imagination of the earliest circles of Christ's adherents. It is not at all unreasonable to suppose that this memory shaped eucharistic practice in particular and in part accounts for the formation and cohesion of communities devoted to preserving the memory of Jesus and for the widespread observance of the banquets in Jesus' memory that Smith's work documents.

The Synoptics agree in dating the institution of the Lord's Supper to the Passover festival that Jesus celebrated with his disciples before his betrayal and crucifixion. It is often suggested that such an association with Passover is lacking in the Pauline account. There are, however, several points of agreement between the Pauline and Synoptic accounts, which commend the conclusion that the tradition Paul reports recalled Jesus instituting the memorial banquet during a celebration of Passover: (1) Jesus' blessings over bread and wine are recalled as having taken place "on the *night* in which he was handed over" (cf. Mark 14:17), in accordance with the requirement that the Passover be eaten after sundown (Exod 12:8,18, 42; Deut 16:4, 6; *m. Pesaḥ.* 10:1). This was crucial enough to conveying the significance of the narrative that Paul, like his predecessor tradent(s), retained this otherwise trivial temporal detail. (2) Paul associates the institution with eschatological anticipation (1 Cor 11:26; cf. Mark 14:25). This fits well in the context of the expectations of eschatological deliverance associated in the Second Temple period with Passover, the festival that commemorated God's deliverance of Israel from slavery in Egypt, and in which eschatological deliverance from present oppression was also anticipated (cf. Josephus *BJ* 4.402; 5.99; *Ant.* 2.313; 2.317; 3.248; 17.213).[22] (3)

---

21. Sanders and Davies, *Studying the Synoptic Gospels*, 324; cf. 329.

22. Josephus details the results when some Jews went beyond hope and prayer to act on their convictions (as in *BJ* 5.98–105) and Rome responded with the ferocity she thought necessary to secure her imperial interests (*BJ* 6.420–434).

Words of interpretation over the elements of an ordinary supper might be surprising, but they are more intelligible at a festal meal, and especially at Passover, where some interpretation of the elements was expected (cf. Ex 12:26–27; Deut 16:3; *m. Pesaḥ.* 10:4–5), even if the interpretation attributed to Jesus was novel and striking. (4) The suggestion that the offering of Christ's body has atoning effect (τὸ σῶμα τὸ ὑπὲρ ὑμῶν, 1 Cor 11:24) also commends a Passover context, although it is often taken to count on the other side of the argument. While commentators frequently remark that the Passover was not an atonement sacrifice in the Hebrew Bible or in later Judaism, Jon Levenson observes that "the unclassifiable passover sacrifice of Exodus 12 . . . [has] much in common with a sin offering, for it is through the blood of the lamb that lethal calamity is deflected, as the mysterious Destroyer is prevented from working his dark designs upon the Israelite first-born (vv 21–23)."[23] (5) This mention of atoning death in connection with the bread stands in parallel with the reference to a "covenant" over the cup; the Pauline and Marcan forms of the tradition allude, respectively, to Exod 24:8 and Jer 31:31–34. Either allusion invites a parallel between Jesus' impending death and God's covenant with Israel initiated in the Passover deliverance and codified at Sinai. All these details of the tradition that Paul recalls commend the conclusion that Paul's prior catechesis presented Jesus' last supper to his converts as a Passover meal and drew significance from that identification.

Besides these indications within the tradition itself, Paul has earlier primed his readers to pick up on these paschal associations through his exhortation, "Cleanse out the old leaven that you may be a new lump, just as you are unleavened. For indeed our pascal lamb has been sacrificed, even Christ. Let us therefore celebrate the festival, not with old leaven nor leaven of malice and evil, but with unleavened loaves of sincerity and truth" (1 Cor 5:7–8), a remarkably brief and rhetorically complex invocation of the Passover tradition.[24] An audience that Paul characterizes as composed of former devotees of pagan cults (ὅτε ἔθνη ἦτε πρὸς τὰ εἴδωλα τὰ ἄφωνα ὡς ἂν ἤγεσθε ἀπαγόμενοι, 12:2; cf. 6:9) is nonetheless presumed to recognize

---

23. Levenson, *Death and Resurrection of the Beloved Son*, 208–9. Levenson further suggests that "in the heated apocalyptic Judaism that served as the matrix of Christianity, the Destroyer [could easily have been] transmuted into a personification of the Israelites' own mortal sins, and the blood of the paschal lamb . . . seen as effecting not only escape from death, but purification from moral pollution as well."

24. On this brevity, characteristic of Paul's summary epitomes of his preaching in 1 Corinthians, see Mitchell, "Rhetorical Shorthand in Pauline Argumentation," 70–72.

at once the association between Passover and unleavened bread (5:8), and also to recognize in Jesus' death the sacrifice of "our" paschal victim Christ, in contrast, presumably, to the Passover celebration that unites "Israel according to the flesh" (10:18). Similarly, in 10:1–13, Paul presupposes that his pagan converts will now recognize the Exodus as an experience of "our fathers" (10:1), and that the details of this narrative will be familiar enough that he can allegorize them straightaway.

These passages strongly suggest that the Exodus narrative and its fulfillment in Christ were among the traditions that Paul had impressed on the Corinthians in the course of his earlier formative instruction of the community. When we recall that in 1 Cor 15:3–4 Paul reminds his converts of the message that he had preached to them as having focused on Christ's death "for our sins in accordance with the Scriptures" and his resurrection "on the third day in accordance with the Scriptures," it seems plausible that Pauline missionary preaching (the foundation that he laid, in the image of 1 Cor 3:10–11) inculcated in converts a narrative of Jesus' death and resurrection as a universal Passover offering that sealed God's eschatological covenant and inaugurated the fulfillment of prophetic hopes for a new exodus in which gentiles would participate as well as Jews. Moreover, Paul does not present this complex of ideas and the practices in which they were embodied as his creation, or his unique possession; he rather ascribes them to the tradition he inherited from those who preceded him in the faith and in the apostolate, and in the case of 1 Cor 11:23–25 ultimately to Jesus himself on the occasion of his final Passover celebration.[25]

Sources antedating the destruction of the temple supply an incomplete picture of the details of Passover observance. Smith observes, however, that the form prescribed in the Mishnah (ca. AD 200) follows the pattern typical of the Mediterranean banquet and argues that "some of its basic features" were likely in place in the earlier period.[26] As Smith shows, an ancient banquet typically involved two stages: first came the *deipnon* or supper, beginning with a cup of wine and an appetizer course, followed by the main course and dessert course; followed by a second cup of wine and

---

25. See further Peterson, "Christ Our Pasch," 133–44.

26. Smith, *From Symposium to Eucharist*, 147; he notes that the Mediterranean banquet form is attested in Jewish contexts already in Amos 6:4–7 (134), in Sirach (134–44), and in Tosefta *Berakot* (145, 333 n. 38). McGowan similarly suggests that "as a banquet in specifically Jewish circles, the Seder remains especially important for the discussion of early Christian meals" and notes that the "meal proper had three courses, as it might have done in pagan circles" (*Ascetic Eucharists*, 53).

the *symposion*, a festive period of fellowship in wine, discourse, chanting, or other less respectable forms of entertainment.[27]

For the Passover, a festal banquet in a Jewish domestic setting, Mishnah *Pesaḥim* prescribes that no dessert course be served (*m. Pesaḥ.* 10:8) and that a minimum of four cups of wine be drunk (*m. Pesaḥ.* 10:1), with the basic elements arranged in the following sequence (*m. Pesaḥ.* 10:1–9):

1st cup mixed (with benedictions over day and wine [Shammai], or over the wine and day [Hillel])
Hors d'oeuvres
Unleavened bread, lettuce, *harosheth* (fruit/nut paste)
Passover lamb (cf. 10:5)
2nd cup mixed (introducing the "program" of haggadic conversation and praise)
"Why is this night different from all other nights?"
"He begins with the disgrace and he ends with the glory."

- Deut 26:5 ("A wandering Aramean was my father.")
- Exod 12:27 ("It is the sacrifice of the LORD's passover, for he passed over the houses of the people of Israel in Egypt, when he slew the Egyptians but spared our houses.")
- Exod 12:39 ("They baked unleavened cakes of the dough which they had brought out of Egypt, for it was not leavened, because they were thrust out of Egypt and could not tarry, neither had they prepared for themselves any provisions.")
- Exod 1:14 (The Egyptians "made their lives bitter with hard service, in mortar and brick, and in all kinds of work in the field.")
- Singing of *Hallel*: Pss 113(–114)
- Benediction for redemption from Egyptians

3rd cup mixed (no dessert; benediction over meal)
4th cup mixed (singing of *Hallel*: Pss 114[115]–118)

We need not suppose that the precise order outlined in *Pesaḥim* was followed in all first century Passover observance to find in it the general outline of a banquet appropriate to celebrating Israel's deliverance from

---

27. Smith, *From Symposium to Eucharist*, 27–31.

Egypt; a comparison with the Pauline and Synoptic accounts of Jesus' final Passover celebration yields a number of elements in common.

Only Luke mentions a cup before bread (Luke 22:17), corresponding to the first cup of the Seder (*m. Pesaḥ.* 10:2).[28] In the tradition recalled in 1 Cor 11:23–25, after the first cup (unmentioned by Paul, as by Matt and Mark), Jesus blesses the unleavened bread (cf. *m. Pesaḥ.* 10:3), identifying it with his body which he will offer on behalf of his dining companions. "After dining" on the Passover lamb (1 Cor 11:25; cf. *m. Pesaḥ.* 10:3–5), Jesus blesses the second cup, declaring it God's new covenant sealed with his blood, rather than the lamb's blood. Mark and Matt likewise quote Jesus' words over the breaking of the bread and the (second) cup (Mark 14:22–25 // Matt 26:26–29), with the intervening main course featuring the Passover lamb not mentioned explicitly but clearly implied (cf. esp. Mark 14:12, 14, 16).

Mark and Matt refer to the singing of a hymn (Mark 14:26 // Matt 26:30), corresponding to the chanting of the *Hallel* (*m. Pesaḥ.* 10:6–7). This element of the Passover celebration may well have supplied Paul the "church-planter" with a model for his converts' service of praise in which "each one has a hymn, has a lesson, has a revelation, has a tongue, has an interpretation" (1 Cor 14:26). This was likely also the case with other Jewish apostles working among both Jewish and Gentile communities (cf. 1 Cor 9:1–6; 15:5–11), as Paul assumes that the church in Rome engaged in similar praise and mutual edification in the context of a meal (Rom 8:15–16, 26; 15:4–14).[29]

The case for the originality of the shorter text of Luke 22:17–20 is strong.[30] On this reading, Luke has reshaped the tradition attested in Paul,

---

28. Pursuing the plausible suggestion that the Last Supper accounts reflect the liturgical practice of churches known to the Evangelists, Bradshaw implausibly suggests that the shorter text of Luke betrays knowledge of a bread-cup eucharistic order observed "in a Gentile environment unfamiliar with Passover meals" (*Eucharistic Origins*, 5). On the contrary, the inclusion of a cup before the bread and the subsequent main course (implied in Luke 22:8, 11, 13, 15) likely reflects Luke's conversance with the Passover as a banquet served in courses.

29. The last passage cited follows closely on exhortation regarding communal strife that Smith plausibly locates at the Roman Christians' meal gatherings (*From Symposium to Eucharist*, 177).

30. Ehrman, *Orthodox Corruption of Scripture*, 197–209. As Ehrman shows, the atoning significance ascribed to Jesus' body and blood in the longer Lucan text is otherwise absent from the presentation of Christ's death in Luke–Acts (including the Lucan parallels to Mark 10:45 and 15:39). The longer text is explicable as a scribal harmonization of

Mark, and Matt with comparatively minor variations to express his theological and hortatory priorities. In the Lucan account, Jesus reclines with his disciples (22:14), opens the festive meal with a brief remark anticipating eschatological woe and joy (22:15–16), and offers words over the first cup, which continue in the same vein (22:17–18). Then over the bread, he says, "This is my body, but behold, the hand of the one delivering me up is with me on the table. For the Son of Man goes in accordance with what has been determined, but woe to that man by whom he is delivered" (22:19–22), to the astonishment of the Twelve (22:23).

Luke's reformulation of the narrative emphasizes the contrast between Jesus' noble gift of himself to the uttermost and the treachery of the one motivated by Satan to betray him (cf. 22:3), who has just received from Jesus' own hand his very body in the form of bread broken and shared with his disciples.[31] After the ironic quarrel over greatness and Jesus' response to the group (22:24–30), the machinations of Satan return in Jesus' exhortation to Peter (22:31–32) and his prediction of Peter's denial (22:33–34). The scene concludes with more conversation anticipating the coming tribulation until the party departs for Olivet (22:35–39). The meal has presumably proceeded, but Luke's focus has turned to Jesus' final, heartbreaking interactions with his disciples before he "accomplishes his exodus" (cf. 9:31).

Like Paul's catechetical recollection in 1 Cor 11:23–25, the Last Supper accounts of the Synoptic Gospels are instructional in nature; they recall events remembered as taking place that gave significance to the activities of the gatherings in which the Gospels were read. The accounts are not, strictly speaking, liturgical, as they do not prescribe actions or words to be done or said in the conduct of the communities' meetings.[32] Also shared by the Pauline and Synoptic accounts is the emphasis on the binding fellowship formed by sharing in the meal, which now commemorates not only the original Passover and deliverance of Israel in Egypt, but also the escha-

---

Luke's distinctive narrative with the other NT accounts (especially 1 Cor 11:23–25) and with the liturgical tradition developing in interaction with them. It is difficult to hypothesize a satisfactory motivation for a scribe to shorten the longer, more familiar account.

31. John 13:21–30 might be read as a revision of this pericope, drawing its implications out into the open.

32. In another sense, the Synoptic accounts *are* liturgical, in that they were written for recitation (in whole or in part) in the gatherings of the community, as is suggested by references to the "lector" (ὁ ἀναγινώσκων, Mark 13:14//Matt 24:15); Luke does not reproduce this reference, but he presumably anticipated for his Gospel a use and audience comparable to that for Mark (see Bauckham, *Gospels for All Christians*, 12–13).

tological sacrifice of "our paschal lamb, even Christ," who was remembered as presenting his disciples that interpretation of the feast when he offered them a share in the bread that was his body, and the wine that was his covenant-sealing blood, in the non-Lucan accounts.

The Evidence of the *Didache*

As noted above, the *Didache* is often treated as a liturgical anomaly in its order of cup before bread and its lack of an institution narrative, or of other reference to Jesus' body and blood or death and resurrection in relation to the elements. We are now, however, in a position to see that the eucharistic practice prescribed in this text fits surprisingly well into the symposial pattern reflecting the Passover observance that the Pauline and Synoptic texts present, probably reflecting eucharistic celebration in a Jewish milieu, often located in Syria.[33] Chaps. 9–10 offer models for the prayers of blessing to be said in the conduct of the weekly eucharistic banquet, following the instructions for baptism. Chaps. 11–13 offer guidance on the discernment whether an itinerant teacher or emissary or prophet should be "welcomed" to the eucharistic banquet, and chap. 14 suggests measures to ensure the spiritual purity of the whole community that assembles on "the Lord's own day."[34]

The first cup of wine provides the occasion for an initial thanksgiving "for the holy vine of your servant David, which you have made known to us through your servant Jesus," concluding in a brief benediction (9:1–2).[35] Then, over the broken bread, there is a second thanksgiving for "the life and knowledge" made known through God's *pais* Jesus, which runs on into a petition for the gathering of the church into God's kingdom as grains of

---

33. See Niederwimmer, *Didache*, 53–54. Niederwimmer's derivation of the *Didache*'s eucharistic prayers from the domestic blessing over meals (ibid., 143–45) and the influence of the Passover celebration are not mutually exclusive hypotheses, inasmuch as the paschal festival was observed in the domestic setting.

34. Such an understanding of the flow of the text seems preferable to the attempt to distinguish the meals of chaps. 9–10 and chap. 14, not least because of the occurrence of εὐχαριστεῖν in 9:1–3, 5; 10:1–4, 7; and 14:1; I am grateful to Professor Jerry L. Sumney of Lexington Theological Seminary for comment on an earlier version of this essay that helped me recognize this point, among others. For κατὰ κυριακὴν δὲ κυρίου as referring to Sunday, despite its partial obscurity, see Bauckham, "The Lord's Day," 227–31.

35. For παῖς here as meaning "servant" and not "child," see Niederwimmer, *Didache*, 147.

wheat are gathered into a loaf of bread, culminating in a second benediction (9:3–4). Finally, after a restriction of participation in "your Thanksgiving" to "those baptized in the name of the Lord," the text calls for an expansive prayer of thanksgiving "after being filled" (μετὰ δὲ τὸ ἐμπλησθῆναι, 10:1; cf. μετὰ τὸ δειπνῆσαι, 1 Cor 11:25). The second cup that one would expect from the Pauline and Marcan/Matthaean accounts is not mentioned explicitly but might be presupposed at this point; the *Mishnah* similarly calls for a "benediction over the meal" to be said with reception of the third cup of wine (*m. Pesaḥ.* 10:7). Allowing for the more modest consumption appropriate to a weekly observance rather than an annual festival, such might also have been felt appropriate to offer upon reception of the second cup.

The text continues with instructions concerning itinerant prophets, teachers, and apostles; the Eucharist remains in view, as the instructions for these functionaries often concern their conduct in relation to the churches' meal assemblies, as do the later instructions concerning bishops and deacons. Thus, prophets are accorded latitude in the wording of prayers (10:7). Teachers are to be heeded if they agree with the preceding instructions, disregarded if not (11:1–2). Itinerant apostles are to be welcomed for one day or two at most, and then supplied only with bread upon their departure (11:4–6); as in the Pauline assemblies (of which the guidelines laid down for the Spirit-inspired *symposion* in 1 Cor 14 afford the clearest picture), prophets are to be respected while speaking in the Spirit (11:7; cf. 1 Thess 5:19–20; 1 Cor 14:31), but their words should also be evaluated (11:8; cf. 1 Cor 14:29; 1 Thess 5:21–22). The prophet who "appoints a table" (11:9), fails to practice what he preaches (11:10), or requests money (11:12) disqualifies himself. Visitors who bring the Lord's name on their lips in greeting are to be welcomed for two or three days; skilled workers may be welcomed permanently, but only admitted to communal meals if they work (12:1–5). "True" prophets and teachers are to share in the food and other goods of the community (13:1–7; cf. Gal 6:6).

Assembly on the Lord's Day is for breaking bread and the "giving of thanks," or "celebration of Eucharist" (κατὰ κυριακὴν δὲ κυρίου συναχθέντες κλάσατε ἄρτον καὶ εὐχαριστήσατε, 14:1) and requires that estranged members be reconciled before they participate, in order that the community's "sacrifice" (θυσία) may be pure (14:2–3; cf. Matt 5:23–24). Resident bishops and deacons (in distinction from the itinerant teachers, apostles, and prophets considered in chaps. 11–13) order the life of the community that gathers thus (15:1–2) in its life of reconciliation and good works (15:3–4).

Readiness for the end times requires frequent assembly to fortify one's soul (πυκνῶς δὲ συναχθήσεσθε ζητοῦντες τὰ ἀνήκοντα ταῖς ψυχαῖς ὑμῶν, 16:2) and readiness to endure eschatological distress (16:3–5) so as to persevere until the Lord is seen coming on the clouds (16:6–8).

Whatever the prehistory of its individual units of tradition, the *Didache* survives as a unified guide to life in the community gathered at the table whose hallmark is thanksgiving to God for the life and knowledge he has revealed in the holy vine of David through his servant Jesus Christ. The text opens with the ethical instructions that are to prepare for initiation (chaps. 1–6; cf. 7:1) and then offers instructions for baptism (chap. 7) and fasting and prayer (chap. 8) before turning to the Eucharist, the communal observance to which the remaining sections of the text relate.

Nor can it be maintained that "[t]he eucharistic prayers of the *Didache* . . . could well be assigned to the heirs of the community of Q" as they "do not imply an interpretation of Jesus' death."[36] Certainly this cannot be sustained for the prayers in their present literary context, as the *Didache* first prescribes baptism "in the name of the Father and of the Son and of the Holy Spirit" (7:1) and then refers to baptism "into the name of the Lord" (9:5). In view of the immediately following verbatim citation from Matt 7:6 attributed to "the Lord," ὁ κύριος should clearly be taken as a reference to the Lord Jesus here (cf. "the Lord commanded in his Gospel," 8:2; also 14:1; 15:4; 16:1, 7–8). This suggests an understanding of Jesus as exalted, which in turn implies his prior death and resurrection, the former perhaps alluded to in the "broken bread" of the prayer for the eschatological gathering of God's *ekklēsia* into his kingdom (9:4; cf. Matt 26:26 et parr.).

Such an exalted station for Jesus is likely also implied in the ascription to God of "the glory and the power through Jesus Christ forever" (9:4), in the prospect of itinerants coming "in the name of the Lord" and being designated *christianoi* (12:1, 4), in the assembly "on the Lord's own day,"[37] in the directions that the community order its life "as you have it in the Gospel of our Lord" (15:4; cf. 8:2; 11:3; 15:3), and in the concluding anticipation of an eschatological sign and trumpet preceding the resurrection of the dead and the coming of the Lord on the clouds of heaven in the company of all his saints (16:6–8).

---

36. Koester, "The Sayings Gospel Q," 349.

37. This designation for Sunday likely alludes to the resurrection, as can be argued on the basis of Rev 1:10; Acts 20:7; Luke 24; and 1 Cor 16:1, perhaps a bit more conclusively than in the informative discussion by Bauckham, "The Lord's Day," 227–40.

Even viewed in isolation, the *Didache*'s eucharistic prayers give thanks for God's revelation of the (messianic) vine of David (*Did.* 9:2) and the "knowledge and faith and immortality" (*Did.* 10:2) revealed through his servant Jesus.³⁸ Crossan among others recognizes in the use of *pais* an allusion to Isa 53 and concludes that the death of Jesus, "explicitly present in 1 Cor 10–11, is implicitly present even in *Didache* 9–10."³⁹ The case for an allusion to the Isaianic servant can be strengthened by noting that, like the narrators of various psalms, at least metaphorically the Isaianic Servant dies (Isa 53:8–9), but "the Lord wills . . . to show him light and to form him in knowledge" (βούλεται Κύριος . . . δεῖξαι αὐτῷ φῶς, καὶ πλάσαι τῇ συνέσει, Isa 53:11 LXX). This prayer thus presupposes the same exalted role for Jesus that we find in the rest of the *Didache*, and this allies its eucharistic celebration with the circles in which the Pauline letters and the Synoptic Gospels were circulated, rather than the supposed communities that were solely or principally centered on an early version of the hypothetical *Sayings Gospel Q* or the equally hypothetical antecedents of the *Gospel according to Thomas*. Likewise linking the eucharistic traditions in Paul and the *Didache* are the acclamation *Marana tha* (*Did.* 10:6; 1 Cor 16:22) and the "fencing" of the table, though this is given different verbal expression (*Did.* 9:5; 1 Cor 16:22).⁴⁰

Conclusion

The eucharistic prescriptions of *Didache* 9–10 appear so different from Paul's institution narrative in 1 Cor 11 and its Synoptic parallels because the *Didache* proposes only the forms of prayer to be offered over the elements of the meal, rather than rehearsing the catechetical narrative that provided the foundational rationale and model for the observance, but which was likely not routinely rehearsed in early eucharistic assemblies. In its lack of an institution narrative for the Eucharist, the *Didache* agrees with later Syrian liturgies, whose framers clearly knew the NT's eucharistic narratives.⁴¹

---

38. On the vine as an image of eschatological salvation, see Niederwimmer, *Didache*, 146–47.

39. Crossan, *Birth of Christianity*, 441.

40. Ibid., 439–41, 443. The thanksgiving for God's provision of "spiritual food and drink" (πνευματικὴν τροφὴν καὶ ποτὸν, *Did.* 10:3) faintly echoes Paul's reference to πνευματικὸν βρῶμα and πνευματικὸν πόμα (1 Cor 10:3–4).

41. W. D. Davies and Dale Allison offer a compressed form of this argument: "[In]

Further, Paul presents 1 Cor 11:23–25 as a reminder of his founding catechesis and gives no indication that it was used regularly in the Corinthian observances. In Austin Farrer's words, "it is more natural to suppose [the Corinthians] forgetful of their catechism than deaf to their liturgy."[42]

Rather than assuming that the Pauline and Synoptic evidence, on the one hand, and the *Didache*, on the other, attest entirely disparate traditions of eucharistic practice, the evidence supports the possibility that the sort of catechetical narrative Paul "received" and passed on to his converts was also formative for the communities for which the *Didache* was written, and that the blessings offered in the *Didache* approximate what was said in the meal gatherings of the Pauline churches, as well as in the meals of churches in Jerusalem, Antioch, and Rome that the Pauline evidence brings into view.

Bibliography

Bauckham, Richard, ed. *The Gospels for All Christians: Rethinking the Gospel Audiences*. Grand Rapids: Eerdmans, 1998.

———. "The Lord's Day." In *From Sabbath to Lord's Day: A Biblical, Historical and Theological Investigation*, edited by D. A. Carson, 227–40. Grand Rapids: Zondervan, 1982.

Bradshaw, Paul F. *Eucharistic Origins*. Oxford: Oxford University Press, 2004.

Crossan, John Dominic. *The Birth of Christianity: Discovering What Happened in the Years Immediately after the Execution of Jesus*. San Francisco: HarperSanFrancisco, 1998.

Dahl, Nils Alstrup. *Jesus in the Memory of the Early Church: Essays*. Minneapolis: Augsburg, 1976.

Davies, W. D., and Dale Allison. *The Gospel according to Saint Matthew*. Vol. 3. ICC. T. & T. Clark: Edinburgh, 1997.

Ehrman, Bart D. *The Orthodox Corruption of Scripture: The Effect of Early Christological Controversies on the Text of the New Testament*. Oxford: Oxford University, 1993.

Farrer, Austin. *A Study in St Mark*. Westminster, UK: Dacre, 1951.

———. "The Eucharist in 1 Corinthians." In *Eucharistic Theology: Then and Now*, edited by R. E. Clements, 15–26. London: SPCK, 1968.

Ferguson, Everett. "Lord's Supper and Love Feast." *Christian Studies* 21 (2006) 27–38.

Koester, Helmut. "The Sayings Gospel Q and the Q of the Historical Jesus: A Response to John Kloppenborg." *HTR* 89 (1996) 345–49.

Levenson, Jon D. *The Death and Resurrection of the Beloved Son: The Transformation of Child Sacrifice in Judaism and Christianity*. Cambridge: Harvard University Press, 1993.

Didache 9–10 . . . there are eucharistic prayers but no words of institution. But the same is true of the later Anaphora of Addai and Mari, which cannot be ignorant of those words" (*Gospel according to Matthew*, 467 n. 88).

42. Farrer, "Eucharist in 1 Corinthians," 19. See also McGowan, "Is There a Liturgical Text," 77–80.

McGowan, Andrew. *Ascetic Eucharists: Food and Drink in Early Christian Ritual Meals.* Oxford: Clarendon, 1999.

———. "'Is There a Liturgical Text in This Gospel?' The Institution Narratives and Their Early Interpretive Communities." *JBL* 118 (1999) 73–87.

———. "Naming the Feast: The Agape and the Diversity of Early Christian Meals." In *Studia Patristica* 30:314–18. Leuven: Peeters, 1997.

Mitchell, Margaret M. "Rhetorical Shorthand in Pauline Argumentation: The Functions of 'the Gospel' in the Corinthian Correspondence." In *Gospel in Paul: Studies on Corinthians, Galatians and Romans for Richard N. Longenecker,* edited by L. Ann Jervis and Peter Richardson, 63–88. JSNTSup 108. Sheffield: Sheffield. Academic, 1994.

Niederwimmer, Kurt. *The Didache: A Commentary.* Translated by Linda M. Maloney. Hermeneia. Minneapolis: Fortress, 1998.

Peterson, Jeffrey. "Christ Our Pasch." In *Renewing Tradition: Studies in Honor of James W. Thompson,* edited by Mark W. Hamilton, Thomas H. Olbricht, and Jeffrey Peterson, 133–44. PTMS 65. Eugene, OR: Pickwick Publications, 2006.

———. "Redeeming the Time: The Christian Year and Life in the Risen Christ." *Christian Studies* 26 (2013–14) 33–45.

Sanders, E. P., and Margaret Davies. *Studying the Synoptic Gospels.* London: SCM, 1989.

Schleuter, Carol. *Filling Up the Measure: Polemical Hyperbole in 1 Thessalonians 2:14–16.* JSNTSup 98. Sheffield: JSOT Press, 1994.

Smith, Dennis E. *From Symposium to Eucharist: The Banquet in the Early Christian World.* Minneapolis: Fortress, 2003.

10

Before There Was a Eucharist
Worship in the House *Ekklesia*

—*Dennis E. Smith*

My approach in this paper will be to reconstruct a moment in the origins of Christianity before there was a Eucharist. As a working hypothesis, I am presupposing that there was such a time. The argument in this paper will serve to support that working hypothesis.[1]

We will begin with an investigation into the nature and form of ritual in the earliest Christian communities for which we have evidence, primarily the Pauline communities. In order to understand the ritual underpinnings of these communities, we will begin by reconstructing the setting where those gatherings took place. Since the Pauline letters consistently

---

1. This is a revised version of a paper first presented at a conference in honor of Everett Ferguson, whom I consider to be a mentor and friend. Back in the 1960's, while an undergraduate and graduate student at ACC, I took several courses with Dr. Ferguson. One course in particular, New Testament Backgrounds, made a strong impact on me. The collection of sources that began with that course formed the basis for his 1987 book, *Backgrounds of Early Christianity*, now in its 3rd edition (2003). Readers will recognize in this paper that I am still at work pursuing questions that first began to take shape for me in that long-ago course with Everett Ferguson.

identify the place of the gathering as the house,[2] our analysis will concentrate on how the ancient house functioned as a context for the ritual life of ancient peoples.

The House as Ritual Space
The Social Protocols of the Roman House.

Entering an ancient house meant that one left behind the ritual zone of the outside world and entered a ritual zone that centered on the hearth and related shrines to household deities, such as the shrine to the Lares which was common in Roman houses.[3] All members of the household would, by definition, be connected in some way to the household deities. Household members all had their socially prescribed roles, as we know from the household codes. Paul attempted to suppress the codes, but they were reinstated after his death.[4]

There were separate ritual expectations for outsiders who entered the house. One zone of the house would often be set aside for public business of some kind. Some of the smaller houses in Pompeii included workshops in the front portion of the house and the private quarters in the back.[5] In the Roman-style atrium house, householders of the elite class served as patrons for a variety of clients in their world. They would receive these clients in the *tablinum*, which would function as the public space of the house where the business of the householder would be conducted.[6]

Special guests to the house would be invited to the dining room. In the Roman atrium house, the dining room itself was not considered a public space that anyone could enter, although sometimes it was designed so that others could observe what took place within.[7]

---

2. E.g., 1 Cor 16:19; Rom 16:3–5; Phlm 2; Col 4:5. See Smith, "House Church," 1–6; see also Lampe, *From Paul to Valentinus*, who proposes up to seven different groupings of Christians in Rome as indicated by the greetings in Romans 16, which is best accounted for as separate house churches (359, 374–76, 379–80).

3. See Clarke, *Houses of Roman Italy*, 6–11.

4. Note how Paul's baptismal triad, "neither Jew nor Greek, slave nor free, male or female" (Gal 3:27–28), tracks so well with the household code categories: "wives/husbands, children/parents, slaves/masters" (Eph 5:21—6:9; Col 3:18—4:1).

5. See Oakes, *Reading Romans in Pompeii*, 1–45.

6. Clarke, *Houses of Roman Italy*, 2–6.

7. Ibid., 12–18.

The definitive cultural expectation at all levels of society, whether elite or non-elite, was that when outsiders were welcomed into one's home, they were invited into the dining room. This correlates with the data in Paul's letters, in which we find their gatherings regularly described as meals. For example, in 1 Corinthians "when you come together as an *ekklesia*" and "when you come together to eat" are used to describe the same gathering (11:18, 33; 14:26). Therefore the house and its dining room can be assumed to be the default ritual context for all gatherings of the Pauline communities and most other early Christian communities.

The term ἐκκλησία is often translated "church" in our literature,[8] but that is a misleading translation for the letters of Paul, since it leads us to assume a social form which would be anachronistic for the time of Paul. In Paul's day, ἐκκλησία was not yet a technical term. It was a generic term for a group meeting, and was used by Paul while he was in process of forming such groups. What distinguished the groups he founded from similar groups in the culture is that the Pauline groups were an "*ekklesia* of the God [of Israel]"(1 Cor 1:2). This is in contrast with *ekklesiai* of Bacchus, or of Zeus, or of some other patron deity commonly honored in other group meetings, such as those of associations.[9] In this paper, I will avoid the term church and either use the transliteration *ekklesia* or the translation "gathering."

When the *ekklesia* came together in a house, we should not assume they considered the house to be temporary quarters, as a stand-in for the day when they could build a suitable church building. After all, at this time church buildings did not yet exist, either physically or conceptually. Rather we should assume that the *ekklesia* was fully embedded in the house and its rituals.

The Ritual of the Invitation, or How the Gathering Came to be "Gathered"

a) *The invitation.* The invitation is a component of the basic ritual process of the meal as indicated in symposium literature and confirmed by the discovery of dozens of papyri which preserve written invitations to a meal.

---

8. See especially 1 Cor 11:18, "When you come together as a church . . ." (NRSV).

9. On the use of *ekklesia* as a term for an association gathering, see Harland, *Associations*, 106, 182; Kloppenborg and Ascough, *Greco-Roman Associations*, 29.

According to literary references, invitations were also extended in a variety of oral forms.[10]

In the gospels, the invitation to the meal plays a major literary and theological role. The classic text is Mark 2:15–17. In this story, Jesus creates a scandal by eating with "tax collectors and sinners." He explains, "I did not come to invite the righteous but rather to invite the sinners." Here the meal gathering has become a symbol for the community of God; Jesus' invitation is tantamount to being invited into the kingdom. The term for invite in this text is καλέω, which is used here as a pun; it is a normal term for an invitation to a meal (see examples among papyri).[11] It can also mean "summon" or "call," which is the other operative meaning in this story: the invitation to the meal is at the same time a "summons" into the community of God.[12]

Paul also used καλέω as his standard term for what we translate as the Christian "calling."[13] To the extent that Paul implies an experiential meaning to the sense of calling, it is quite possible that Paul used it as a pun as well. A connection with the meal invitation is especially suggested in 1 Cor 1:9, "Faithful is God, by whom you were called (or invited; Greek: καλέω) into *koinonia* with his son Jesus Christ our Lord." As Paul makes clear in 1 Cor 10:16–17, *koinonia* with the Lord Jesus is experienced when bread and wine are shared at the meal. ("The cup of blessing that we bless, is it not *koinonia* with the blood of Christ? The bread that we break, is it not *koinonia* with the body of Christ?"). Therefore, in the case of 1 Corinthians 1:9, the experience of "calling" can be interpreted as embedded in the ritual of the meal.

b) *Responsibilities of the host.* The invitation was traditionally extended by the host, who, in most cases, would also be the householder of the house where the group gathered. The social role of the ancient host required that he or she provide a banquet that honored the guests according to standard

---

10. Smith, *From Symposium to Eucharist*, 22–25. An example of a papyrus invitation is the following: "Chaeremon requests you to dine at the banquet of the Lord Sarapis in the Sarapeion tomorrow, the 15th, at the 9th hour" (POxy 110, 2nd CE; ibid., 23). See also Clarke, *Houses of Roman Italy*, 17.

11. Smith, *From Symposium to Eucharist*, 23. An example is: "The god invites (καλεῖ) you to the banquet which takes place in the sanctuary of Thoeris" (PColon. inv. 2555, from Koenen, "Einladung").

12. BDAG 502–04 has a definitive discussion of this term. For another example from early Christian literature, see also Rev 19:9, "Blessed are those who are invited (κεκλημένοι) to the marriage supper of the Lamb."

13. See, for example, 1 Th 2:12; Gal 1:6, 5:13; Rom 8:30; see especially "called" to different roles in the community in 1 Cor 7:17.

banquet protocol. This included such things as carefully placing the guests according to rank so as not to offend anyone as well as providing a sumptuous and well-ordered meal. As "patron" of the event, the host received honor by means of his having conducted a well-ordered meal.[14]

Paul identifies house *ekklesiai* by the name of the householder/host of the gathering. The standard references to house *ekklesiai* occur in the greetings sections of the letters of Paul, for example: "Greet Prisca and Aquila . . . Greet also the *ekklesia* in their house" (Rom 16:3, 5). Other house *ekklesiai* in Rome were hosted by Phoebe, Aristobulus, Narcissus, a group of "brothers and sisters," and a group of "saints" (Rom 16:1, 10, 11, 14, 15). In Corinth, house *ekklesiai* were hosted by Chloe, Stephanas, and Gaius (1 Cor 1:11, 16:15; Rom 15:23), as well as Prisca and Aquila before they went to Rome (1 Cor 16:19). In Colossae, a house *ekklesia* was hosted by Philemon (Phlm 1–2). The cultural expectation for such individuals was that they serve the social role of host, which Paul affirms when he labels one such individual, Gaius, with the technical term "host" (ὁ ξένος, Rom 16:23). Furthermore, consistent with societal expectations, by singling out the householder/hosts for commendation, Paul gives them the honor they were due as benefactors of the gathering.[15]

The Ritual of Hospitality.

a) *As a cultural ideology.* The concept of hospitality to the stranger was a shared value throughout ancient Mediterranean culture. It can be characterized by two versions of a popular story motif which set forth the hospitality theme. The Jewish version of this tradition is expressed in the story of Abraham and Sarah at the Oaks of Mamre (Gen 18–19). In this story, Abraham and Sarah offer hospitality to three traveling strangers by serving them a sumptuous meal of the best they have. Only after they have served the meal do they discover that the strangers are actually divine guests disguised as ordinary humans. The guests then reward Abraham and Sarah for their

---

14. Smith, *From Symposium to Eucharist*, 33–34, 55–58.

15. Note that inscriptions of associations regularly gave honor to their patrons or benefactors; see Danker, *Benefactor*, 32–35, nos. 2–24; Harland, *Associations*, 97–101, 152–60; Kloppenborg and Ascough, *Greco-Roman Associations*, no. 27. Paul's letters are in a genre different from the association inscriptions, but his naming of the benefactors of local church gatherings accomplished the same task, namely, giving honor to patrons.

hospitality. They next go to Sodom and Gomorrah to test their hospitality (Gen 18:16–21), and when these two cities fail the test, they are destroyed.

In the Greco-Roman tradition one of the better-known versions is Ovid's story of Baucis and Philemon (*Metamorphoses* 8). Here an elderly couple of simple means offer the best meal they can muster, meager though it is, to two strangers who knock on their door. They then discover they have entertained divine guests, Zeus and Hermes, who are disguised as ordinary humans. The couple is rewarded for their hospitality while the village that surrounds them perishes in a flood because no one else in the village would offer hospitality to the strangers.

Such stories about the offering of hospitality to divine beings disguised as ordinary strangers were widely known in the ancient world and were frequently referenced in NT texts.[16] The "stranger" in these stories is the archetypal "other," generally someone who is from a distant land or another culture. Hospitality is shown here to be embedded in Mediterranean culture as a ritual means for resolving tension with the displaced "other" by peaceful rather than violent means. It is signified by hosting the stranger in a meal in which he/she is treated as guest of honor and is feted with the finest that the host has to offer.[17]

b) *As a ritual practice.* Hospitality functioned as a corollary to the ritual of the invitation. In the Greek language, hospitality was most commonly identified with the Greek term ξενία, a term which emphasized its nature as a ritual interaction between the host and the stranger. When Paul identifies Gaius as a host to the entire *ekklesia* in his house (ὅλης τῆς ἐκκλησίας, Rom 16:23), he refers to him with the term ξένος, a term from the semantic world of hospitality. It refers broadly both to the host who invites the stranger and

---

16. See Heb 13:2, "Do not neglect the practice of hospitality, for it is in this way that some have unknowingly provided hospitality to divine messengers" (author's translation). By using the indefinite "some" (τινές), the author implies that many such stories were well known in the culture. Acts 14:11–14 makes a specific reference to the Baucis and Philemon story when the author recounts how Paul and Barnabas were assumed to be the disguised deities Hermes and Zeus by the citizens of Lystra. Matt 10:14–15 makes a specific reference to the hospitality theme in the Sodom and Gomorrah story: "If there are some who will not welcome you nor listen to your words, depart from that house or city and shake the dust from your feet. Truly I tell you, it will be more tolerable for the land of Sodom and Gomorrah on the day of judgment than for that city."

17. For a full discussion of hospitality in the Mediterranean world, see Arterbury, *Entertaining Angels*.

to the stranger who receives hospitality.[18] Consequently, Paul embeds the ritual process of the "gathering" in hospitality tradition.

Paul also utilizes the hospitality motif as a metaphor for the event of grace. The key text is Rom 15:7: "Welcome one another in the same way as Christ has welcomed you."[19] Paul uses several metaphors for grace in Romans, such as justification, redemption, expiation, and reconciliation. Hospitality differs from these other metaphors in that, through the ritual process referenced by this metaphor, grace could be *experienced*. That is to say, the welcome of Christ was experienced by the members when they gathered through the ritual act of hospitality that brought them together at the "table of the Lord" (1 Cor 10:21). In the context of Romans, this motif is used in reference to issues at a mixed table of Jews and Gentiles in the Roman Christian community (Rom 14:1–15:13). At the Roman Christian community table, it appears that some were following Jewish dietary laws, presumably the Jewish Christians, while others were not, presumably the Gentile Christians. Paul's advice is to practice hospitality in the same manner as they had received it. The weighty theology embedded in the phrase "welcome one another as Christ has welcomed you" is here applied specifically to the act of ritually accepting the other at the Christian gathering by not raising questions about diet regardless of differences in dietary restrictions.

How the invitation was extended in the name of Christ is not entirely clear, but an interesting parallel is found in the official invitations from the sanctuary of Zeus Panamaros in which a standard phrase is "the god invites you to the sacred feast."[20] Such invitations imply that not only the feast but also the invitation itself were considered to be under the patronage of the deity. Note that in the Pauline communities, Paul extended the responsibil-

---

18. *BDAG* 684. I have argued elsewhere that the reference to Gaius hosting the entire *ekklesia* in Corinth might better be read as "everyone is welcome at the house of Gaius," rather than implying that Gaius had a house large enough for the entire group of believers in the city. This is more consistent with the non-elite nature of the earliest Christian communities and their benefactors. See Smith, "House Church," 12; "Hospitality," 108.

19. Romans 15:7 (Διὸ προσλαμβάνεσθε ἀλλήλους, καθὼς καὶ ὁ Χριστὸς προσελάβετο ὑμᾶς εἰς δόξαν τοῦ θεοῦ.) The term translated "welcome" in this text is *proslambanomai*, which in this context means "to extend a welcome or receive into one's home or circle of acquaintances" (*BDAG* 883). It is used elsewhere by Paul in Philemon 1–2 and 17 to refer to Philemon's obligations to offer hospitality as host to the *ekklesia* in his house.

20. ὁ θεός ὑμᾶς ἐπὶ τὴν ἱερὰν ἑστίασιν καλῖ; from Caria, Asia Minor, second-century CE; Hatzfeld, "Inscriptions," 74, no. 14; Smith, *From Symposium to Eucharist*, 80–84. See also note 10 above.

ity for hospitality to the entire community (Rom 14:1–15:13) as well as the host (e.g., Rom 16:23).

The Dining Room as Ritual Space

Sacred and Secular in the Dining Room.

Ancient banquets partook of the integrative nature of sacred and secular that was characteristic of all ancient culture. The rituals of dining intertwined secular and sacred, or to put it differently, the banquet as a social occasion always had a religious component. Consequently, since the Christian meal in Corinth was fully embedded in banquet tradition it too was both a social and religious event.

2. Dining Styles in Greco-Roman Dining Rooms.

The ancients reclined when they dined at any meal of significance, and dining rooms were designed accordingly.[21] The standard design was the *triclinium*, in which three large couches were placed in a "Π"-shaped arrangement. Each couch was designed to hold three diners resulting in a gathering of nine diners. Figure one illustrates a standard *triclinium* design, showing how couches and diners would be arranged in a dining room.[22] Figure two shows such a room in a first century house in Ephesus. The design on the floor indicates where couches would have been placed and the photo illustrates how diners would have been arranged in the room, although originally they would have reclined not on the floor but on couches.[23] Another popular style of *triclinium* provided built-in couches, as shown in figure three.[24] An alternative to the *triclinium* style was the

---

21. See Smith, *From Symposium to Eucharist*, 14–18; "Greco-Roman Banquet," 21–27; Dunbabin, *Roman Banquet*; Roller, *Dining Posture*.

22. Figure 1: An artist's rendition of a Roman *triclinium* banquet; from Smith, *From Symposium to Eucharist*, 17. (All Illustrations are collected at the end of this essay.)

23. Figure 2: A dining room in Terrace House 2, Room 24, Ephesus. Note that the dining room dates from the early first century but the mosaic floor was added in the early third century. Photo by Dennis Smith.

24. Figure 3: A dining room in the Clubhouse of the Guild of the Builders in Ostia, second to third century CE. Photo by Dennis Smith.

stibadium whereby the diners reclined in a semicircular arrangement as shown in figure four.[25]

All meals of Jesus in the Gospels are described as reclining banquets.[26] Early Christians were not part of the patrician class and so would not likely be meeting in the house of an elite member of society.[27] In archaeological studies of the ancient house, elite houses dominate the data, primarily because they have been so well preserved. Accordingly, the data presented thus far in this paper has primarily been based on elite houses. More modest domestic quarters have also been found but have not been given much discussion in scholarly literature.[28] The question then becomes how to imagine a reclining banquet in a modest house.

In the Gospel of Mark the setting for the Last Supper is described as "a large room upstairs, furnished and ready" (14:15 NRSV). The term translated "furnished" is στρώννυμι, which literally means "spread something." While it could mean to furnish couches with pillows, it could just as likely mean to spread the floor with cushioning. Figure five shows such a setup: a *stibadium* scene in which the cushioning was apparently placed on the floor.[29] Such a style fits well with the presumed lower class level of the Markan community:[30] It requires no furniture and could easily be provided in any available room in the house, even in the most modest of houses.

Since the Gospels are narrative texts they use descriptive terminology for the setting of the meals of Jesus. In contrast, Paul's letters never describe the setting. However, since the meals referenced in Paul are meals of significance held in a house, with a symposiac division between *deipnon* and symposium (see below), they would most likely be reclining banquets.

---

25. Figure four: Mosaic design of a *stibadium* dining scene pictured on the floor of a *triclinium* dining room in a third century house in Sepphoris of Galilee. Photo by Dennis Smith.

26. See, for example, Mark 2:15, 6:39–40, 8:6, 14:3, 14:18, and parallels.

27. On the lower class level of early Christians, see Friesen, "Poverty" and "Wrong Erastus."

28. A notable exception is Oakes, *Reading Romans in Pompeii*.

29. Figure five: A wall painting showing reclining diners in a *stibadium* arrangement, from the Large Columbarium of the Villa Doria Pamphili. Early Augustan (about thirty to twenty BCE). Rome, Palazzo Massimo. Photo by Dennis Smith.

30. In an unpublished paper, I have argued that the Markan community was self-identified as the poor. See, for example, Mark 4:18–19, in which the "lure of wealth" chokes off the word like a seed planted among the thorns, and 10:17–23, in which the wealthy can only enter the kingdom of God if they sell off all their possessions and give the proceeds to the poor.

What then are we to make of the reference to one "sitting" during the worship service in 1 Corinthians 14:30, the only reference to posture at the gathering? Here Paul is addressing the protocols of the service: who gets to speak and who is to stay silent. Recall that reclining was traditionally a mark of status; if lower status individuals were present, such as slaves, they might be required to sit while their betters reclined.[31] Thus I would translate 1 Corinthians 14:30 as follows: "If a revelation is made to one who is sitting, *even someone in the position of honor should be silent* (ἐὰν δὲ ἄλλῳ ἀποκαλυφθῇ καθημένῳ, ὁ πρῶτος σιγάτω).[32]

The Christian Gathering as a Greco-Roman Banquet

a) *The Last Supper story*. The Jesus story Paul adapts in 1 Cor 11:23–25 includes references to the order of the Greek banquet. First there was a bread ceremony: "[Jesus] took bread, gave thanks, broke it, and said . . ." Then "after the *deipnon* (μετὰ τὸ δειπνῆσαι, 11:25) he took a cup *in the same way* [e.g. gave thanks] and said . . ." Thus the bread ceremony took place as a ritual component of the first course of the meal, the *deipnon*, and the cup ceremony marked the beginning of the *symposion*, or the drinking course, during which the entertainment of the evening would take place. Consequently, 1 Cor 11:23–25 describes an adapted version of a standard Greco-Roman banquet.[33] The adaptation meant giving a meaning *distinctive to this gathering* to the pre-existing banquet ritual; no creation of a new ritual was required. For example, the wine ceremony corresponded to the standard libation with which a symposium normally began. In this case, however, the libation is dedicated to the Lord Jesus rather than the Lord Zeus, or Lord Jupiter, or Lord Dionysus, or Lord Caesar.[34] Theologically, this was a ritual practice whereby the meal became "table/cup of the Lord" as opposed to "table/cup of demons" (1 Cor 10:21). The rituals would be the same; the difference would be the deity with whom the meal is associ-

---

31. See especially examples from Lucian *Symposium* 8, discussed in Smith, *From Symposium to Eucharist,* 44; and Suetonius *De Poetis* fragment 11, discussed in Roller, *Dining Posture*, 1–2.

32. Compare the term πρωτοκλισία, "position of honor at a banquet" (BDAG 892), in Matt 23:6; Mark 12:39; Luke 14:7–11, 20:46.

33. Smith, *From Symposium to Eucharist*, 27–31; Smith, "Greco-Roman Banquet," 24–25.

34. Smith, *From Symposium to Eucharist*, 29–30; Taussig, *In the Beginning was the Meal*, 130–35.

ated and to whom the rituals are directed. The sharing of bread and wine, Paul notes, is normally understood in the culture as a means of creating and experiencing *koinonia* with a deity or divine figure (1 Cor 10:16–21). In this case, *koinonia* is with the Lord Jesus (1 Cor 10:16–17). The meal ceremony here is so fully embedded in cultural models that, when Paul points out what is distinctive about the Christian meal, it is not the ritual itself to which he refers but to its patron deity: "You cannot drink the cup of the Lord and the cup of demons. You cannot partake of the table of the Lord and the table of demons" (1 Cor 10:21).

b) *Worship*. In 1 Cori 14:26–31, Paul describes what corresponds to the "entertainment" at the symposium of the *ekklesia* of the Lord Jesus:[35] "When you come together, each one has a hymn, a lesson, a revelation, a tongue, or an interpretation." As with other groups in the ancient world, the symposium had become the context for the kinds of activities that today we would identify with worship. Every item named here can be paralleled with activities commonly found at meals of a variety of ancient groups, most notably meals of associations.[36] There is no reason to think that the Christian *ekklesia* would have adjourned to another room or another format in order to engage in their worship. Rather, it should be noted that the ambience of their worship betrays that fact that they are still reclining at the table. That is to say, the idea that everyone should bring a contribution ("When you come together, each one has a hymn, a lesson, a revelation, a tongue, or an interpretation") is a common characteristic of meal gatherings.[37] Similarly, the ethical tradition that Paul references here also derives from symposium ethics. When he urges that each take his/her turn to speak so that all can benefit from what is said ("Let all things be done for building up . . . For you can all prophesy one by one, so that all may learn and all be encouraged" [1 Cor 14:26c, 31), he makes direct reference to an ethical tradition of the ancient banquet, in which the entire occasion is to be one in which all share

---

35. On entertainment at the symposium, see Smith, *From Symposium to Eucharist*, 34–38. At a philosophical banquet, the entertainment tended to be philosophical conversation (Plato *Symposium* 50–54). At Jewish banquets, the entertainment tended to be conversation about Torah. See Smith, *From Symposium to Eucharist*, 138–38; Sir 39:8.

36. See especially the catalogue of activities at the banquets of various kinds of clubs and associations in Smith, *From Symposium to Eucharist*, 87–131; Taussig, *In the Beginning was the Meal*, 67–85, 104–113.

37. See especially Lampe's discussion of the term ἔρανος, which he defines as the ancient version of a "potluck dinner" ("Korinthischer Herrenmahl," 192–97). See also the practice of each diner bringing a topic of conversation to a philosophical banquet (Aulus Gellius *Noctes Atticae* 7.13.1–4; cited in Smith, *From Symposium to Eucharist*, 201).

equally, and as a group, in the food, wine, conversation, and other forms of entertainment.[38] Finally, as pointed out above, the meal from the very beginning of its ritual has defined the table as a zone in which the deity is fully present and fully engaged in *koinonia* with the meal participants. With the deity fully present and the community fully formed at table, what we call "worship" fits perfectly in the ritual context of the table.

Conclusion

The ritual process embedded in the house, its dining room, and its banquets provided the context and source for the ritual practice of early Christians. The ritual life of the Corinthian *ekklesia* was therefore, as far as we can reconstruct it, virtually the same as the ritual life of other groups in their day. The difference is in the adaptation of the content of the rituals, not in their practice. There is no reason to think that Paul installed any of the ritual activities at the gatherings of the Corinthian *ekklesia*. Rather he took what was already present in the culture and redefined its content. The ritual worked because its power was already established in the culture. Paul's innovation was that he was a close student of ritual and a genius at harnessing it as the means to create out of a diverse and motley collection of people a new community of God. If we ignore or devalue the ritual complexity of the house and dining room, we lose the context for early Christian social and identity formation.

Bibliography

Arterbury, Andrew. *Entertaining Angels: Early Christian Hospitality in Its Mediterranean Setting*. New Testament Monographs 8. Sheffield: Sheffield Phoenix, 2005.
Clarke, John R. *The Houses of Roman Italy, 100 B.C.–A.D. 250: Ritual, Space, and Decoration*. Berkeley: University of California Press, 1991.
Danker, Frederick W. *Benefactor: Epigraphic Study of a Graeco-Roman and New Testament Semantic Field*. St. Louis: Clayton, 1982.
Dunbabin, Katherine M. D. *The Roman Banquet: Images of Conviviality*. Cambridge: Cambridge University Press, 2003.
Friesen, Steven J. "Poverty in Pauline Studies: Beyond the So-Called New Consensus." *JSNT* 26 (2004) 323–61.
———. "The Wrong Erastus: Ideology, Archaeology, and Exegesis." In *Corinth in Context: Comparative Studies on Religion and Society*, edited by Steven J. Friesen, Daniel N. Schowalter, and James C. Walters, 231–56. NovTSup 134. Leiden: Brill, 2010.

38. Smith, *From Symposium to Eucharist*, 51–64.

PART 2: PRESENTED ESSAYS

Harland, Philip A. *Associations, Synagogues, and Congregations: Claiming a Place in Ancient Mediterranean Society*. Minneapolis: Fortress, 2003.

Hatzfeld, J. "Inscriptions de Panamara." *BCH* 51 (1927) 57–122.

Kloppenborg, John S., and Richard S. Ascough, eds. *Greco-Roman Associations: Texts, Translations, and Commentary. 1. Attica, Central Greece, Macedonia, Thrace*. BZNW 181. Berlin: de Gruyter, 2011.

Koenen, Ludwig. "Eine einladung zur Kline des Sarapis." *ZPE* 1 (1967) 121–26.

Lampe, Peter. *From Paul to Valentinus: Christians at Rome in the First Two Centuries*. Translated by Michael Steinhauser. Edited by Marshall D. Johnson. Minneapolis: Fortress, 2003.

———. "Das korinthische Herrenmahl im Schnittpunkt hellenistisch-römischer Mahlpraxis und paulinscher Theologia Crucis (1 Kor 11,17–34)." *ZNW* 82 (1991) 192–97.

Oakes, Peter. *Reading Romans in Pompeii: Paul's Letter at Ground Level*. Minneapolis: Fortress, 2009.

Roller, Matthew B. *Dining Posture in Ancient Rome: Bodies, Values, and Status*. Princeton: Princeton University Press, 2006.

Smith, Dennis E. *From Symposium to Eucharist: The Banquet in the Early Christian World*. Minneapolis: Fortress, 2003.

———. "The Greco-Roman Banquet as a Social Institution." In *Meals in the Early Christian World: Social Formation, Experimentation, and Conflict at the Table*, edited by Dennis E. Smith and Hal Taussig, 21–33. New York: Palgrave Macmillan, 2012.

———. "Hospitality, the House Church, and Early Christian Identity." In *Mahl und religiöse Identität im frühen Christentum*, edited by Matthias Klinghardt and Hal E. Taussig, 103–117. TANZ 56. Tübingen: Francke, 2012.

———. "The House Church as Social Environment." In *Text, Image, and Christians in the Graeco-Roman World: A Festschrift in Honor of David Lee Balch*, edited by Aliou Cissé Niang and Carolyn Osiek, 3–21. PTMS 176. Eugene, OR: Pickwick Publications, 2012.

Taussig, Hal. *In the Beginning Was the Meal: Social Experimentation and Early Christian Identity*. Minneapolis: Fortress, 2009.

Figure 1

Figure 2

Figure 3

Figure 4

Figure 5

11

Wait for One Another
The Significance of the Eucharist for a Theology of Patience

—Arthur M. Sutherland

> There have been those (such as the Sandemanians) who thought that following apostolic example required taking communion in an upstairs room. But there is no historical evidence supporting the idea that this was normal practice, and no doctrinal meaning is given in the New Testament to the place of observance.[1]

ONE OF EVERETT FERGUSON'S great academic virtues is his ability to place into context small moments in the history of Restoration Theology. There is little doubt the Sandemanians have already faded into time past, but Ferguson would remind us that the struggle to align orthodoxy with orthopraxy will not soon lose its importance. Just like the followers of Robert Sandeman up and down the coastline of mid-Eighteenth century New England, certain types of Protestants today are adamant that the best hope for a true *ekklesia* will only be found in the house church. In their view, with plain and unadorned worship, with cheeks by jowls on sagging couches, the wind of the Spirit will arrive in time to plop down on the last available folding chair. However, anyone who tries to actually worship with a house church will quickly find out that simpler is not necessarily better.

1. Ferguson, "Lord's Supper and Love Feast," 30–31.

Let us imagine for a moment an enthusiastic contemporary house church striving to replicate the experience of the early church. They do this by making the celebration of the Eucharist, rather than the sermon, the center point of their worship experience. Then they go further, back to the "real" church, by incorporating a potluck supper. One can then imagine what might happen on a snowy day when one of the members is unable to arrive at the start of the meal. Upset that the others have gone ahead without him, and even worse, that only edges of the twice baked tuna casserole he had eagerly anticipated remain, he opens his Bible to 1 Cor 11:33, reads to them, "So then, my brothers and sisters, when you come together to eat, wait for one another"[2] and flatly announces the whole bunch to be in sin because they had not stuck it out long enough for him to finish shoveling out his car. Chastened, the others resolve to do better the next time. They are mindful that they rejected the modern church with its hard pews and straight rows in the first place because it is too driven by the mantra, "We need to get out on time if we have any prayer of beating the Baptists to the cafeteria."

I think you can see that in my parable, our disgruntled church member has read "wait for one another" as though waiting for one another only meant "don't watch the clock." But I would suggest that neither the underfed brother nor my satisfied sisters have really grasped the theological potential of Paul's exhortation. Instead of pointing them to their wrists or to their stomachs, Paul's exhortation points them back to the Eucharist as the foundation of Christian patience.

Fellowship, whether fancy or free, is sustained by deepening relationships and increasing consideration for others. Although it is true that we must acknowledge the contributions that space, furniture, and eating together make toward corporate worship, our sense of place, and belonging, the most significant factor in determining what really constitutes fellowship is who we are and what we are towards each other in view of Christ's life, death, and resurrection. This is the reason Paul says to that most dissembled of all assemblies, the house church of Corinth, "When you come together, it is not really to eat the Lord's supper" (1 Cor 11:20). The Eucharist is not as Ignatius of Antioch described it "the medicine of immortality" but is instead medicine *for* mortals. It awakens, stirs, and forms our desire for Christlikeness. To paraphrase Nietzsche, the Eucharist is for those whose impatience makes them "human, all too human."

2. All quotations are from the NRSV.

The Corinthian Meal

Who ate the Lord's Supper in Corinth, what they eat, where they met, what the sitting arrangements were, who had enough, and who had little, are continuing concerns of New Testament scholars. Mark Surburg summarizes scholarly debate about the order of the meal this way: "One line of interpretation has maintained that at Corinth a meal *preceded* the celebration of the Lord's Supper (the sacramental bread and cup). Another position has argued that the Corinthians celebrated a meal *between* the sacramental bread and the sacramental cup."[3] The first position is offered by a school of scholars who follow Günther Bornkamm and Joachim Jeremías.[4] The second position follows the work of Gerd Theissen.[5]

Theissen's interpretation puts significant weight on the distinction between ἴδιον δεῖπνον (his own meal, vs. 21) and κυριακὸν δεῖπνον (the Lord's Supper, vs. 20). His own meal is meal that an individual Christians brings to the gathering and is not shared with those who have nothing (μὴ ἔχοντες); the Lord's Supper is the meal shared by all.[6] He says,

> Some of the wealthier Christians have made the meal itself possible through their generosity, providing bread and wine for all. What was distributed is declared by means of the words of institution to be the Lord's and given to the congregation. Thus, in conjunction with this common meal there could take place a private meal because the starting point of the Lord's Supper was not regulated, and up to this starting point (that is, until the words of institution) what had been brought and provided was private property. More importantly, this distinction was possible because wealthier Christians ate other food in addition to the bread and wine, and the words of institution made no provision for sharing this with the fellowship.[7]

A.J. Malherbe argued that Theissen's interpretation of the situation in Corinth was not always convincing,[8] but I would like to highlight Theissen's

---

3. Surburg, "Situation at the Corinthian Lord's Supper," 1.

4. Bornkamm, "Lord's Supper and Church in Paul," 123–60; Jeremias, *Eucharistic Words of Jesus*.

5. Theissen, *Social Setting*, 143–74.

6. Ibid., 148.

7. Ibid., 160.

8. Malherbe, *Social Aspects*, 84.

suggestion that "the Lord's Supper did not have a regulated starting time."[9] If he is correct then it is easy to understand that the inception of the meal in Corinth could be hurried along by the impatient who said to one another, "Although not everyone is present, we have a good enough quorum to get the meal started."

Actually, when the stomach takes over it would not matter whether it was the wealthy or the poor Corinthians who arrived first. There is nothing in the text that would requires believing that those who had plenty were necessarily waiting for their own kind anyway. What makes us think that any of the Corinthians rich or poor, early arriving or late coming, host or guest, were any more patient in pronouncing "come and get it" than we are today? However this debate is resolved among New Testament scholars, theologians and ethicists must step in and say that the answer must also grapple with the fact that Paul sets his answer to the Corinthian problem to the tune of relationship language: "Wait one for another."

Heresies, House Churches, and Hosts

In the letters of the New Testament, the Greek word for "one another" (ἀλλήλων) appears fifty-eight times. For example, Christians are to love one another (Rom 13:8), bear with one another (Eph 4:2), admonish one another (Col 3:16), and instruct one another (Rom 15:14). Husbands and wives submit to one another (Eph 5:21) and do not deprive each other (1 Cor 7:5). In 1 Corinthians, they are to care for one another (12:25) and greet one another (16:20).

The one another phrases give a command or an instruction that are intended to modify behavior. They should stop doing one thing and begin to do another thing. This is Paul's intent in 1 Cor 11:33. In sum, although it is difficult to imagine the Corinthian situation in reverse, i.e. that the poor brought plenty of food and dived in before the hungry wealthy arrived, mutuality and reciprocation is still the hallmark of authentic Christian community.

Paul's exhortation gains even more weight when we remember that the church in Corinth is marked by σχίσματα (divisions) and αἱρέσεις (factions).[10] The distinction between divisions and factions is not immediately clear. The separate groups in 1 Cor 1:10, those who follow Paul, or

9. Theissen, *Social Setting*, 151.
10. 1 Cor 1:10; 11:18,19.

Apollos, or Cephas, could be based on personality, or theology, or ethnicity. Certainly they had room to divide over incest, lawsuits, slavery, marriage, food, or Paul's authority. In any case, it is worth noting that these divisions are not mentioned again in Paul's discussion of the meal controversy. Whatever the divisions were, it did not stop them from "coming together" (συνέρχομαι) in 11:17, 18, 20, 33. Where they came together, of course, is what triggers all of this conflict, manifest in the common meal.

Although the homes of Christians are an important part of the New Testament[11] there are only four mentions of the church in "their house" (1 Cor 16:19; Rom 16:5) or "her house" (Col 4:15) or "your house" (Phlm 2). The Colossian letter tells us that Christian groups meet in Laodicea, Hierapolis, and Colossae (4:13), but only the Laodicean church has a patron (the woman Nympha), and Paul singles out for mention the church that meets in her house. Mentioning her name either recognizes her status or elevates it, perhaps both. One wonders if this indicates that her leadership and authority in the church is on par with Paul's mention of "Chloe's people" in 1 Cor. 1:11. The mention of Nympha as the host of "her church" along with the plea from Paul that letters to Colossae and Laodicea should be exchanged point us to the importance of one another relationships between churches.

We can say more about the one another relationship found in 1 Cor 16:19 which reads, "The churches of Asia send greetings. Aquila and Prisca, together with the church in their house, greet you warmly in the Lord." Paul is writing from Ephesus but he met Aquila and Prisca in Corinth (Acts 18:2). They allow him to board with them (18:3). Luke takes pains to mention that Aquila is a Jew from Pontus who fled Rome because of the imperial edict by Claudius against his kind. When Paul leaves Corinth in Acts 18:18–19 they travel with him as far as Ephesus and remain there for some time.

Apparently they returned to Rome after the death of Claudius because when Paul sends his letter to the church at Rome he asks his readers to greet Prisca and Aquila and "the church in their house" (Rom 16:3). They are important to Paul and not just because they had a spare room. No, "they risked their necks for my life" and "all the churches of the Gentiles" give thanks for them (Rom 16:4).

---

11. Acts 2:46; 9:17; 10:30; 12:12; 16:15, 31–32, 34, 40; 17:1, 4–5; 18:1, 7–8; 19:9–10; 20:20; 28:30–31; Rom 16:5; 1 Cor 16:19; Col 4:9; Phlm 1–2; 2 John 10. For fuller study, see Banks, *Paul's Idea of Community*.

It is not clear how or when Aquila and Prisca converted to Christianity. Being tentmakers together was the first bond between Paul and the couple (18:3). Luke tells us nothing about their evangelistic work with Paul, and the start of Paul's activity in Corinth is the synagogue (18:4). But once the couple took on the role of host to Paul in Corinth, they would have been the first to learn of Paul's traditions and to practice them. All manner of early theology could have been worked out in their home: the meaning of Christian marriage, reading the scripture under the canopy of an unfolding eschatology, the development of church governance, or how new churches begin across town (18:7–9). Since they were tentmakers, a trade that Paul considered slavish and demeaning (1 Cor 9:19; 2 Cor 11:7),[12] they would have slowly come to understand along with Paul how Christian commitment upends vocation.[13] Whether in Corinth, Ephesus, or Rome house churches had to struggle with (have patience with) an evolving Christianity and the Christians that came along with it. It is a lot easier to be patient with ideas than with people. Was it from their house that Paul worked out his metaphor of the church as the body of Christ (1 Cor 12:12–13), the *locus classicus* of one another theology and which follows immediately after Paul's discussion of the Eucharist?

Time, Waiting, and Patience

The situation in Corinth is the impatience of members with one another; the solution, says Paul, is a change of mind that brings about a change of habit: "So then, my brethren, when you come together to eat, wait for one another." The word translated "wait" is ἐκδέχομαι, and it or one its forms occurs seven times in the New Testament.[14] However the word need not have so much the meaning waiting for the passing of chronological time (like reading a newspaper in the train station) as it may have the more emotional sense of "expecting." The blind and sick keep track of water's movement in (John 5:3) because they anticipate healing; the hopeful farmer looks twice for the first growth (Jas 5:7).[15] Fitzmyer tries to bring out a bit more of

---

12. Hock, "Paul's Tentmaking," 564.
13. Still, "Did Paul Loathe Manual Labor?", 793.
14. 1 Cor 11:33; Jas 5:7; 1 Cor 16:11; John 5:3; Heb 10:13; Acts 17:16; Heb 11:10
15. Bruce Winter notes the appearance of ἐκδέχομαι in places outside of the New Testament that feature hospitality argues that "receive one another" rather than "wait for one another" is the better translation. Winter, "Lord's Supper at Corinth," 79–80.

this by translating 11:33 as "Consequently, my brothers, when you meet together to eat, await the arrival of one another."[16] Roman dinners, at least, were usually held in the late afternoon or early evening and were often delayed until after a visit to the baths.[17] The behavior of guests and hosts in the first century is illustrated by Pliny and Juvenal. In Juvenal's satire *An Invitation to Dinner*, the host reminds his guest that everything he is serving comes from his own farm and not the marketplace—so much the better a reason to come on time.[18] Pliny feigns a hot and angry letter to an invited dinner guest who stood him up and ate instead with another host.[19] An example within earshot of the Corinthian offense is found in Pliny's letter to his friend Avitus. In this letter he refers to a meal he attended where the host did not know the difference between good and bad manners, between pretense and sincerity.

> I . . . dined at the house of an individual who thought himself refined and attentive, but was in my eyes mean and extravagant; for he served himself and a few of us with choice fare, but the rest with cheap food and tiny portions. He had further separated out small flasks of wine into three categories, not to offer the possibility of choice, but to forestall the right to refuse. The first category was for himself and for us, the second for his friends of lesser account (for he ranks his friends at different levels), and the third for his freedmen and ours. The man reclining next to me noticed this, and asked if I approved. I said no. 'What is your practice?' he asked. 'I put the same food before all,' I replied, 'for I invite them for dinner, not for disgrace. Those whom I have made equal at table and on the couches, I make equal in all respects.' 'Even the freedmen?' he asked. 'Yes, the freedmen too, for then I regard them as fellow guests, not freedmen.' He rejoined: 'That costs you a packet!' 'Far from it,' I replied. 'How come?' he asked. 'Because, I suppose, my freedmen do not drink what I drink; no, I drink what they drink.'[20]

These references are about the expectations of individual hosts and guests, but in the ancient world voluntary associations like the *collegium*, *secta*, *factio*, *koinon*, *ekklesia*, and *synodos* also hosted meals and banquets.[21]

---

16. Fitzmyer, *First Corinthians*, 448.
17. Fagan, *Bathing in Public*, 221.
18. Juvenal, "Satire 11," 405.
19. Pliny, *Complete Letters*, 18.
20. Ibid., 34–35.
21. Wilson, "Voluntary Associations: Overview," 1.

Walker-Ramisch says, "It was primarily the experience of conviviality and *communio* provided by the collegia which drew people together, and this is reflected in the names they gave to their societies—'Mates and Marble Workers,' 'Brother Builders,' 'The Comrade Smiths,' 'The Late Drinkers.'"[22]

With smallish memberships of a hundred or less, associations tended to be composed of the urban poor, slaves, and freedmen, were often sustained by wealthy patrons, were sometimes suppressed by Imperial command, frequently had members that belonged to more than one association, and reflected the ever changing mix of people who made up the Mediterranean basin.[23] Associations became the "socially constructed replacement for the family."[24] Everybody got to be somebody. Walker-Ramisch approves of Wayne Meek's pronouncement, "Evidently, besides conviviality, the clubs offered the chance for people who had no chance to participate in the politics of the city itself to feel important in their own miniature republics."[25] He goes on to say that, "abusive, slanderous, disruptive, or dishonest behavior was strictly prohibited, and offending members punished by the imposition of fines or be expulsion.[26] The voluntary associations, just as our similar gatherings today, considered manners and etiquette to be social codes useful for self-governance.

It is not hard to believe that impatience for latecomers or imposing on the good will of others by arriving late would be understood by the Corinthians as violations of the community social code. At the same time it helps us to understand the depth of Paul's dislike for the way the impatient are dispensing shame upon the latecomers. In chapter 11, the language of shame fills Paul's entire description of the misbehaving Corinthians: "In the following instructions, I do not commend you" (vs. 17); "What! Do you not have homes to eat and drink in? Or do you show contempt for the church of God and humiliate those who have nothing" (vs. 22); "When we are judged by the Lord, we are disciplined so that we may not be condemned along with the world" (vs. 32). He says, "I am writing to you not to associate with anyone who bears the name of brother or sister who is sexually immoral or greedy, or is an idolater, reviler, drunkard, or robber. Do not even eat with such a one" (1 Cor 5:11).

22. Walker-Ramisch, "Graeco–Roman Voluntary Associations," 133.
23. McRae, "Eating with Honor," 170.
24. Ascough, "Question of Death," 510.
25. Walker-Ramisch, "Graeco–Roman Voluntary Associations," 133.
26. Ibid.

Time That Counts

Paul would have empathy for the grievance of my disgruntled, hungry, and shamed house church goer not simply because others ate without him, but because he was disregarded. He was shut out from the meaningfulness of their time together. The difference is this: installing an instrument to count decaying atoms, or melting sticks of wax, or dripping water into bowl work will all get the job done if all you need to do is measure time. Time is measured not just by its passing but also by how it is experienced as in: we had a "beautiful time," a "horrible time." Further, we can speak of "the right time" or "the appropriate time." When we do this, we indicate our appreciation for order and control. Clocks, says Danielle Allen, were used by the Greeks because they knew:

> Human passions, especially anger, could vary the flow of time for each individual, making time always relative to personal experience. It was this very knowledge, I believe, that helps to explain why the Athenians made clocks a central tool of civic life. By imposing a more reliable external measure for the passage of time, they were trying to moderate the passions, and bring a due measure of order to their city.[27]

Waiting is the intersection of time and expectation. It is a multi-disciplinary phenomenon (there is a psychology of waiting, an anthropology of waiting, and other sciences of time). According to Lahad, the construct of waiting also emerges as a relational sociological phenomenon.

> Waiting is often associated with fear and anxieties about the future, yet it can also be a time of anticipation, hope, and excitement. Hence, waiting has multiple facets: it can be tranquil or anxious, patient or impatient, a waste of time or an important and meaningful interval in our lives . . . In that sense, the ascribed meaning of waiting . . . is not an unconditional phenomenon but contingent on collective timetables and changing discursive understandings.[28]

Ultimately, waiting is a complex idea that involves the distribution of power.[29] The rich and celebrated are seated at restaurants without delay. Likewise an ill-treated "waiter" can deliberately let a hot food order chill in the pick-up window as a way of reordering the relationship to his customer.

27. Allen, "Flux of Time," 62–63.
28. Lahad,"Sociology of Time," 165.
29. Schwartz, *Queuing and Waiting*, 5.

The entire dynamic of Jesus' life and ministry is based upon the principle of disrupting expectations and assumptions about time, waiting, and the patience required to do so: "For who is greater, the one who is at the table or the one who serves? Is it not the one at the table? But I am among you as one who serves" (Luke 22:27).

A Eucharistic Theology of Patience

The problem in Corinth and the problem with my imagined house church around the corner is that they have not considered how the heart of the service, the Eucharist, becomes a service of the heart. A eucharistic theology of patience begins with the belief that participating in the Lord's Supper implies, in fact demands, an ethical posture. As Richard Hays has said, "the issue of the Lord's Supper . . . comes down in the end to the matter of 'rightly discerning the body'—i.e., recognizing that the Lord's Supper is a sign of the unity of the Body of Christ, and behaving accordingly."[30] Similarly, Victor Paul Furnish stresses the communal context of Pauline ethics by saying that: "The believer's life and action are always in, with, and for 'the brethren' in Christ. For him, moral action is never a matter of an isolated actor choosing from among a variety of abstract ideas on the basis of how inherently 'good' or 'evil' each may be. Instead it is always a matter of choosing and doing what is good for the brother and what will upbuild the whole community of brethren."[31]

Second, a eucharistic theology of patience does not separate remembering the suffering of Jesus from remembering the life of Jesus. In 1 Cor 11:23–25, Paul aligns his tradition of the Last Supper with that of Luke's by including the words "do this in remembrance or me" (Luke 22:19). This remembrance is proclamation of the Lord's death (1 Cor 12:26). There is no doubt that remembering the death of Christ is a remembering of the suffering of Christ. Without placing an extraordinary weight on the distinction between the two, we should note that Paul actually says to remember "the Lord Jesus" (11:23), not Christ. I take this to be a signal that the humanity of the Lord is the pillar of the Supper. If it is his humanity, then it is also a humanity lived out under conditions of patience and impatience.

Remembering the life of the Lord Jesus is remembering the crowds who waited for him to return to Galilee after his trip to the Gerasenes (Luke

---

30. Hays, "Ecclesiology and Ethics," 40..
31. Furnish, *Theology and Ethics*, 203

8:40). In fact the text says "they welcomed him" (ἀπαεδέξατο αὐτὸν) because "they were all waiting for him" (πάντες προσδοκῶντες αὐτόν)—phrases that give the opposite of the Corinthian experience. This should be held in contrast to Luke 11:54 where the hostile Pharisees are said to be lying in wait for him, to catch him in something he might say (ἐνεοντες αὐτόν θηρεῦσαίδρεύ). We should remember how his wait by the well with the woman from Samaria at noon, tired, hungry, and thirsty (John 4:6) becomes a two day stay, an interruption accepted with patience, because the hour now is (4:40). The most dramatic instance is in John 8:6 where Jesus writes in the dust while he waited for an answer to his question, and then waits more until "one by one" all of the accusers walk away (John 8:9).

Third, a eucharistic theology of patience is one that ventures outside of the boundaries imposed by clock watching and embraces the richer concepts of endurance, forbearance, and suffering, what the New Testament would call μακρουθμία,[32] ὑπομονή,[33] and ἀνεχόμενοι.[34] While it is often very difficult to see always clear differences between the three, each has Christological significance. Each are recalled in the Eucharist. The "body broken for you" becomes personal when I Tim 1:6 reminds the reader, "for that very reason I was shown mercy so that in me, the worst of sinners, Christ Jesus might display his unlimited patience" (I Tim. 1:6).

Finally, a eucharistic theology of patience is derived from God's decision to enter into the world "at the right time" (Rom 5:6) at the *kairotic* moment. There is no doubt and no escape from the fact that we are indeed ruled by clocks, that we are ruled by sunrises and sunsets. Yet, our gathering for worship, and the patience we demonstrate with each other, ought to be in view of God's patience just as much as it is with God's mercy and justice. Karl Barth, the theologian from the land of clocks and clockmakers says:

> We define God's patience as His will, deep-rooted in His essence and constituting His divine being and action, to allow to another—for the sake of His own grace and mercy and in the affirmation of His holiness and justice—space and time for the development of its own existence, thus conceding to this existence a reality side by side with His own, and fulfilling His will towards this other in such

---

32. Col 1:11; 3:12; 1 Tim 1:16; 1 Pet 3:20; Rom 2:4; 9:22; 2 Cor 6:6; Gal 5:22; Eph4:2; 2 Tim 4:2; Jas 5:10; 2 Tim 3:10; Heb 6:12; 2 Pet 3:15.

33. Luke 21:19; Rom 5:3; 15:4,5; 2 Cor 6:4; Heb 10:36; 12:1; Rev 2:2,3,19; 3:10; 13:10; 14:12.

34. Eph 4:2; Col 3:13; 2 Thess 1:4; 2 Tim 4:3; Matt 17:17; Mark 9:19; Luke 9:41; 1 Cor 4:12; 2 Cor 11:19,20: Heb 13:22.

a way that He does not suspend and destroy it as this other but accompanies and sustains it and allows it to develop in freedom.[35]

Theology has overlooked the theological significance and potential of Paul's exhortation. It is extremely difficult to find more than a passing acknowledgment in biblical commentaries or theological works to Paul's small phrase or that it even exists in the text. No one has had time for it.

It is likely as well that the phrase is overlooked because the nature of our worship has changed so radically from the early centuries. It is not just the loss of the shared meal, it is also the development of sacrificial and performative notions of the Eucharist in early Catholicism, the Protestant tendency to celebrate the Eucharist only on "communion Sundays," the emphasis in modern worship on efficiency and convenience, the institutionalized clergy, and the triumph of individualized and private piety that has sent the both the rich and the poor, to use the King James rendering of Luke 1:53, "empty away." If this is the case, then perhaps we should listen to the complaint of our house church goer and ask what are have we lost and what are we losing by either the tyranny of our timepieces or the greed of our stomach? It would not hurt us a bit to tarry a little longer. In his small text *Rediscovering the Lord's Supper*, Markus Barth refocuses the supper when he says about waiting for others, "Much more than condescending tolerance is meant . . . Love for one's neighbors is not only an ethical corollary or implication of the Lord's Supper; it is the form and substance of the celebration of Christ crucified, who loved us and gave himself for us."[36]

Bibliography

Allen, Danielle S. "The Flux of Time in Ancient Greece." *Dae* 132.2 (2003) 62–73.
Ascough, Richard S. "A Question of Death: Paul's Community-Building Language in 1 Thessalonians 4:13–18." *JBL* 123 (2004) 509–30.
Banks, Robert J. *Paul's Idea of Community*. Grand Rapids: Eerdmans, 1980.
Barth, Karl. *Church Dogmatics*. Vol. II/1. Edinburgh: T. & T. Clark, 1975.
Barth, Markus. *Rediscovering the Lord's Supper: Communion with Israel, with Christ, and among the Guests*. Atlanta: John Knox, 1988.
Bornkamm, Günther. "Lord's Supper and Church in Paul." *Early Christian Experience*, 123–60. Translated by Paul L. Hammer. New York: Harper & Row, 1969.
Fagan, Garrett G. *Bathing in Public in the Roman World*. Ann Arbor: University of Michigan Press, 1999.
Ferguson, Everett. "Lord's Supper and Love Feast." *CS* 21 (2005) 27–38.

---

35. Barth, *Church Dogmatics*, II/1, 409–410.
36. Markus Barth, *Rediscovering the Lord's Supper*, 70.

Fitzmyer, Joseph A. *First Corinthians: A New Translation with Introduction and Commentary.* AB 32 New Haven: Yale University Press, 2008.

Furnish, Victor Paul. *Theology and Ethics in Paul.* Nashville: Abingdon, 1968.

Hays, Richard B. "Ecclesiology and Ethics in 1 Corinthians." *ExAud* 10 (1994) 31–43.

Hock, Ronald F. "Paul's Tentmaking and the Problem of His Social Class." *JBL* 97 (1978) 555–64.

Jeremias, Joachim. *The Eucharistic Words of Jesus.* Translated by Norman Perrin. New York: Scribner, 1966.

Juvenal. "Satire 11." In *Juvenal and Perisus*, edited by Susanna Morton Braund, 400–418. LCL. Cambridge: Harvard University Press, 2004.

Kaster, Robert A. "The Taxonomy of Patience, or When Is 'Patientia' Not a Virtue?" *CP* 97 (2002) 133–44.

Lahad, Kinneret. "Singlehood, Waiting, and the Sociology of Time." *SocF* 27 (2012) 163–86.

Malherbe, Abraham J. *Social Aspects of Early Christianity.* 2nd ed. 1983. Reprinted, Eugene, OR: Wipf & Stock, 2003.

McRae, Rachel M. "Eating with Honor: The Corinthian Lord's Supper in Light of Voluntary Association Meal Practices." *JBL* 130 (2011) 165–81.

Pliny. *Complete Letters* [in English]. Oxford World's Classics. Oxford: Oxford University Press, 2006.

Schwartz, Barry. *Queuing and Waiting: Studies in the Organization of Access and Delay.* Chicago: University of Chicago Press, 1975.

Still, Todd D. "Did Paul Loathe Manual Labor?: Revisiting the Work of Ronald F. Hock on the Apostle's Tentmaking and Social Class." *JBL* 125 (2006) 781–95.

Surburg, Mark P. "The Situation at the Corinthian Lord's Supper in Light of 1 Corinthians 11:21: A Reconsideration." *Concordia Journal* 32 (2006) 17–37.

Theissen, Gerd. *The Social Setting of Pauline Christianity: Essays on Corinth.* Edited, translated, and introduction by John H. Schütz. Philadelphia: Fortress, 1982.

Walker-Ramisch, Sandra. "Graeco-Roman Voluntary Associations and the Damascus Document." In *Voluntary Associations in the Graeco-Roman World*, edited by John S. Kloppenborg and Stephen G. Wilson, 128–45. London: Routledge, 1996.

Wilson, S. G. "Voluntary Associations: An Overview." In *Voluntary Associations in the Graeco-Roman World*, edited by John S. Kloppenborg and Stephen G. Wilson, 1–15. London: Routledge, 1996.

Winter, Bruce W. "Lord's Supper at Corinth: An Alternative Reconstruction." *RTR* 37 (1978) 73–82.

12

The Koinonia of Christians—and Others
I Corinthians 10: 14–22

—Wendell Willis

IN ADDITION TO THE challenge of the overall meaning of 1 Cor 10:14–22, the passage contains some significant and debated words. These key words cannot all be treated equally in a single paper so for the present study I will focus on the meaning of one word in the passage, κοινωνία, and how it shapes this pericope. It appears that investigations of the pericope tend to emphasize either κοινωνία or σῶμα χριστοῦ and which one takes priority greatly shapes the conclusion. While the second phrase must considered, this essay will focus on the former word (κοινωνία). One question that is often asked in approaching this passage is: "Is "κοινωνία" equal to 'holy communion'?" In the words of the British essayist, C. E. M. Joad, "It all depends on what you mean . . ." It is one of the many cases in which Paul's meaning as conveyed by translations both *reflects* and *effects* theological understanding.

With respect to the passage under consideration, Paul's use of the common Greek word, κοινωνία, which is not very prominent in the New Testament and used chiefly by Paul is the key.[1] While one must begin with

---

1. Of seventeen uses in the NT, fourteen are by Paul. A good, succinct review of the

the common meanings assigned to this noun, that in itself is not sufficient to locate Paul's point. It seems clear that Paul carefully chose this word to describe the Christian common meal, but for understanding how Paul employs κοινωνία here, in my view, one should not look to non-Pauline texts as the guide to his meaning.

Let me begin by recalling two ways the latter mistake has occurred. One is roughly a century back *die Religionsgeschichte Schule* applied what they understood (wrongly in my view) to be the meaning of cultic meals in the mystery religions in which the worshippers believed that they consumed their deity in a substantial way (the ὠμοφαγία). This earlier interpretation has been sufficiently challenged in subsequent scholarly works that it does not need refutation here.[2] But similar is an approach that takes other Christian writings that perhaps—it is debatable,—allude to the Eucharist as a guide to Paul's meaning in 1 Cor 10. It might be that the Gospel of John has a "presence" view of the relationship of Christ to the Eucharist (John 6). What this essay will question is that such a view is present in 1 Cor 10.

Κοινωνία: The range of meanings

While context always must decide the meaning of word usage, it is appropriate to begin with a short review of the range of meanings proposed to understand how various scholars have interpreted κοινωνία in this passage.

Κοινωνία, the abstract form from κοινός and κοινωνεῖν, can carry the meaning of "having a share," or "partnership," or "association." (The distinctions often represented in German as between "*Anteilhaben*" and "*Gemeinschaft*.")[3] Wilfried Sebothoma suggests these two meanings represent two poles of the range of meaning, and both are included in the word communion. "The term communion seems to approximate

---

difficulty in interpreting the word, and especially finding a good English translation, is Thiselton, *Corinthians*, 103–105. In commenting on 1 Cor 1.9 he argues for "communal participation." Of course, κοινωνία, like all words, derives specific meaning from the context in which it appears. Both in 1 Cor 1.9 and 10.16 it is precisely emphasized that this κοινωνία is grounded in Jesus Christ. However, what exactly Paul meant by that is of much greater dispute.

2. For a good balanced review of this approach, now largely abandoned, see Klauck, "Presence," 57–60.

3. See the review of these standardized German words by Thiselton, *Corinthians*,761–763. He refers to Seesemann, *Begriff Koinonia*, 34–56. Thiselton, *Corinthians*,762, gives another option, *Mitteilsamkeit*.

both participation in something, e.g., Christ, and the bond between the participants."[4] Κοινωνία appears in a variety of contexts in Greek literature, including marriage, associations of business, military and friendship. Basically it refers to two or more persons who have something in common or who share something. The thing shared is most often put in the genitive case, as it is in these usages of 1 Cor 10.[5] The key question is in a given usage whether the emphasis is on *those who share* or *the thing shared*. That both are possible foci is important for consideration of the 1 Cor 10 passage. It is the mutual, sustained sharing that most distinguishes κοινωνία from μετέχειν, although they are sometimes used interchangeably.[6]

To keep this essay in manageable length, this must serve as a general linguistic review, and the attention turn to a too forgotten work that is important for the present analysis, the unpublished dissertation of 50 years ago by Dr. Stuart Currie. Done at Emory under the supervision of William Beardslee, Currie asks the questions which the current study asks, and fortunately for this paper, arrives at a place close to the same conclusion. In his survey, Currie concludes: "To sum up: koinonia does not have any intrinsic implication of inward, emotional involvement. It simply specifies an action or a condition of relationship more or less continuous or extensive. Similarly koinonein . . . does not itself carry a religious freight."[7]

Currie further argues that Paul's uses of κοινωνία can be organized into three groups: First is the collection for the poor saints in Jerusalem (Rom 15:26; 2 Cor 8:4; 9:13); secondly usages which are connected to either πνεῦμα or υἱός (I Cor 1:9; 2 Cor 13:13 and Phil 2:1); finally exemplified in the passage of focus in the present study, where κοινωνία is related to the Christian meal, as well as those of others (1 Cor 10). While all usages

---

4. Sebothoma, "Koinonia," 243. I agree with his observation that here "to have a share" (*Anteilhaben*) really presumes a community (*Gemeinschaft*).

5. Hollander, "Idea of Fellowship," 461–464 gives a careful discussion of the role of the genitive with κοινωνία and then applies it to 1 Cor 10.14–22. As will be seen in this essay, I am in basic agreement with Hollander, and often invoke his study for support.

6. Paul only uses μετέχω five times, all in 1 Cor 9 and 10. Conzelmann, *I Corinthians* 172, says that μετέχειν ἐκ explains the meaning of κοινωνία, but he does not say how. If there is a diffference, it may be that μετέχειν describes the specific physical action of taking something. Hollander, "Idea of Fellowship," 467, 468 argues that μετέχειν is used absolutely, and refers to the participants, and thus is more or less synonymous with κοινωνεῖν. He paraphrases: "on the basis of the fact that there is one bread we are all partners (in our belief in Jesus Christ)."

7. Currie, *Koinonia*, 9.

cannot be fully examined, some general observations of the first two categories are relevant for understanding the latter.

With regard to the collection for the poor in Jerusalem, G. W. Peterman, writing about the use of κοινωνία in Rom 15:26 argues that the phrase κοινωνία ποιήσασθαι should be rendered "establish fellowship" because in Greco-Roman social conventions the giving and receiving of goods or services is an essential part of relationships.[8] It is important that this giving and receiving has a religious base in that the Roman Christians had been given to share (ἐκοινώνησαν) in spiritual blessings from the believers in Jerusalem (Rom 15:27). In 2 Cor 9:13, also about Paul's collection, the addition of καὶ εἰς πάντας, points to a relationship among Christians that extends beyond this immediate benevolence need. This supports the view that joint participation establishes, or maintains, a significant relationship between those who are κοινοί. With respect to the participation in the pagan meal—this is the presenting problem of 1Cor 10:14–22—it warns of a relationship with the demons that believers must avoid. Similarly, κοινωνία with the body and blood of Christ is about a relationship established and maintained with others in the body of Christ.

The second group of passages are more difficult to interpret. In 2 Cor 13:13 does ἡ κοινωνία τοῦ ἁγίου πνεύματος mean "have a share of the Holy Spirit," (partitive genitive) or "participation in the Holy Spirit" (note the concluding phrase μετὰ πάντων ὑμῶν, "with all of you")? Most probably the second meaning is intended. Phil 2:1 would seem to be very similar. The more uncertain passage is I Corinthians 1:9 in which the genitive qualifier is τοῦ υἱοῦ αὐτοῦ Ἰησοῦ Χριστοῦ τοῦ κυρίου ἡμῶν. In all three passages it appears that it is the association with and the shared participation in life with the Spirit and with Christ which is meant. Paul would certainly not say the Corinthians "have a part" of Christ. Indeed, he argues strongly that Christ is not parceled out among the believers (1 Cor 1:13).

This brings us to the passage now under study, 1 Cor 10:14–22. In addition to how one should understand κοινωνία, here there is the additional complication of the reference to the "body and blood" of the Lord. The proper interpretation of σῶμα χριστοῦ is a minefield of its own, apart from the eucharistic reference in our passage.[9] While it is obviously necessary to consider the body and blood objects of κοινωνία in 10:16f., rather than begin with these two terms, I propose to start with larger context. In my un-

8. Peterman, "Romans 15:26," 457–63.
9. See the review by Thiselton, *Corinthians*, 768–70.

derstanding, the larger argument of 8–10 (Christian participation in meals associated with idols) as well as the three-fold use of κοινωνία in 10:16, 18, and 20 with respect to three different meals, really focuses upon Christian interaction with other religious communities.[10] That means that the references to κοινωνία with respect to Israel and the idolaters in 10:16–20 are not illustrations in support of a view of the Christian κοινωνία; rather this is an argument against believers being involved in meals associated with idols. This view rejects Sebothoma's summary of the usage, but accepts his observation, "for Paul κοινωνία and cognates seem to be fundamental to religion in general whether one thinks of it with reference to the pagan, Old Testament, or the New Testament worlds."[11] With the three usages found in the same brief context and with such similar referents, should not one expect that κοινωνία should have the same meaning?

Κοινωνία in the Context of 10:14–22[12]

What is the commonality being pointed to by these uses of the word κοινωνία in this passage? Whatever κοινωνία means in this context should be applicable to all three manifestations of it. It is necessary to repeat that one must keep in focus that Paul's concern is really with the κοινωνία of demons manifested in the cultic meals of idolaters. Both the Christian example and the example of Israel are appealed to in order to stress the danger of the κοινωνία of demons. Perhaps as a parallel rhetorical design one could look at Gal 3:28. There Paul is really concerned about "Jew nor Greek" and the references to slave nor free, male and female are rhetorical examples, not direct concerns.

Edgar Hainz says, "The special character of Pauline usage is always emphasized in the exegetical literature and its religious character is always

---

10. As Smit, "'Do Not Be Idolaters,'" 41 says, "With regard to 1 Cor. 10:14–22 it is regularly noticed that participation in the Lord's Supper is not Paul's main subject matter, but that he puts this to use in rejecting participation in sacrificial meals as a form of idolatry."

11. Sebothoma, "Koinonia," 245.

12. Smit, "Do not Be Idolaters," 40–53, rightly points to 10:1–22 as a complete rhetorical unit, and demonstrates how Paul's retelling of Israel's experience described in Deut 32 is given as an exemplum parallel to his discussion of the present situation in Corinth. Smit makes his case by his careful rhetorical analysis. I agree with his overall assessment, with a couple of caveats discussed later in the paper, which may be my failure rightly to understand him.

emphasized. However, the neutral rendering, 'participant,' 'participate,' 'participation,' is overwhelmingly preferred."[13] Paul's broad concern is with Christians participating in pagan meal occasions.

The Larger Context

The correct understanding must begin with the broader context, 1 Cor 8–10, a discussion of Christians[14] who chose to eat εἰδωλοθύτων (his argument assumes that some Corinthians are doing so and therefore Paul is seeking to stop an existing practice). Apart from the details, including the passage considered at present, the broad context of the three chapters should not be forgotten. The earlier analysis by Weiss and others locating parts from two or more letters in these chapters has largely been abandoned. That means a correct explanation must search for the flow of the entire three chapters as conceived by Paul. In 1 Cor 8 Paul replies to arguments of some Corinthians who insist on their right (ἐξουσία) to eat at meals related to non-Christian sacrifice, in spite of the impact on other Christians who are injured by the practice. In chapter 9 Paul sets forth himself as an example of one who does not use rights he legitimately has. In the first half of chapter 10 he warns those who defend their participation in pagan meal occasions[15] that the history of Israel is an example (for them!) against over confidence in the relationship to the jealous God by involvement with other worship communities.

The larger concern of at least chapters 8 to 14 is the internal relationships of the Christian community at Corinth. Thus the emphasis (manifested in the topics of sacrificial meat, the participation of women in worship, the Eucharist and the exercise of spiritual gifts) is about community formation and life. This larger purpose accords well with the view that in 10:14–22 Paul's concern is to discourage Christians from κοινωνία in the

---

13. Hainz, "Κοινωνία," 304.

14. I acknowledge Mark Nanos' extensive and repeated arguments that the ἀσθενής are not "weak" Christians, but refers to non-Christ-believers who are pagans. Among several essays, see Nanos, "Why the 'Weak,'" 386–404. While I am not persuaded of his conclusion about the "impaired" [Nanos' term], the decision on their identity does not directly affect the focus of the current study.

15. On the varied possible contexts for pagan sacrificial meals, see my *Idol Meat*, 13–17. I did not consider a possible specific influence from the Imperial cult, as is suggested by Winter, "Achaean Federal Imperial Cult," 169–78. For the present discussion of the Christian κοινωνία, the specific pagan cult involved is not a necessary concern.

meals of idols, because the relationship in the Christian meal is exclusive of other associations. Smit accepts this focus, but repeatedly insists that it is "theological" and not "social."[16] This distinction seems to me ill advised, because it is in fact both. I would call Paul's focus here "ecclesiological" and insist that it combines both theology and social life. The "theological" reality of being part of the Christian "society" cannot be acceptably maintained if one joins the "social" occasions of pagan cult meals. I concur with Hollander, "The basis for the prohibition of idolatry is Paul's understanding of Christian Fellowship. Christians share in the worship of God and cannot share with pagans in the worship of pagan deities as well. The key in this passages seems to be the κοινωνία/κοινωνός word group."[17]

The Structure of 1 Cor 10:14–22

10:14–15 Warning[18]

Paul begins with an imperative instruction "Therefore, my dear friends, flee from the worship of idols." Thus the key concern of the passage is clearly not to explain the Christian cult meal, but to argue that those who do share in it must stay away from idolatry, that is not from "idolaters" per se, but from their actions of worship (λατρεία). Paul then proposes to give information that should lead the Corinthians to act on this warning—if they are wise.[19] Thus for proper interpretation this means 10:16–21 must be read as a series of arguments in support of the admonition to avoid worship of idols. 10:22 is the final warning, consisting of two rhetorical questions which imply that to participate (even implicitly) in pagan cults is to provoke the Lord.[20]

16. Smit, "Do not be Idolaters," 43, "It is my considered opinion that in I Cor. 10:1–22 Paul exclusively deals with the theological side of the case." And he continues, 45, "For, verse 17 is not, as is generally accepted, a brief social excursus, but a theological statement." He does contrast this with "social."

17. Hollander, "Idea of Fellowship," 457.

18. On where to begin the pericope, see the discussion in Thiselton, *Corinthians*, 754–55.

19. It is debated whether Paul uses φρονίμοις in a sarcastic manner, a tactic that seems clearly employed elsewhere in the letter. Fitzmyer, *First Corinthians*, 389, thinks not, rather Paul is flattering those he seeks to change. For the present argument, this question is not important.

20. Παραζηλοῦμεν, otherwise only in Rom 10: 19; 11:11, 14. Bailey, *Paul*, 275, argues for a chiastic arrangement in the section. It appears at least the bracketing parallels of 10:14 and 10: 22 highlights the function of the pericope.

Therefore the pericope is bracketed by warnings of the danger of association with pagan meals.

10:16—21 Three Examples to Consider

It is notable that Paul gives three paralleled examples in support of his imperatival instruction: φεύγετε ἀπό τῆς εἰδολολατρίας. The first is that of Christians, with respect to the cup and bread of the Lord. The second is the κοινωνία of Israel according to the flesh in their sacrifice and altar, which he had already mentioned in chapter 9 (18); third is the κοινωνία of those who sacrifice to demons (19–20). Since the primary concern of the pericope is that the Corinthians avoid idol worship, not to explain the Christian meal, it would be expected that κοινωνία would have the same meaning in all three examples. "One enters into partnership with the powers to which the sacrifices are dedicated and with those who share in the offerings. According to Paul, what takes place at the Lord's Supper is not *fundamentally different* [my italics] from what takes place in Jewish and Gentile sacrifices."[21] That is, in this argument the word κοινωνία should carry the same concepts, and therefore the Christian κοινωνία must be a genuine parallel to those of Israel and the idol worshippers.

1 Cor10:18 The Κοινωνία of Israel

Because the meaning of the Christian κοινωνία is the goal of the investigation and has received by far the most scholarly attention, it will be postponed for now and the study turns to the two other examples given of κοινωνία. The first is that of Israel κατὰ σάρκα, that is physical Israel, as in Rom 9:8, 11:14, and Gal 4:23, rather than "spiritual Israel"[22] as Paul sees the church. From the gospels and from the LXX it is clear that the θυσιαστήριον was the altar on which sacrifices were placed. In most sacrifices those who offer the sacrifice, share in the meat (they are κοινωνοί), a point made by Paul a chapter earlier in 9:13.[23] Gardner argues Paul intends a close connection to the

---

21. Hainz, "Κοινωνία," 305; Smit, "Do not be Idolaters," 51, "The disjunctive syllogism which Paul develops in this passage requires that he presents the Lord's Supper and pagan sacrificial meals as similar, but opposite realities."

22. Paul does not use this designation, but Gal 6:16 is similar, and the allegory of Gal 4:21–31 also supports such an interpretation.

23. Coutsoumpos, *Community, Conflict*, 84 argues Paul is alluding to Deut. 14:22–27

first half of chapter 10, specifically the episode of the Golden Calf, and that the sin of Israel is being stressed.[24] This is a key, decisive comparison for interpreting 10:16,17 because it is improbable that Paul thought that Israel saw God as present in the sacrifices. While Israel was certain that their God was aware of and valued these sacrifices, it is unlikely that Israel believed God was in some special, personal way present at the sacrifice,[25] certainly not in a realistic sense. (If so, what would happen to God in the "whole offering"?)[26] Rather, as Thiselton says, "The participant and the participant's group or community appropriate the reality or influence which the altar of sacrifice [θυσιαστηρίον] represents and conveys."[27]

1 Cor 10:19-20 The Κοινωνία *of Demons*

Jews were of two opinions about the idols worshipped by their pagan neighbors. On the one hand, idols were examples of human irrationality and thus easy to lampoon. For example, Isa 44:13-17 makes fun of a man who cuts down a tree and uses part of it to cook the meal, but carves and paints the other part and worships it! How dumb!

The other view was that idols are really just front men for demons. The deceived worshippers of course, do not realize this truth; rather, they

---

regarding Jewish cult meals. See also Panikulam, *Koinonia*, 28.

24. Gardner, *Gifts*, 111--34. Connecting with 10:1-13 he thinks it is specifically "sinful Israel" whom Paul has in mind. He succinctly states, 155f.: "In terms of the structure of Paul's argument we shall contend that there are not three meals discussed here (Christian, Israelite and pagan) but one: the Israelite—briefly illustrated by the Christian meal." Indeed, 166-167, he does not think pagan meals are discussed, based on rejecting τὰ ἔθνη as part of the original text. See also Smit, "Do not be Idolaters," 43-44, 49-51.

25. Klauck, *Herrenmahl*, 265, 266 says that nowhere in the OT is the idea presented that in a sacrificial meal a table fellowship [*Tischgemeinschaft*] between men and God is formed. He does think that there was such an idea in Hellenistic religious meals where the demons [demi-gods] are present at the table fellowship.

26. On Jewish strictures about pagan sacrifices, see Tomson, *Paul and the Jewish Law*, 154-176. Hollander, *Idea of Fellowship*, 458, gives a useful comparison with the criticism seen in *Joseph and Aseneth*.

27. Thiselton, *Corinthians*, 772. Hollander, *Idea of Fellowship*, 460, "What Paul wants to underline here is that when Israelites or Jews eat together for the glory of God they are a close-knit community, or in his words 'partners in the altar', that is, partners who share in the food on the altar and who consequently share the same cult." Similarly, Panikulam, *Koinonia*, 28, says "those who ate from the altar became κοινωνοί of the altar; this is an allusion to the cultic unity of Israel."

regard the idols as gods.[28] This is important in understanding the passage's argument. While the idols are either frauds or demonic (although their worshippers do not consider them such of course), to join in their worship (again, even if only implicitly) is to become κοινωνοί of demons. Δαιμόνιον in Greek texts does not necessarily describe beings which might be associated with Dante's *Inferno*, specifically the various graphic versions. It can, perhaps even here does, only mean "minor" or "unnamed" deity.[29] The reference to the cup of demons represents the contrast to the cup shared by Christians. As Goppelt says the point is: "It is thus impossible to drink both the cup of the Lord and the cup of demons (10:21)."[30] Klauck, and many others, have suggested the pagan meals in question were connected to the shrine of Asclepius or Demeter and Kore in Corinth.[31] Since it is unlikely that Christians would take part in what was explicitly worship to idols, it is more probable that Paul is referring to social gatherings, such as birthday or family celebrations, which perhaps began with a sacrifice and continued with a meal from the sacrifice.[32] It is probable that the dining was done in one of the dining rooms associated with temples, since Paul gives other instructions for meals in a private home (10:27–31).[33]

While it seems obvious to heirs of the Enlightenment that idols and idol sacrifices have no ontological reality, that was not a common assumption of Paul's day, and therefore in their social construction of reality they did exist and decisively shaped lives of the worshippers and what they

---

28. Klauck, *Herrenmahl*, 266–68 gives an instructive discussion of the understanding of demons in Greco-Roman thought. They stand between heroes and gods, and in that way are gods in a sense, as well as representing the gods. Because the demons subsist from the sacrificial meals, they are in a sense meal partners and associate with men at the sacrificial meal.

29. *Didache* 6:3 terms them "worship of dead gods."

30. Goppelt, "Ποτήριον," VI.157.

31. Klauck, "'Leib Christi,'" 15–21.The problem with these locations has been surveyed by Winter, *Seek the Welfare*, 169–173. Excavators have recently expressed doubts about the possible continuity of the cults into the Roman colonial period. For the present purpose the location of pagan sacrificial meals in Corinth is unimportant, but many opportunities surely existed.

32. For an argument of the primarily social significance of pagan cult meals to the participants, see Willis, "Table of Demons," II. 799–813. Also Fisk, "Eating Meat," 49–70.

33. Winter, "Identifying the Offering," II. 815–36 seeks to show that the particular "demons" Paul has in mind are related to Roman Imperial cults. This specificity is not significant for the present argument.

considered as "true."³⁴ Although based on assumptions other than these, Paul makes a similar observation—whatever idols are or are not (10:20), their worship created an empirical community—a κοινωνία to use Paul's term. Paul evaluates the sacrificial gatherings of the pagans as analogous to the worship of the Golden Calf as portrayed in Deuteronomy32 and specifically in Deut 32.17 with the Song of Moses, "They sacrificed to demons and not to God [LXX ἔθυσαν δαιμονίοις καὶ οὐ θεῷ]."³⁵ For Christians to be in these sacrificial associations is to become members of their community, even if believers know these pagan gods are not real (1 Cor 8.4–6).³⁶ Again Thiselton explains well: "the reality of social construction means that idolatry *involves* the **communal participants** (i.e., those who enter the 'projected world' at issue) in *actually* becoming κοινωνοὺς τῶν δαιμονίων."³⁷ The impossibility of Christians being included in these communal gatherings is stressed in v. 21 which summarizes the point of the whole argument: "You cannot drink the cup of the Lord and the cup of demons. You cannot partake of the table of the Lord and of the table of demons!" Note Paul does not say "should not" but "cannot" the implication is the two κοινωνοί are fundamentally exclusory of each other. "He [Paul] does not seem to consider the 'table of the Lord' and the 'table of demons' as altars on which sacrifices were offered in honour of God or demons but rather as tables³⁸ at which people were eating together, either as Christians in remembrance of the death of Jesus Christ or as pagans for the glory of pagan deities."³⁹

34. Thiselton, *Corinthians*, 773–74, has an insightful discussion of the role of social constructs in relation to the pagan worship.

35. Smit, "Do not be Idolaters," 43, 44, 47.

36. Klauck, *Herrenmahl*, 271, suggests perhaps the Corinthian Christians, being persuaded that the pagan deities were non-beings, felt no danger in participating in the pagan meals.

37. Thiselton, *Corinthians,* 774. The italics are Thiselton's. Martin, *Corinthian Body*, 184–89 argues Paul's opposition to Christian involvement with meals of pagans is based on a fear of "pollution" by the δαιμονίων. I am arguing that the pollution is with the pagan participants, by becoming κοινωνοί of their community. It is the group of co-eaters, who because of their religious commitments, are outside the bounds for the Christian community.

38. Klauck, *Herrenmahl*, 269, notes that it is because the pagan meal had no precise equivalent to the bread in the Christian cult meal that Paul uses the term τραπέζα, as the antitype to the bread. So it is not the pagan altar that is the key comparison, but the table from which the worshippers had a share. However, 270, the two were not always clearly distinguished.

39. Hollander, "Idea of Fellowship," 459: "these meetings are to be characterized as *convivia* or *symposia*; social gatherings at which food and wine were offered to the gods

Evaluating the function of this example, Smit rightly says, "Paul's most important move in this respect is that he reduces to the same denominator the contrary relationships brought about by the two meals: participation in the Lord's Supper as communion (κοινωνία) with the blood and body of Christ is diametrically opposed to being participants in sacrificial meals as a communion (κοινωνοί) with demons (vv. 16–17, 18–20).[40]

1 Cor 10:16, 17 The Κοινωνία of Christians

It seems to be certain that in regard to the altar sacrifices of Israel and the sacrifices made to demons, the emphasis is upon being part of a κοινωνία. With respect to 10:16–17 the most discussed concern is what is meant by the κοινωνία of the body and blood of Christ.[41] Klauck speculates that the phrasing in v. 16 may well represent language from catechesis.[42] Fitzmyer finds three ways Paul uses σῶμα χριστοῦ: the historical body of Jesus crucified, the ecclesiastical body of Christ (1 Cor 12:27), and "liturgically of the Eucharistic body of Christ" (1 Cor 10:16 and 11:27).[43] His understanding of the meaning of κοινωνία here is clear when he says of the Lord's Supper κοινωνία: "Do not we Christians share in the life-blood of the crucified Christ, when we partake together of the contents of the cup in the liturgical celebration of his death (11:26)?"[44] However that this experience is

and at which like-minded people ate and drank together."

40. Smit, "Do not be Idolaters, 52.

41. On the possible backgrounds for Paul's selection of σῶμα Χριστοῦ see the survey by Dunn, "Body of Christ," 146–62. Dunn, 150, makes the important observation that in each of the Pauline letters uses it is always the "body of Christ" (also in Colossians and Ephesians, whether or not they are by Paul). This distinguishes Paul's use from the Stoic use of "body" which is clearly metaphorical with respect to the universe as body, although Dunn thinks that such civic use is the source of Paul's reference to the body image (156). With respect to Paul's usage, Dunn emphasizes the charismatic body of Christ, as empowered by the Spirit.

42. Klauck, *Gemeinde*, 332.

43. Fitzmyer, *I Corinthians*, 391; Sebothoma, "Koinonia," 247, noting that all three examples describe a sacrifice, thinks this implies a sacrificial character of the Christian Eucharist. This is to miss the real emphasis of κοινωνία in this pericope, the group gathering itself, the community which Christians should avoid (i.e. the gathering of idolaters or in an idol temple). It is noteworthy that Sebothoma, like most interpreters, has little to say about the κοινωνία of the idol temple, although making interpretive connections with the κοινωνία of Israel.

44. Fitzmyer, *Corinthians*, 389. Similarly, Coutsoumpos, *Community, Conflict*, 83, "So, we can conclude that κοινωνία means participation in the body and blood of Christ

a means of being intimately united with the Lord, while possible, is not explicit. Prout says that "What is striking in this passage, however, is the use of 'body' in two senses: (1) the physical body of Christ which was nailed to the cross and (2) the spiritual body of Christ which is his church."⁴⁵ That Paul speaks of the σῶμα χριστοῦ as the "eucharistic body of Christ," is only asserted to be here and in 11:27. Whether that is true of 11:27 is strongly debated, and the subject for another paper (a few comments below), but that it is asserted here seems improbable.⁴⁶ It is certainly possible that Paul says less here than he believes about the Eucharist (more in chapter 11 of course), but in the immediate context the Eucharist is set forth as an example of the formation of an association or fellowship in a way parallel to the altar of Israel and the meals of idol worshippers. Jerome Murphy-O'Connor says that Paul is arguing *from* the Eucharist towards implications for Jewish and pagan meals. While certainly the Eucharist has a significance that Paul would not grant for the parallel meals referenced, I am not persuaded it is the focus here because the first and last two verses of the pericope deal with avoidance of "idolatry" which also is the overall concern of chapters 8 and 10.⁴⁷ Fitzmyer does acknowledge that: "Although this verse teaches some important effects of the Lord's Supper . . . the participation now mentioned is meant to provide the background for Paul's argument against Christians taking part in meals in pagan temples and consuming meat sacrificed to idols."⁴⁸ The "cup of blessing" is probably an allusion to the Jewish Passover

---

and thus union with the exalted Christ." Also Hofius, "Gemeinschaft," 173, "Nach 1 Kor 10,16 empfangen also die zum Tisch des Herrn Kommenden in den sakramentalen Gaben von Brot und Wein Anteil an dem für sie dahingegebenen Leib Christi und an seinem für sie vergossenen Blut . . ."

45. Prout, "One Loaf," 79.

46. Dunn, "'Body of Christ,'" 151, reviewing all Pauline uses, concludes "such variation strongly suggests that the point being made is not one of dogmatic precision, but of metaphorical imprecision. . ." Käsemann, *Essays*, 108–135, argues "body of Christ" means the church. Similarly, Gardner, *Gifts of God*, 165. Hofius, "Gemeinschaft," 176, rejects this: "Paulus spricht also an unserer Stelle keineswegs von der Kirche als dem 'Leib Christi' und von der Eingliederung in dem ekklesiologischen Christusleib."

47. As argued by Murphy-O'Connor, "Eucharist and Community," 56–69. I think the comparison runs the other way. However his later comment, 59, "The eating of the bread (10:17) and the drinking of the cup (11:27–28) is a real participation in the body and blood of Christ. This is possible only if the bread and wine are *in fact* [my italics] the body and blood of Christ." At least in 10:14–22 the question of Jesus's "presence" in the communion does not arise.

48. Fitzmyer, *Corinthians*, 391. Similarly, Smit, "Do not Be Idolaters," 48, "He [Paul] introduces baptism and the Lord's Supper in his exposition as a means to exclude

cup, although here it clearly references Christian practice.[49] But what is the meaning of this cup? Is it that Christians who partake are "united with the Lord in intimacy undreamed of by the OT worshipper" as Fitzmyer says, quoting E. F. Siegman, "The Blood of Christ in St. Paul's Soteriology."[50] It is very important to recall the purpose for which Paul employs the description of the Eucharist as κοινωνία.

Stuart Currie has shown that with respect to κοινωνία in 1 Corinthians 1:9 it designates not "fellowship," or "companionship" (indicating camaraderie or collectivity) but alliance, covenant relationship, as is indicated in 1:10 that the church be in agreement and not divided.[51] He points to the parallels of 10:16 and 11:24f., which equate the κοινωνία with the covenant established in Christ.[52]

	1 Cor 10:16		1 Cor 11:24f.
ποτήριον	= κοινωνία τοῦ αἵματος	=	ἡ καινή διαθήκη ἐν τῷ ἐμῷ αἵματι
ἄρτος	= κοινωνία τοῦ σώματος	=	τὸ σῶμα τὸ ὑπέρ ὑμῶν

The cup and bread refered to in 1 Cor 10:16,17 are the signs of the new covenant, and the formation of the new covenant people. It assumes and advances the OT covenant practice of sacrifice that accompanied the making of covenant. It is the one body of the risen Lord manifested in the community of believers. Hainz asserts:

> κοινωνία in Io:16ff., especially in contrast to μετέχω, which in Greek can be synonymous with κοινωνέω, but which in Paul expresses only the concrete receiving of a share, but not the most decisive aspect, which is the 'partnership' in the body of Christ effected at the Lord's Supper through 'participation in' the body of

---

participation in sacrificial meals for believers."

49. Goppelt, "ποτήριον," 156. notes the addition "which we bless" is not pleonistic, but differentiates the Christian cup from the Jewish one. On the cup of blessing, see Thiselton, *Corinthians,* 756–60. Gardner, *Gifts of God,* 164, rightly says, "The significance of the cup lay in the proclamation of Christ's death (11:26) as the inauguration of that [new] covenant."

50. Fitzmyer, *I Corinthians,* 394. I have not seen Siegman's study.

51. Currie, *Koinonia,* 40. Similarly, Gardner, *Gifts of God,* 162, says, "If κοινωνία refers to sharing in the results of the Gospel message, then a κοινωνία in the blood and body of Christ may mean a sharing in the results of Christ's sacrificial death. In this epistle these specifically have to do with the formation of a 'new Covenant' (11:25) and the forming of a unified community."

52. Currie, *Koinonia,* 44.

the exalted Christ, the Church, i.e., the partnership with the other partakers in the meal. The explication of 10:16 is in 10:17[53] and the larger context, in which the concern is the various relationships between those who partake at the table of the Lord, and those who partake at the altar, i.e., at the table of demons (10:18).[54]

Summary and Conclusion

In regard to the focus of this colloquy, this passage is important to me for two reasons. One is that after having made frequent forays into the topic of idol meat and Paul's responses to it this is familiar territory. But second is the focus of this colloquy. In these verses there is a vital intersection of Eucharist and ecclesiology. Paul's concern in the larger discussion of I Corinthians 8–10 is the involvement of Christians with other religious communities by sharing their meals. It is clear from the end of I Cor 10:2–30 that the meat itself is not the problem, but the occasions in which it is eaten. Neither, in fact, is it the danger present in "so-called" gods, represented in idols. They are really "nothings" although used by demons to deceive their worshippers. In short, it is not "what you eat" but "with whom you eat—and why."

There has been a tendency in examinations of this pericope to focus on the genitive nouns which specify the κοινωνία being considered: Israel, the idols/demons and blood/body of the Lord. However, to follow the argument—and I think to find the pulse—the focus should be on κοινωνία / κοινός. It is the communities, the associations, the partnerships formed by those who take part in the three dining occasions which is Paul's interest. Hainz rightly comments, "κοινωνία is in Paul a designation for various community relationships that come into being through (common) participation

---

53. Suggs, "Koinonia," 359, says that the participation effects the unity of the church. Similarly Mitchell. *Paul and the Rhetoric*, 254–256. While I Corinthians is very concerned about unity, that major issue is not directly concerned here.

54. Hainz, "Κοινωνία," 304, 305; Smit, "Do not Be Idolaters," 46, "In 10:16,17 he demonstrates that by taking part in the Lord's Supper they enter into communion with the body and blood of the Christ, a communion which, at that, is exclusive." My agreement with this statement depends on what precisely Smit means by "communion with the body and blood of the Christ." In this pericope the communion is with the gathered believers, based on their belief in the ultimate significance of Jesus' death, and their commitment to him. Note that in the comparison of v. 18 the "table of the lord" does not equal "table of demons."

and are seen in reciprocal giving and taking of a portion," . . . "Κοινωνοί are persons who stand in a relationship of community because they have a common share in something."[55] Making this point well is Anthony Thiselton's paraphrase of κοινωνία "communal participation."[56] The Christians who take part (become κοινωνοί) at the tables of demons, their sacrifices, are implicitly abandoning the Christian community (read church) because they join another. The God of Jesus and of his followers is a "jealous" God who will not share loyalties with other deities. As Hollander says, "Both the references to κοινωνία in v. 16 (cf. vv. 18 and 20) and the phrases in v. 17 should be understood ecclesiologically, denoting 'partnership' rather than 'participation.' The entire passage vv. 14–22 centres on the idea of the unity and solidarity of the Christian community."[57]

It could be said that this analysis of 1 Cor 10:16 and 17 diminishes the importance of the Eucharist—in fact, that was said in several reviews of my published dissertation of 30 years ago. If so, perhaps it is because I have not adequately articulated my understanding. The comments were often that my book presented a social understanding of the Eucharist, and denied a theological one. This seems to me confused, as if Christian (and pagan) social interactions could not be theological *and* social. My argument in this essay is that the groups gathered for worship (Jewish, pagan and Christian) constitute specific religious communities. The Christian one Paul usually calls the ἐκκλησία. Thiselton in his section heading for 1 Cor 10:14–22 says it well, "Exclusive Loyalty to God: Covenantal Allegiance in Sharing in the Lord's Supper."[58]

Klauck says because of the meaning of the pagan sacrificial meals with which Paul compares with the Eucharist one cannot avoid the belief that Paul classifies the Lord's Supper indirectly as a type of sacrificial meal.[59] While that may be a reasonable conclusion of the comparison, I am not persuaded it is one Paul makes. Klauck concludes, also from the comparison with pagan meals and the meaning of the κοινωνία language as he explains both in 1 Cor 10:16–20 as well as "the distinctively realistic-sounding argumentation of Paul in 1 Cor 11:27–30" that Paul is speaking

---

55. Hainz, "Κοινονία," 304.
56. Thiselton, *Corinthians*, 761.
57. Hollander, *Idea of Fellowship*, 469–70.
58. Thiselton, *Corinthians*, 750.
59. Klauck, *Herrenmahl*, 271,

of a "bodily real presence."[60] This is possibly the understanding of (some) Corinthians based on their previous understanding of religious meals, however, there is no access to their inner thoughts. It is possible also this would be Paul's understanding as well, but again we have no unambiguous description from Paul about his understanding (although, of course, many interpreters would insist that is precisely what is present in 1 Cor 10 and 11). What this essay seeks to establish is that in the rhetoric of the pericope, the concern is focused on those who partake, and with whom they partake and where. Paul is insisting upon a strong boundary between the believers and the pagan neighbors at religious meals.

I am comfortable about speaking of a vertical dimension, in the sense that this community is gathered around and grounded in a common faith in the risen Christ, but in I Cor 10:16–17 the focus is upon their mutual relationship which excludes their participation in other religious communities.[61] Also, as many have noted, it is a relationship grounded in the death of the Lord Christ, which is much more than a voluntary association.[62] I believe that what my analysis does is point very strongly to the boundary function of the Eucharist, in that it binds in solidarity those who partake, and does so in such a way as to prohibit their involvement in other communities of worship. This is most clearly, and dramatically, articulated when Paul labels the meals associated with pagan idols the "κοινωνία of demons." The main point of Paul's mention of the eucharistic is to insist upon its significance for ecclesiology.[63] In a time of the sharp decline of church participation in the Western world, the essential role of the church for the Christian faith may be the most important, yet most under discussed, doctrine.

60. Klauck, "Presence," 72.

61. Suggs, "Koinonia," 159, says "What emerges in this passage on any interpretation, is a κοινωνία with a vertical dimension, a participation in a religious symbol with a transcendent reference. It is participation in the transcendent which effects communal wholeness." Thiselton, *Corinthians*, 751, says "the κοινωνία is primarily 'vertical' and then by inference also 'horizontal.'" With Paul's ecclesiology, that is a distinction that he would not make.

62. Prout, "One Loaf," 78–81; Klauck, *Herrenmahl*, 260–26, thinks that Paul took the word κοινωνία from the prior pagan uses. See also Klauck's comments in "Presence in the Lord's Supper," 72, 73 where he suggests Paul makes implicit connections to mystery religions which taught theophagy.

63. Hollander, "Idea of Fellowship," 469–70, summarizes, "In the light of ancient parallels, it is concluded that the references to κοινωνία in v. 16 (cf. vv. 18 and 20) should be understood ecclesiologically, denoting 'partnership' rather than 'participation.'"

Bibliography

Bailey, Kenneth. *Paul through Mediterranean Eyes.* Downers Grove, IL: IVP Academic, 2011.

Conzelmann, Hans. *1 Corinthians.* Translated by James W. Leitch. Hermenia. Philadelphia: Fortress, 1975.

Coutsoumpos, Panayoytis. *Community, Conflict, and the Eucharist in Roman Corinth.* Lanham, MD: University Press of America, 2006.

Currie, Stuart D. "Koinonia in Christian Literature to 200 A. D." PhD diss., Emory University, 1962.

Dunn, James D. G. "The 'Body of Christ' in Paul." In *Worship, Theology and Ministry in the Early Church: Essays in Honor of Ralph P. Martin,* edited by Michael J. Wilkins and T. Paige, 146–62. JSNTS 87. Sheffield: JSOT Press, 1992.

Fisk, Bruce. "Eating Meat to Idols: Corinthian Behavior and Pauline Response in I Corinthians 8–10." *TJ* 10 (1989) 49–70.

Fitzmyer, Joseph A. *First Corinthians.* AB 32. New Haven: Yale University Press, 2008.

Gardner, Paul Douglas. *The Gifts of God.* Lanham, MD: University Press of America, 1994.

Goppelt, Leonhard. "Ποτήριον." In *TDNT* 6:148–58.

Hainz, Edgar. "Κοινωνία." In *EDNT* 2:303–5.

Hofius, Otfried. "Gemeinschaft am Tisch des Herrn: Das Zeugnis des Neuen Testaments." In *Einheit der Kirche im Neuen Testament,* edited by Anatoly, A. Alexeev, Christos Karakolis and Ulrich Luz, 169–85. WUNT 2/218. Tübingen: Mohr/Siebeck, 2008.

Hollander, Hann W. "The Idea of Fellowship in 1 Corinthians 10.14–22." *NTS* 55 (2009) 456–70.

Käsemann, Ernst. *Essays on New Testament Themes.* SBT 1/41. 1964. Reprinted, Philadelphia: Fortress, 1982.

Klauck, Hans-Josef. *Gemeinde, Amt, Sakrament: Neutestamentliche Perspektiven.* Würzburg: Echter, 1989.

———. *Herrenmahl und Hellenistischer Kult.* Münster: Aschendorf, 1982.

———. "'Leib Christi'—Das Mahl des Herrn in I Kor 10—12." *BK* 57 (2002) 15–21.

———. "Presence in the Lord's Supper: 1 Corinthians 11:23–26 in the Context of Hellenistic Religious History." In *One Loaf, One Cup,* edited by Ben F. Meyer, 57–60. New Gospels Studies 6. Macon, GA: Mercer University, 1991.

Martin, Dale B. *The Corinthian Body.* New Haven: Yale University Press, 1995.

Mitchell. Margaret M. *Paul and the Rhetoric of Reconciliation.* Louisville: Westminster John Knox, 1992.

Murphy-O'Connor, Jerome. "Eucharist and Community in First Corinthians." *Wor* 50 (1976) 370–85; 51 (1977) 56–69.

Nanos, Mark D. "Why the 'Weak' in I Corinthians 8–10 Were not Christ-believers." In *Saint Paul and Corinth,* [Greek title: *ΑΠΟΣΤΟΛΟΣ ΠΑΥΛΟΣ ΚΑΙ ΚΟΡΙΝΘΟΣ*], edited by Constantine J. Belezos, 2:385–404. Athens: Psichogios, 2009.

Panikulam, George. *Koinonia in the New Testament: A Dynamic Expression of Christian Life.* Analecta Biblica 85. Rome: Biblical Institute Press, 1979.

Peterman, G. W. "Romans 15:26: Make a Contribution or Establish Fellowship?" *NTS* 40 (1994) 457–63.

Prout, Elmer. "One Loaf . . . One Body." *RQ* 23 (1982) 78–81.

Sebothoma, Wilfried. "*Koinonia* in I Cor 10,16: Its Significance for Liturgy and Sacrament." *QL* 70 (1959) 243–50.

Seesemann, H. *Der Begriff Koinonia in NT*. BZNW 14. Giessen: Töpelmann, 1933.

Smit, J. "'Do not Be Idolaters': Paul's Rhetoric in First Corinthians 10:1–22." *NovT* 39 (1997) 40–53.

Suggs, M. Jack. "*Koinonia* in the New Testament." *Mid-Stream* 23 (1984) 351–69.

Thiselton, Anthony C. *The First Epistle to the Corinthians*. NIGT. Grand Rapids: Eerdmans, 2000.

Tomson, Peter. *Paul and the Jewish Law: Halakha in the Letters of the Apostle to the Gentiles*. Compendia rerum Iudaicarum ad Novum Testamentum III/1. Minneapolis: Fortress, 1990.

Willis, Wendell. *Idol Meat in Corinth*. SBLDS 68. 1985. Reprinted, Eugene, OR: Wipf & Stock, 2005.

———. "The 'Table of Demons': Pagan Sacrifice and Christian Eucharist." In *Saint Paul and Corinth* [Greek title: *ΑΠΟΣΤΟΛΟΣ ΠΑΥΛΟΣ ΚΑΙ ΚΟΡΙΝΘΟΣ*], edited by Constantine J. Belezos, 2:799–813. Athens: Psichogios, 2009.

Winter, Bruce. "The Achaean Federal Imperial Cult II: The Corinthian Church." *TynBul* 46 (1995) 169–78.

———. "Identifying the Offering, the Cup and the Table of the 'Demons' in I Cor 10:20–21." In *Saint Paul and Corinth* [Greek title: *ΑΠΟΣΤΟΛΟΣ ΠΑΥΛΟΣ ΚΑΙ ΚΟΡΙΝΘΟΣ*], edited by Constantine J. Belezos, 2:815–36. Athens: Psichogios, 2009.

———. *Seek the Welfare of the City: Christians as Benefactors and Citizens*. Grand Rapids: Eerdmans, 1984.